COMPENSATION FUNDS IN COMPARATIVE PERSPECTIVE

COMPENSATION FUNDS IN COMPARATIVE PERSPECTIVE

Edited by
Thierry VANSWEEVELT
Britt WEYTS

INTERSENTIA
Cambridge – Antwerp – Chicago

Intersentia Ltd
8 Wellington Mews
Wellington Street | Cambridge
CB1 1HW | United Kingdom
Tel.: +44 1223 736 170
Email: mail@intersentia.co.uk
www.intersentia.com | www.intersentia.co.uk

Distribution for the UK and Ireland:
NBN International
Airport Business Centre, 10 Thornbury Road
Plymouth, PL6 7PP
United Kingdom
Tel.: +44 1752 202 301 | Fax: +44 1752 202 331
Email: orders@nbninternational.com

Distribution for Europe and all other countries:
Intersentia Publishing nv
Groenstraat 31
2640 Mortsel
Belgium
Tel.: +32 3 680 15 50 | Fax: +32 3 658 71 21
Email: mail@intersentia.be

Distribution for the USA and Canada:
Independent Publishers Group
Order Department
814 North Franklin Street
Chicago, IL 60610
USA
Tel.: +1 800 888 4741 (toll free) | Fax: +1 312 337 5985
Email: orders@ipgbook.com

ISBN 978-1-78068-942-5
D/2020/7849/30
NUR 820

British Library Cataloguing in Publication Data. A catalogue record for this book is available from the British Library.

ACKNOWLEDGEMENTS

On 7 June 2016 the Antwerp Liability Law and Insurance Chair (ALLIC)[1] organised an international conference on compensation funds at the University of Antwerp. Experts from several European universities were asked to shed light on this fairly recent phenomenon of compensation law in their respective countries. This book is the result of this conference and further inter-university collaboration between Professors Michael Faure, Ton Hartlief, Gerrit van Maanen (Maastricht University), Jonas Knetsch (Jean-Monnet University Saint-Étienne), Ken Oliphant (University of Bristol), Post-Doctoral Researcher Rosa M. Garcia-Teruel (Rovira I Virgili University) and Doctoral Researchers Larissa Vanhooff and Kim Watts (University of Antwerp).

Since the 2016 conference, there has been no halt to the continued development of compensation funds. Yet there remains a pressing need for further analysis and definition of this field, to better inform the development of these hybrid systems. The contributions within this book are updated to December 2019, and therefore capture the most recent compensation fund developments within the selected jurisdictions.

The importance of compensation funds as a subject is also reflected in two ongoing PhD research projects at the University of Antwerp's Faculty of Law. These projects are funded by ALLIC and the FWO (Research Foundation – Flanders). Larissa Vanhooff is preparing her doctoral thesis on the nature, function and legality of Belgian compensation funds. Kim Watts is preparing her doctoral thesis on comprehensive no-fault compensation funds from a comparative law perspective. Both theses will be written in English and are expected to be completed in late 2021. We are pleased that further research is being undertaken to address important and unresolved questions in the continually evolving field of compensation funds.

The editors would like to thank the authors for their ongoing collaboration and their valuable contributions to this book.

---

1 For more information on the chair's activities and research see: <https://www.uantwerpen.be/en/faculties/faculty-of-law/chairs-and-funds/allic/>.

CONTENTS

LIST OF CONTRIBUTORS

Michael Faure
Professor of Comparative Private Law and Economics and Academic Director of METRO, Maastricht University, the Netherlands; Member of the Rotterdam Institute of Law and Economics, Erasmus University Rotterdam, the Netherlands.

Rosa M. Garcia-Teruel
Postdoctoral Researcher in the UNESCO Housing Chair, Department of Private, Procedural and Tax Law, Rovira i Virgili University, Catalonia, Spain.

Ton Hartlief
Advocat-General at the Hoge Raad (Dutch Supreme Court); Professor of of Private Law, Maastricht University, the Netherlands.

Jonas Knetsch
Professor of Civil and Comparative Law, Faculty of Law, Jean-Monnet University Saint-Étienne, France; Fellow of the European Centre of Tort and Insurance Law (ECTIL).

Ken Oliphant
Professor of Tort Law, University of Bristol, United Kingdom.

Larissa Vanhooff
Doctoral Researcher at the Research Foundation – Flanders, University of Antwerp, Belgium.

Gerrit van Maanen
Professor of Private Law, Maastricht University, the Netherlands; Part-Time Judge in the Court of Appeal, s'Hertogenbosch, the Netherlands.

Thierry Vansweevelt
Full Professor in the Faculty of Law and Joint Chairperson of the Antwerp Liability and Insurance Chair, University of Antwerp, Belgium; Advocate at Dewallens & partners.

Kim Watts
Doctoral Researcher, University of Antwerp, Belgium.

Britt Weyts
Full Professor of Private Law and Joint Chairperson of the Antwerp Liability and Insurance Chair, University of Antwerp, Belgium; Advocate at Verbist & Vanlerberghe Omega Law.

AN INTRODUCTION TO COMPENSATION FUNDS

Current Trends and the Questions We Need to Ask

Thierry VANSWEEVELT and Britt WEYTS

1. BACKGROUND

The general concept of a compensation fund, in most jurisdictions, is that it is a redress structure that provides compensation to victims of accidents and other misfortune where tort law, insurance law or social security law provide no or insufficient compensation.[1] Beyond that common reference point, there are vast differences in the shape and categorisation of compensation funds around the world.[2] For example, in some European civil law jurisdictions, compensation funds can be divided into two main categories: the so-called guarantee funds on the one hand and damage funds on the other hand.[3] Their approach is different. Guarantee funds, such as motor guarantee funds, function as a safety net that complements

---

1 W.H. van Boom and M.G. Faure, 'Introducing "Shifts in Compensation Between Private and Public Systems"' in W.H. van Boom and M. Faure (eds), *Shifts in Compensation between Private and Public Systems* (Springer 2007), pp. 13–14.

2 S. Porchy-Simon, 'Panorama générale et typologie des fonds' in GRERCA (ed.), *La socialisation de la réparation; fonds d'indemnisation et assurances* (Bruylant 2015), pp. 119–131.

3 L. Clerc-Renaud, *Du droit commun et des régimes spéciaux en droit extracontractuel de la reparation* (th. Chambéry 2006), pp. 402–403.

tort and insurance law. In short, they intervene in case the tortfeasor cannot be retrieved or is un(der)insured. On the contrary, so-called damage funds, e.g. Belgium's Asbestos Compensation Fund, compensate the victim when no liability can be established, for example due to a lack of fault.[4] By way of contrast in the common law world, the UK has taken an erratic approach to compensation funds that does not fit a set pattern, yet New Zealand operates a comprehensive universal compensation fund that eclipses refinements such as 'damage' and 'guarantee'.

2. THE ORIGINS AND GROWTH OF COMPENSATION FUNDS

As shall be seen, compensation funds are created because of perceived gaps of coverage or shortfalls in the compensation offered by the three other, traditional, sources of compensation, i.e. tort law, private insurance and social security.[5] Due to budgetary constraints, the social security system cannot cover all the damages of a victim of an accident. Tort law and private insurance are said to be too slow, too costly and unfair, because the victim generally bears the burden of proving negligence of the tortfeasor.[6] Moreover, where accident insurance is available it generally only offers a lump sum. As a result, victims of harmful events often remain fully or partially uncompensated. However, victims as a group in society no longer find it acceptable to carry their own loss. Instead, they may claim to be entitled to damages, regardless of whether they find a person accountable for the damage.

In recent decades compensation funds have emerged to tackle these problems. It is indeed hard not to see the many advantages of compensation funds: they offer compensation to victims who do not bear a heavy burden of proof, in an easy, fast and administrative way of providing redress, and victims are not obliged to go to court. It is thus not surprising that the number of compensation funds is growing rapidly. In Belgium and France, there is an abundance of compensation funds with

---

4 E. De Kezel, *Asbest, gezondheid en veiligheid. Ontwikkelingen in het aansprakelijkheidsrecht* (Intersentia 2013), pp. 511–515.

5 S. Macleod and C. Hodges, 'An introduction to the Schemes' in S. Macleod and C. Hodges (eds), *Redress Schemes for Personal Injuries* (Hart Publishing 2017), pp. 3–4.

6 L. Vanhooff, T. Vansweevelt and B. Weyts, 'So many funds, so many alternatives: compensation funds as a solution for liability issues in Belgium, the Netherlands and the United Kingdom' (2016) 3/4 EJCCL 41.

different functions. Meanwhile, New Zealand is at the extreme end of the spectrum in the realm of compensation funds. In Spain, compensation funds are still relatively unknown. In the United Kingdom (UK), the idea of compensation funds has been explored but there has been legislative reluctance to implement them. In between these extremes are countries such as the Netherlands and Germany that have a few funds but seem reluctant to go further in that direction. What is more, compensation funds also transcend borders: they have been created at the European Union (EU) level (e.g. the EU Solidarity Fund) and at the private and public international law level (e.g. International Oil Pollution Compensation Funds). The EU as well as the Council of Europe have a key role in the foundation of certain funds on a national level, such as Motor Insurance Bureaus of the different Member States[7] and Victim Compensation Funds.[8]

Compensation funds are growing, both on the national and on the international level, and more and more victims will come into contact with them as their importance increases. That is why it is important to know more about the way these funds operate and assess their merits and their flaws. The positive and negative traits of compensation funds is not self-evident, because there is a lot of variation within the general field of compensation funds. In fact, every single fund has its own characteristics, often dictated by the needs of a particular case. Despite their increasing number, little research has been conducted to their function, legality and nature. The countries in this book have been chosen because they portray different pictures of the role of compensation funds, which translates into a conceptual variety of approaches. The countries represent a mixture of jurisdictions:

- jurisdictions that are more (Belgium, France, New Zealand) and less (UK, Spain, the Netherlands, Germany) familiar with compensation funds;
- jurisdictions from the common law (UK, New Zealand) and civil law (Belgium, France, Germany, Spain, the Netherlands) traditions; and
- jurisdictions with a preference for structural (Belgium, France, Spain, New Zealand) and ad hoc (the Netherlands and the UK) compensation funds.

7 Second Council Directive 84/5/EEC on the approximation of the laws of the Member States relating to insurance against civil liability in respect of the use of motor vehicles [1983] OJ L8/17, art. 1(4).

8 European Convention on the Compensation of Victims of Violent Crimes [1983] <http://www.coe.int/en/web/conventions/full-list/-/conventions/rms/0900001680079751>.

The authors believe this colourful sampling can bring insights into both the versatility of compensation funds and into the difficulties of determining their proper doctrinal place in each jurisdiction. Whether compensation funds find a fertile soil in a legal system depends on the nature of funds as much as it depends of the particularities of the jurisdiction. The contrast between common and civil law jurisdictions is a giveaway yet this does not necessarily mean that compensation funds thrive equally in similar legal systems, as demonstrated by the contrast between Spain and France, for example. The unique New Zealand system also breaches the general reluctance of common law systems towards socially inspired compensation mechanisms.

More particularly, the contributions focus on the following aspects:

- The function of compensation funds: in which domains of disasters, accidents and wrongs can they be found?
- Their purpose and the motivation given for their establishment: for what reason was the creation of a compensation fund necessary?
- The funding of compensation funds.
- The level of compensation that victims can receive.

Apart from exploring these common focus points, the authors highlight important details about their jurisdiction that further clarify the position of compensation funds for the international legal reader. K. Watts gives an in-depth look into the past and the future of the New Zealand ACC Scheme and shows the limits of the system. L. Vanhooff and J. Knetsch add a more dogmatic take on compensation funds by searching for a precise definition and by analysing different types of compensation fund found in Belgium and France. J. Knetsch contrasts funds against social security and insurance, an approach which is typical of civil law jurisdictions. J. Knetsch and L. Vanhooff also question the legality of compensation funds vis à vis human rights. Fundamental issues concern access to the court, procedural safeguards of victims pursuing compensation before a compensation fund and equal treatment of victims. R.M. Garcia-Teruel includes other compensation mechanisms to give a more complete view of compensation law in Spain. This helps us understand the more limited role of compensation funds in Spain and the preference for using public aids and other instruments. K. Oliphant takes us behind existing laws and shows us several rejected proposals for new compensation funds in the UK, but also reflects on the possibilities of future funds that might be more successful.

M. Faure, T. Hartlief and G. Van Maanen offer a critical view on compensation law in the Netherlands, considering the advantages and disadvantages of tort and social security, and the merits of establishing compensation funds as well as other alternatives.

3. OBJECTIVES OF THIS BOOK AND SOME KEY IDEAS

What are the objectives of compensation funds and in what way do they differ from insurance and social security? And to what extent are compensation funds effective in realising these objectives? As compensating victims is one of the main tasks of funds, it is important to assess the relevant compensating procedures and to compare them to a civil court action and an efficient insurance claim structure. The objectives of each compensation fund are traditionally procedural clarity, accessibility and offering compensation to victims that would otherwise end up empty-handed if they had to rely on general compensation law. Or in other words, the most recurring issues that funds are meant to redress are the inefficiency, expense and unpredictability of a court procedure. The impossibility of an individual insuring him or herself against every kind of misfortune is also a motivation for the creation of compensation funds. Compensation funds are established to avoid situations where certain classes of victims will have to bear their own damages.

Even if compensation funds have a laudable goal of efficiently and equitably compensating victims, they are not beyond criticism. In Belgium for example, more and more decisions of the Medical Accidents Compensation Funds are contested in court.[9] One could also point out the difficulty of coordinating between the different legal doctrines and regulatory frameworks of tort law, private insurance, social security and compensation funds. The fund landscape lacks a clear direction which affects the coherence of the compensation system. Every fund has its own set of rules which leads to difficulty in ascertaining a proper overview of the development of compensation law. This could lead to a lack of awareness among the public about compensation funds as a redress mechanism.

---

[9] W. Buelens, *Het medisch ongeval zonder aansprakelijkheid* (Intersentia 2019), pp. 475–476.

Possible solutions for defogging compensation funds and their relationship with other compensation sources vary from creating a single window to a new, comprehensive compensation fund, as exists already in New Zealand. Each of the jurisdictions present adapted measures for simplifying or clustering (existing) compensation funds.

Another point of interest is the financial aspect of compensation funds and more specifically the question of who endows them or who should endow compensation funds: the government, the private sector or a combination of both. When the government subsidises a fund via direct government spending, the financial burden eventually lies with the taxpayer. The government can also intervene by redirecting social security income to a fund. In that case, the respective group of employers or employees bears the burden. In most cases, funds receive compensation from the government via government spending ('national solidarity') or a share from social security income.

This therefore begs the question of which model of solidarity we wish to pursue.[10] Do we prefer a system of pure national solidarity that is financed via all taxpayers (public spending) and that resembles the insurance model (contributions are paid by citizens that might not need to make an appeal to the fund), or are we proponents of a system that corresponds to the liability mechanism, where a specific group of the population contributes to the solidarity (based on the idea of repartition, 'the polluter pays')? Can lessons be learnt from jurisdictions such as New Zealand which operate a mixed private-public approach to funding?

Many questions, many ideas, but still too few answers. We hope that this book will be a useful contribution to legal scholars and practitioners in multiple jurisdictions who seek to better understand the nebulous world of compensation funds.

---

10 N.F. Van Manen, 'De paradox van individualisering en collectivisering' in N.F. Van Manen and R.H. Stutterheim (eds), *Wie draagt de schade? De allocatie van risico's in het recht* (Ars Aequi Libri 1998), pp. 95–98.

COMPENSATION FUNDS IN BELGIUM

Larissa VANHOOFF

1. INTRODUCTION

Belgian citizens who have suffered damage of any kind and who seek compensation would probably write to their insurer or the wrongdoers (if any). Additionally, they can receive supplementary compensation via social security (Belgian social security is very generous compared to certain other countries). Maybe they would even sue the liable person, if they deemed their chances real. However, not all of the abovementioned options are available at all times for victims. Sometimes the tortfeasor is irretrievable or insolvent. On other occasions, the damage has occurred without liability. Even when victims can rely on compensation from insurance, social security or the tort system, this compensation can be insufficient. However, this is not the end of the story. In a growing number of cases another compensation source is available for the victim: a compensation fund.

Indeed, next to the three 'classic' compensation sources (liability law, social security and insurance law) a fourth one is emerging: compensation funds. Recently created funds are proof of the legislature's trust in funds, which considers that funds offer more than a mere marginal solution to compensation issues.

More significantly, these funds represent a change in mentality. Citizens have become more reluctant to accept that they have to bear (the costs of) damage. To the contrary, they expect the Government to support them financially in one way or another. An example is the Fund for Medical Accidents. This fund intervenes (under certain conditions) when a medical accident has occurred without liability of the medical practitioner. In this situation, under the general rules of liability law, no damages can be received from the medical practitioner, which means that a victim would end up empty-handed. Instead, the Fund now grants the patient a certain level of compensation.

In other words, the adage 'the loss lies where it falls', referring to the rule that any person has to cover his or her own damage unless he or she can appoint a liable person, is slowly fading away.[1] Compensation funds seem to reverse this old rule by offering financial relief in situations where victims would otherwise have to bear their costs themselves.

Compensation funds are, together with no-fault liability systems and other no-fault compensation schemes part of the shift towards compensation.[2] Notwithstanding their increasing number and importance in Belgian compensation law, little research has been done towards the system of compensation funds.

That is why it is important to investigate these alternative compensation schemes more in-depth. This chapter introduces the reader to Belgian compensation funds by clarifying where they come from and how they work. In the last section the funds are assessed briefly by comparing their merits to their flaws. As a result, the reader will have a better view on these interesting constructions of law.

2. DEFINITION AND CLASSIFICATION OF COMPENSATION FUNDS

2.1. DEFINITION

Many legal bodies and structures in Belgium are known as a 'fund' but they each represent a different kind of fund. Therefore, defining a compensation fund is not clear-cut, yet necessary. In its most basic meaning, a fund is 'a sum of money saved or made available for a purpose'.[3] This encompasses investment funds, government budget, the Fund for Alimony Claims, purely private funds, as well as compensation funds.

What separates compensation funds from other funds such as investment funds is mainly their purpose. The purpose of compensation

1 T. Vansweevelt and B. Weyts, *Handboek buitencontractueel aansprakelijkheidsrecht* (Intersentia 2009), p. 25.

2 W.H. van Boom and M. Faure (eds), *Shifts in Compensation Between Private and Public Systems* (Springer-Verlag 2007).

3 *Little Oxford English Dictionary* (Oxford University Press 2006), °fund.

funds is compensating damage that has occurred in a specific circumstance, often described by law, irrespective of the presence of a wrongdoer.[4] As a rule, a body within the fund will assess the request of a victim autonomously, this means, without the influence of the legislative, the executive or the jurisdictional branch of power.

2.2. CATEGORIES OF COMPENSATION FUNDS

Traditionally, Belgian compensation funds are classified into four categories. The two most important categories are the guarantee funds and the 'damage'[5] funds.[6]

Guarantee funds intervene when a tortfeasor is un(der)insured yet identifiable or when an insurance company is no longer able or allowed to perform its duties (e.g. due to insolvency or non-compliance with financial regulations). Thus, there is always a link between liability insurance and a guarantee fund. Only in the case of liability of the wrongdoer does a guarantee fund come into play.

Damage funds intervene on a different level and more specifically in three scenarios: (1) when a tortfeasor is unidentifiable (e.g. hit-and-run cases); (2) when damage has occurred due to human interference but without liability (e.g. medical misfortune); and (3) when damage is caused by a force of nature (e.g. flooding).

The next types of funds are limitation and advance payment funds. They play a lesser role in Belgian national law. However, *limitation funds* are important in international maritime law. Worth mentioning are the oil pollution funds that have been created in order to compensate damage caused by oil spills from ships and rigs, like the Deepwater Horizon Oil Spill Trust Fund that was created after the disaster at the Deepwater Horizon drilling rig.[7]

Advance-payment funds live up to their name as they give a temporary relief to a victim that seeks compensation via court. When the victim's

---

4 J. Knetsch, *Le droit de la responsabilité et les fonds d'indemnisation* (L.G.D.J. 2013), p. 9.

5 This is a literal translation from the Dutch concept of 'schadefonds'. An English counterpart is absent.

6 E. de Kezel, *Asbest, gezondheid en veiligheid* (Intersentia 2013), p. 504.

7 C. McDonell, 'The Gulf Coast claims facility and the Deepwater Horizon litigation: judicial regulation of private compensation schemes' [2011] *Stanford Law Review* 765.

claim is ungrounded, the fund will recover the paid-out sum.[8] Belgium used to have one advance-payment fund, yet it has been dissolved.[9]

Despite this seemingly clear classification, the reader should be aware that some compensation funds have different objectives and that they can be categorised under multiple classes of funds.

3. BELGIAN COMPENSATION FUNDS

What follows is a short enumeration of Belgian's most important compensation funds. It covers the main tasks of each fund.

3.1. BELGIAN COMMON GUARANTEE FUND

The Belgian Common Guarantee Fund, formerly known as the Common Motor Guarantee Fund, was created in post-World War II Europe, parallel to the rise of motor vehicles – and hence traffic accidents.[10] Since 1989, car owners have been obliged to take out an insurance policy to cover their liability and that of their passengers and other drivers in case of an accident.[11] This insurance grants a direct action to the victim against the insurer. The purpose of this fund is to compensate victims that are so unfortunate as to find an un- or underinsured wrongdoer

---

8 H. Bocken, 'Rechtstreekse verzekeringen ten behoeve van derden en andere wisseloplossingen voor aansprakelijkheid en aansprakelijkheidsverzekering. Een typologie' in J. Rogge (ed.), *Liber amicorum René Van Gompel: studies in verzekeringen* (Story-Scientia 1998), p. 29; de Kezel, *Asbest, gezondheid en veiligheid*, above n. 6, pp. 504–505.

9 The advance payments fund for compensation of damage caused by water extraction, wet van 10 januari 1977 houdende regeling van de schadeloosstelling voor schade veroorzaakt door het winnen en het pompen van grondwater, BS 8 februari 1977 [Act of 10 January 1977 on the regulation of compensation for damage by extraction of water, *OB* 8 February 1977].

10 Article 16 wet van 1 juli 1956 betreffende de verplichte aansprakelijkheidsverzekering inzake motorrijtuigen, *BS* 15 juli 1956 [Act of 1 July 1956 on the compulsory liability insurance for motor vehicles, *OB* 15 July 1956]; Waarborgfonds Motorverkeer, *Jaarverslag 2014: 1965–2015: 50 jaar Waarborgfonds motorverkeer*, <http://www.wbf.nl/NL/Organisatie/Paginas/Jaarverslagen.aspx>, p. 6; J.L. Fagnart, 'Recherches sur le droit de la réparation' in J.L. Fagnart (ed.), *Mélanges Roger O. Dalcq* (Larcier 1994), p. 138.

11 I. Boone. 'Coördinatie van aansprakelijkheid en andere vergoedingssystemen' in *Aansprakelijkheid, aansprakelijkheidsverzekering en andere schadevergoedingssystemen, XXXIIIe Postuniversitaire cyclus Willy Delva* (Kluwer 2007), p. 632.

(e.g. in case of theft, which is not covered). It also intervenes when the insurance company goes bankrupt or does not comply with the financial regulations.[12] In these cases, the fund acts as a guarantee fund, hence the name. In two circumstances, however, the fund acts as a damage fund. Firstly, when an accident is caused by an unexpected event or 'act of God'. Secondly, when the tortfeasor is unidentifiable (and thus it is impossible to know their insurer).[13] An example of the first case is a sudden lightning strike that caused a car accident. An example of the second case is a typical hit-and-run accident.[14]

Eventually, the fund received additional tasks concerning the fourth Motor Vehicle Directive of the EU of 2000.[15]

In 2018, the Fund received 8,647 applications for damages (accidents on Belgian soil) and the total cost of the Fund in 2018 was €30,104,881.[16]

In 2014 the Motor Guarantee Fund changed its name to the Belgian Common Guarantee Fund as it received additional compensation duties.[17] More precisely, it plays an important role in the newly created compensation scheme for technological disasters.[18]

3.2. VICTIM COMPENSATION FUND

The Victim Compensation Fund, officially known as the Fund for Redress to Victims of Intentional Offences and to the Occasional Rescuers,

---

12 Article 19-1 *bis*, §1, °1, °2, °4 wet van 21 november 1989 betreffende de verplichte aansprakelijkheidsverzekering inzake motorrijtuigen, *BS* 8 december 1989 [Act of 21 November 1989 on compulsory motor vehicle liability insurance, *OB* 8 December 1989; further on: WAM-wet 1989 [*WAM*-Act 1989]].

13 Article 19-1 *bis*, §1, °3, °7 of the WAM-wet [*WAM*-Act 1989].

14 J. Andre-Dumont, P. Becue, C. De Voet, D. De Laminne De Bex, G. Hullebroeck, A. Junion, C. Schildermans, I. Sollie and P. Vandergeten, (eds), *Kluwer's verzekeringshandboek* (Kluwer *sine data*) *sine loco*.

15 Directive 2000/26/EC of the European Parliament and of the Council of 16 May 2000 on the approximation of the laws of the Member States relating to insurance against civil liability in respect of the use of motor vehicles and amending Council Directives 73/239/EEC and 88/357/EEC (Fourth motor insurance Directive), *Pb. L* 20 July 2000, p. 65.

16 Belgisch Gemeenschappelijk Waarborgfonds, *Jaarlijks verslag 2018*, <http://www.fcgb-bgwf.be/orki/view/8/jaarlijks-verslag.html>.

17 Belgisch Gemeenschappelijk Waarborgfonds, 'Jaarlijks verslag boekjaar 2013', <http://www.fcgb-bgwf.be/orki/view/8/jaarlijks-verslag.html>, p. 3; V. Callewaert, 'Le fonds commun de garantie belge, rapport belge' in GRERCA (ed.), *La socialisation de la reparation: fonds d'indemnisation et assurances* (Bruylant 2015), p. 51.

18 See further below section 3.7.

was created in 1985.[19] This fund gives an equitable compensation to victims of intentional crime and their rescuers to restore their financial situation, under certain conditions. One of these conditions is that it only intervenes as a matter of last resort when no other financial options are available or sufficient enough.[20] In the aftermath of the 23 March 2016 terrorist attacks on Brussels a special chamber was introduced to the fund that focuses on the terrorist attacks only.[21] Additionally, deviations from the general conditions of application were inserted by Royal Decree of 16 February 2017 and by the 2019 amendment of law.[22] It can be qualified as a damage fund as it compensates victims irrespective of the insurance of the wrongdoer.

3.3. ASBESTOS COMPENSATION FUND

The Asbestos Compensation Fund was created in 2006 in order to provide redress to the numerous victims of the lethal asbestos dust.[23] Between 1955 and 1960 the link between asbestos dust and several diseases and cancers (e.g. asbestosis, mesothelioma, lung cancer, pleural plaques) had already been scientifically established. Yet it was only in 2001 that a total ban on the use of the ominous dust was installed (notwithstanding

---

19 Wet van 1 augustus 1985 houdende fiscale en andere bepalingen, *BS* 6 augustus 1985 [Act of 1 August 1985 on fiscal and other matters, *OB* 6 August 1985], further Wet Slachtofferfonds [Victim Compensation Fund Act].

20 Article 31*bis* of the Wet Slachtofferfonds [Victim Compensation Fund Act]; N. Estienne, 'L'aide financière aux victimes d'infractions pénales en Belgique: le Fonds spécial d'aide aux victimes d'actes intentionnels de violence' in GRERCA (ed.), *La socialisation de la réparation: fonds d'indemnisation et assurances*, above n. 17, p. 84.

21 Article 30, §2, laatste lid of the Wet Slachtofferfonds [art. 30, §2, last paragraph of the Victim Compensation Fund Act].

22 Article 2 of the Koninklijk besluit van 16 februari 2017 houdende de uitvoering van artikel 42*bis* van de wet van 1 augustus 1985 houdende fiscale en andere bepalingen, wat de Hulp van de Staat aan de slachtoffers van terrorisme betreft, *BS* 3 maart 2017 [Royal Decree of 16 February 2017 concerning the execution of article 42*bis* of the Act of 1 August 1985 on fiscal and other matters, regarding the Aid of the State to victims of terrorism, *OB* 3 March 2017] and wet van 3 februari 2019 tot wijziging van de wet van 1 augustus 1985 houdende fiscale en andere bepalingen wat de bevoegdheden van de commissie voor financiële hulp aan slachtoffers van opzettelijke gewelddaden en aan de occasionele redders betreft inzake de slachtoffers van terrorisme, *BS* 8 februari 2019 [Act of 3 February 2019 amending the Act of 1 August 1985 on fiscal and other matters, regarding the Aid of the State to victims of terrorism, *OB* 8 February 2019].

23 E. de Kezel, *Asbest, gezondheid en veiligheid. Ontwikkelingen in het aansprakelijkheidsrecht*, (Intersentia 2013) pp. 527 ff.

intermediate small-scale prohibitions).[24] In the meantime, many construction workers and employees in asbestos factories were diagnosed with one of the abovementioned diseases. Citizens whose dwelling was located next to an asbestos factory were also often affected by the dust.

Victims of asbestosis disease (and pleural plaques[25]) and of mesothelioma (cancer) can apply to the fund for compensation.[26] As of 2019, victims of lung and larynx cancer are included to the list of eligible victims.[27] Victims of other diseases, although caused by asbestos dust, do not fall under the scope of this compensation scheme.[28] Instead they have to turn to the court and point out the liable person, which is not an easy enterprise. Chances of success are small, given the very long incubation period of asbestos diseases (up to 20 or even 40 years) and the difficulty of finding the liable person (e.g. a company that went bankrupt, causality issues when the victim has worked for several employers).[29] To date, only one case has been handled by the courts in Belgium. In the *Eternit* case (named after the asbestos factory) the judge was generous to the victims and allowed them compensation, whereas a strict interpretation of the time bar would probably not have allowed for the victims to bring their claim before court.[30] Recently, the Court of Appeal has confirmed this judgment but has diminished the compensation of the victim drastically (€24,820 instead of €250,000).[31]

---

24 AFA, *Het Asbestfonds, 5-jarig bestaan (2007–2012)*, <http://www.afa.fgov.be/pdf/Verslag%205%20jaar%20AFA.pdf>, pp. 11–12; KB van 3 februari 1998, *BS* 21 februari 1998, 4905; KB 23 oktober 2001, *BS* 30 november 2001, 41157.

25 Article 1 of the koninklijk besluit van 11 mei ter uitvoering van hoofdstuk VI, van titel IV, van de programmawet (I) van 27 december 2006 tot oprichting van een Schadeloosstellingfonds voor asbestslachtoffers, *BS* 29 mei 2007.

26 Article 118 of the Programmawet (I) van 27 december 2006, *BS* 28 december 2006 [art. 118 of the Finance Act (I) of 27 December 2006, *OB* 28 December 2006].

27 Wet van 5 mei 2019 tot verbetering van de schadeloosstelling voor asbestslachtoffers, *BS* 22 mei 2019 [Act of 5 May 2019 improving the compensation of asbestos victims, *OB* 22 May 2019]; T. Santens, 'Slachtoffers van asbest krijgen makkelijker vergoeding, maar kritiek op regeling houdt aan' (<https://www.vrt.be/vrtnws/nl/2019/04/03/wetsvoorstel-asbestfonds/>).

28 E. de Kezel, 'Asbestfonds "immuniseert" voormalige asbestwerkgevers' [2007] 5 December 2007 *De Juristenkrant* 8.

29 AFA, *Het Asbestfonds, 5-jarig bestaan (2007–2012)*, <http://www.afa.fgov.be/pdf/Verslag%205%20jaar%20AFA.pdf>, p. 19.

30 Rb. Brussel 28 november 2011, *RABG* 2012,1064; *Juristenkrant* 7 december 2011 (weergave E. de Kezel), p. 3; E. de Kezel, 'Eerste asbestvonnis: moeilijke verjaringshorde gepasseerd' [2011] 7 December 2011 *Juristenkrant* 3.

31 E. de Kezel, 'Hof van beroep bevestigt veroordeling asbestproducent Eternit' [2017] 5 April 2017 *Juristenkrant* 2–3.

However, it is too early to deduce any position of the courts from one single judgment.

This damage fund grants a fixed sum to eligible victims.

3.4. FUND FOR MEDICAL ACCIDENTS[32]

The Fund for Medical Accidents was created in 2010, after a failed attempt to create a further-reaching no-fault compensation scheme in 2007. In that first version of the law (the law already passed the preparatory stage but was never enforced) the road to court would have been replaced by a fund structure. Victims would be more certain about their right to compensation, yet the amount would be limited to a fixed sum (instead of the current full compensation).[33]

The scope of the current fund is more limited than that of its predecessor. Nevertheless, *in globo* it reaches further than most other funds. In short, it compensates damage occurred in the medical sector broadly speaking (e.g. hospitals, general practitioner, abortion clinic).[34] Only two medical practices are excluded from the scope of this law: medical experiments and cosmetic surgery.[35] It acts both as a guarantee fund and as a damage fund.

As a guarantee fund, it intervenes when the medical practitioner's liability is un- or underinsured. It also compensates a patient when the insurer denies its client's liability, or when the insurer agrees on

---

32 For an extensive analysis of the conditions of this fund, the reader can consult the doctoral thesis of W. Buelens, *Het medisch ongeval zonder aansprakelijkheid* (Universitas Cursusdienst 2018).

33 Wet van 15 mei 2007 betreffende de vergoeding van schade als gevolg van gezondheidszorg, *BS* 6 juli 2007 [Act of 15 May 2007 on compensation of damage caused by health care, *OB* 6 July 2007]; T. Vansweevelt, 'De wet medische ongevallen: de krachtlijnen, de filosofie en het toepassingsgebied' in I. Boone and S. Lierman (eds), *Vergoeding van slachtoffers van medische ongevallen* (Intersentia 2011), p. 11.

34 Article 3 of the Wet van 31 maart 2010 betreffende de vergoeding van schade als gevolg van gezondheidszorg, *BS* 2 april 2010 [Act of 31 March 2010 on the compensation of damage resulting from health care, *OB* 2 April 2010], further: Wet Medische Ongevallen [Medical Accidents Act]; S. Lierman, 'Vergoedingsvoorwaarden voor het Fonds voor Medische Ongevallen' in Boone and Lierman (eds), *Vergoeding van slachtoffers van medische ongevallen*, above n. 33, pp. 1586–1588.

35 T. Vansweevelt, 'Hoofdstuk XI' in T. Vansweevelt and F. Dewallens (eds), *Handboek gezondheidsrecht. Volume I. Zorgverleners: statuut en aansprakelijkheid* (Intersentia 2014), pp. 1588–1591.

the determination of liability but makes a financial proposition that is insufficient according to the Fund to cover the damage.[36]

As a damage fund it helps patients who were inflicted with damage by an act of a medical practitioner that was caused by sheer medical misfortune. This is called a medical accident without liability, abbreviated to *moza* in Dutch (*medisch ongeval zonder aansprakelijkheid*).[37] However, a patient cannot ask for compensation for any size of injury. Instead, the conditions for a *moza* are rather strict: the damage has to be severe (25% permanent invalidity, six months of temporary disability, causing severe impact on the victim's way of life, including an economic impact, or death).[38] Victims receive full compensation.[39]

3.5. FEDERAL AGENCY FOR OCCUPATIONAL RISKS *FEDRIS*

Fedris is a recently created umbrella organisation that coordinates two former occupational-risks-related compensation funds, namely the Workmen's Occupational Accidents Fund and the Workmen's Occupational Diseases Fund.[40] Although both funds have merged, and the Workmen's Occupational Diseases Fund has accordingly dissolved, their respective functions and financial structure remain unchanged.

The former Workmen's Occupational Accidents fund, a guarantee fund, was the oldest fund in Belgium, making its first appearance as the '*Steun- en Voorzorgskas*' (the Support and Prevention Fund) in 1890.[41] Today, victims of occupational accidents can rely on *Fedris* in its function of occupational accidents fund for fall-back aid. Employers are obliged to take out insurance for their employees. If they fail to do so, or in the event the insurance does not comply with its own duty, victim-employees can address the fund for compensation.[42]

---

36 Article 4, °2–4 of the Wet Medische Ongevallen [Act on Medical Accidents].

37 Article 4, °1 of the Wet Medische Ongevallen [Act on Medical Accidents].

38 Article 5 of the Wet Medische Ongevallen [Act on Medical Accidents].

39 Article 4 of the Wet Medische Ongevallen [Act on Medical Accidents].

40 Wet van 16 augustus 2016 met betrekking tot de fusie van het fonds voor arbeidsongevallen en het fonds voor de beroepsziekten, *BS* 5 september 2016 [Act of 16 August 2016 on the fusion of the Workmen's Occupational Accidents Fund and the Workmen's Occupational Diseases Fund, *OB* 5 September 2016].

41 Wet van 21 juli 1890, *BS* 22–23 juli 1890.

42 Article 58, §1, 3°of the Arbeidsongevallenwet [art. 58, §1, 3° of the Occupational Accidents Act]; U. Deprez, 'Honderd jaar geschiedenis: van Steun -en Voorzorgkas tot Fonds voor Arbeidsongevallen' [1990] BTSZ 372.

In its role as Occupational Diseases Fund, *Fedris* compensates victims of occupational diseases according to the rules laid down in the Occupational Diseases Act.[43] In fact, this is not characteristic of an actual compensation fund, for its objectives can instead be described as offering an insurance, albeit publicly organised. Indeed, the fund offers primary compensation to the victims of occupational diseases.[44]

Apart from that, the fund has other tasks that are typical for an organ of social security. To name a few: it is the insurer of sailors; it authenticates agreements between the victim of an occupational accident, the insurer and the attending physician; it controls compliance with social law and it takes prevention measures.[45]

3.6. DISASTER FUND

With regular appearances in the media, the Disaster Fund is probably the most well-known fund among the general public. Its two main objectives are to compensate damage to individuals and agricultural damage caused by natural disasters. For example, the Flemish government announced that victims of the heavy rainfalls of 23 July 2016 could submit their file at their local town government.[46]

Formerly the fund was the primary compensation source. However, its role has diminished since the laws of 2003 and 2005. Fire insurance now mandatorily includes insurance against flooding, earthquake and other disaster-related hazards.[47] Yet fire insurance is not a mandatory

43 See for example art. 33 of the Occupational Diseases Act.

44 J. Van Langendonck, *Handboek Socialezekerheidsrecht* (Intersentia 2011), p. 368.

45 Article 58, §1, 1°, 9°, 11° and 13° of the Arbeidsongevallenwet 1971 and Wetten van 3 juni 1970 betreffende de preventie van beroepsziekten en de vergoeding van de schade die uit die ziekten voortvloeit, *BS* 27 August 1970, 8721, *err. BS* 18 September 1970.

46 S. Van Ginneken, 'Het Rampenfonds zit niet in geldnood', *De Standaard* 25 July 2016; <https://overheid.vlaanderen.be/rampenfonds#nieuws>.

47 Wet van 21 mei 2003 tot wijziging van de wet van 25 juni 1992 op de landverzekeringsovereenkomst en de wet van 12 juli 1976 betreffende het herstel van zekere schade veroorzaakt aan private goederen door natuurrampen, *BS* 15 juli 2003 [Act of 21 May 2003 amending the Act of 25 June 1992 on land insurance and the Act of 12 July 1976 on the compensation of certain damage on private property caused by natural disasters, *OB* 15 July 2003]; wet van 17 september 2005 tot wijziging wat de verzekering tegen natuurrampen betreft, van de wet van 25 juni 1992 op de landverzekeringsovereenkomst en de wet van 12 juli 1976 betreffende het herstel van zekere schade veroorzaakt aan private goederen door natuurrampen, *BS* 11 oktober 2005 [Act of 17 September 2005 amending the Act of 25 June 1992 on

insurance itself.[48] Consequently, the fund will only intervene to the extent that the fire insurer does not cover the damage.[49] The fund also has tasks typical of a guarantee fund, being intervening when the fire insurer does not comply with financial regulations and when he becomes insolvent.[50]

The reader should keep in mind that the sixth constitutional reform act has regionalised the former Disaster Fund. This means that since 1 July 2014, the Flemish, the Walloon and the Brussels-Capital region each have their own Disaster Fund.[51] The National Disaster Fund is now abolished.

3.7. 'FUND' FOR TECHNOLOGICAL ACCIDENTS

Technological advancement does not only bring prosperity, it creates a whole new range of risks as well. Sometimes these risks result in catastrophes like the explosion of a gas installation at Gellingen (Belgium) in 2004. This disaster was the immediate incentive to create an alternative compensation scheme – the fund-based mechanism for technological accidents.[52] Contrary to the foregoing schemes, this

land insurance and the act of 12 July 1976 on the compensation of certain damage on private property caused by natural disasters, with regard to the insurance of natural disasters, *OB* 11 October 2005]; I. Durant, 'Belgium' in M. Faure and T. Hartlief (eds), *Financial Compensation for Victims of Catastrophes, a Comparative Legal Approach* (Springer 2006), p. 66; M. Faure, 'Vergoeding voor natuurrampen in Frankrijk, Nederland en België' in I. Boone, I. Claeys and L. Lavrysen (eds), *Liber Amicorum Hubert Bocken. Dare La Luce* (die Keure 2009), p. 343.

48 Faure, 'Vergoeding voor natuurrampen in Frankrijk, Nederland en België', above n. 47, p. 344.

49 Faure, 'Vergoeding voor natuurrampen in Frankrijk, Nederland en België', above n. 47, p. 344; 'Natuurrampen-Het Rampenfonds', <https://overheid.vlaanderen.be/komt-mijn-schade-in-aanmerking>.

50 Article 34-2 of the wet van 12 juli 1976 betreffende het herstel van zekere schade veroorzaakt aan private goederen door natuurrampen *BS* 13 August 1976 [Act of 12 July 1976 on the compensation of certain damage on private property caused by natural disasters, *OB* 13 August 1976].

51 Wet van 6 januari 2014 met betrekking tot de zesde staatshervorming, *BS* 31 januari 2014 [Act of 6 January 2014 on the sixth Constitutional Reform, *BS* 31 January 2014]; L. Lavrysen, 'De "zesde staatshervorming" en de milieubescherming' [2014] TMR 280. The reader can find the links to their respective online portals at: <https://www.belgium.be/fr/logement/problemes_de_logement/catastrophes_naturelles/fonds_de_calamites>.

52 L. Lemmens, 'Slachtoffers technologische ramp binnenkort vergoed', <http://www.jura.be>, p. 3; wet van 13 november 2011 betreffende de vergoeding van de lichamelijke

mechanism functions through both the Belgian Common Guarantee Fund and the Belgian State. The Belgian Common Guarantee Fund intervenes when neither social security, nor the liability insurer of the tortfeasor, the exploiter or owner of the technological construction that caused harm, can pay out to the victims.[53] In case the Belgian Common Guarantee Fund steps in and pays the victim, it will turn to the wrongdoer for recourse afterwards. If it is impossible to determine responsibility, the Belgian Common Guarantee Fund can, on its turn, recover its expenses from the Belgian State.[54] Why the legislature has chosen this rather complicated structure remains vague. According to the preparatory works the lawmaker considered the Belgian Common Guarantee Fund competent for this kind of damage where a liable person is irretrievable or insolvent.[55] Whilst that might be true, one can ponder about any similarity between car accidents and large-scale technological accidents, e.g. gas explosions.

3.8. FUND FOR ENVIRONMENT AND NATURE

Unlike the other funds, the main objective of the Fund for Nature and Environment is not compensatory. Instead, the main focus of the fund is environmental policy as it is the watchdog of environmental regulation (e.g. imposing penalties).[56]

---

en morele schade ingevolge een technologisch ongeval, *BS* 24 February 2012, p.1267; wetsvoorstel (M.-C. Marghem) betreffende de schadeloosstelling van lichamelijke en geestelijke letsels ingevolge een technologisch ongeval. Verslag.,, *Parl. St.* Kamer 2010–2011, nr. 1286/011, 4; K. Bernauw, 'De vergoeding van schade door technologische rampen' [2013] T. Verz. 135.

53 L. Lemmens, 'Slachtoffers technologische ramp binnenkort vergoed', above n. 52, p. 2.

54 Article 18 of the Wet van 13 november 2011 betreffende de vergoeding van de lichamelijke en morele schade ingevolge een technologisch ongeval, *BS* 24 februari 2012 (ed. 2) [Act of 13 November 2011 on the compensation of physical and moral damage caused by a technological accident, *OB* 24 February 2012 (ed. 2); further: Wet Technologische Ongevallen [Technological Accidents Act].

55 Wetsvoorstel (M.-C. Marghem) betreffende de schadeloosstelling van lichamelijke en geestelijke letsels ingevolge een technologisch ongeval. Verslag., *Parl. St.* Kamer 2010–2011, nr. 1286/011, 5.

56 Article 4 of the decreet van 23 januari 1991 tot oprichting van het Fonds voor preventie en sanering inzake leefmilieu en natuur als gewestdienst met afzonderlijk beheer, *BS* 2 februari 1991 [art. 4 of the Decree of 23 January 1991 on the establishment of a Fund for prevention and restructuring of the natural environment and nature as a Regional service with separate administration, *OB* 2 February 1991].

Adjacent to these tasks, it compensates wildlife-related damage as a damage fund. Wildlife (e.g. game and protected species) has per definition no owner or user.[57] When these animals cause damage, no one can be held responsible. As regards damage by game, a special no-fault liability was created in order to avoid a situation where the victim remains uncompensated. According to this specific rule, the owner of the right to hunt will be held liable for damage caused by game on his or her territory.[58] This keeper of the game right will be responsible for 'serious damage' caused by the animal.[59] Yet in some cases, the keeper of the hunting right is not liable, e.g. when that particular species of wild animal was not hunted after the year the damage was caused. In that specific case, the victim can go to the Fund for Environment and Nature for compensation.[60]

As regards protected species, the Flemish government deemed it unfair that citizens, who are not allowed to kill those animals, would have to bear the damage. For that reason, victims can address the fund.[61]

4. ORIGINS OF COMPENSATION FUNDS: WHY WERE THEY CREATED?

4.1. DEFICIENCIES OF LIABILITY LAW AND INSURANCE

The creation of an additional compensation source marks the deficit of the pre-existing compensation sources. Indeed, the preparatory works of most funds reveal that a general feeling of dissatisfaction surrounds the classic compensation sources, especially tort law.

This dissatisfaction is often expressed towards procedural burdens that are intrinsic to classic fault-based liability. Perceived as one of the

57 Vansweevelt and Weyts, *Handboek buitencontractueel aansprakelijkheidsrecht*, above n. 1, p. 556.

58 Ibid, p. 559.

59 Article 24, eerste lid of the Jachtdecreet van 24 juli 1991, *BS* 7 September 1991, 19584; Fagnart, 'Recherches sur le droit de la réparation', above n. 10, p. 147.

60 Article 25 of the Jachtdecreet van 24 juli 1991, *BS* 7 september 1991 [art. 25 of the Hunting Decree of 24 July 1991, *OB* 7 September 1991].

61 Article 52 of the Jachtdecreet van 24 juli 1991, *BS* 7 september 1991 [art. 25 of the Hunting Decree of 24 July 1991, *OB* 7 September 1991]; Voorstel van Jachtdecreet. Verslag namens de Commissie voor Leefmilieu en Natuurbehoud (M. Capoen), *Parl. St.* Vl. Parl. 1990–1991, nr. 481/10, 36.

most burdensome requirements is the need to prove a nexus between the damage and the liable person. This can turn out to be problematic when multiple possible tortfeasors concur, the so-called problem of alternative causation. A good example is asbestos cases where employees have worked in different asbestos factories over the years. It is almost impossible to point out in which factory the asbestos dust affected the victim's body first.[62]

Victims of asbestos-related diseases face another issue: prescription law. Due to the long incubation period (20–40 years for asbestosis and mesothelioma) their action in tort will often be time-barred because the prescription period is limited to five or 20 years (depending on the calculation).[63]

Another problem that victims who seek damages via court can encounter is the determination of liability. Due to either the complete absence of a liable party, or the irretrievability of such party, victims cannot claim damages in the ordinary way. An example of the first case is medical misfortune. An example of the second case is hit-and-run accidents.

Insolvency of the responsible party or their insurer is yet another situation where liability law falls short in guaranteeing (full) compensation to victims.[64]

Liability insurance cannot cope properly with these issues either. Indeed, when, for example, a tortfeasor is unidentifiable, it is not possible to know his or her insurer.

It is exactly those deficiencies and procedural hurdles that compensation funds hope to redress.[65] Funds should also redress the procedural downfalls of a court action such as the costliness, slowness (although

---

62 Vansweevelt and Weyts, *Handboek buitencontractueel aansprakelijkheidsrecht*, above n. 1, pp. 817–819.

63 Article 2262*bis*, §1, 3rd paragraph of the Burgerlijk Wetboek [Civil Code].

64 T. Hartlief, *Anno 2010. Beschouwingen over aansprakelijkheid en verzekering* (deLex 2009), pp. 88, 94–95 and 97–98.

65 T. Hartlief, 'Heeft het aansprakelijkheidsrecht (de) toekomst?' in P. Taelman et al (eds), *Aansprakelijkheid, aansprakelijkheidsverzekering en andere schadevergoedingssystemen 2006–2007* (Kluwer 2007), pp. 851 and (2009), pp. 88, 94–95, 97–98; J.F. Leclercq and D. De Roy, 'Quelques observations sur l'intervention de l'etat dans la reparation de certains prejudices' in J. Rogge (ed.), *Liber Amicorum Jean-Luc Fagnart* (Anthemis 2008), pp. 577–578; H. Bocken, 'Rechtstreekse verzekeringen ten behoeve van derden en andere wisseloplossingen voor aansprakelijkheid en aansprakelijkheidsverzekering. Een typologie' in J. Rogge (ed.), *Liber amicorum René Van Gompel: studies in verzekeringen* (Story-Scientia 1998), pp. 27–28.

some funds themselves deal with delays) and the inimical atmosphere between parties.[66]

4.2. GROWING NATIONAL SOLIDARITY

Underneath the first reason of creation lies a policy-based and moral explanation. Indeed, the question of whether or not to help victims who fall outside the scope of a certain act remains an ethical and political one. The creation of funds shows us that the legislature does not agree with the old principle that the loss lies where it falls. To the contrary, a new sentiment emerges, that of so-called national solidarity. The legislature expresses concern with victims of certain disasters and states that the community as a whole should support them (financially).[67] For example, the preparatory works of the Belgian Common Guarantee Fund mention that the fund aims to give victims as certain level of compensation as fast and as completely as possible.[68] It is in the light of this national solidarity that the government decided to compensate the victims of the Belgian *Softenon* crisis.[69] The drug thalidomide (launched under its commercial name *Softenon*) lessened morning sickness of pregnant women. Sadly enough, it had a grave side effect – malformation of the foetus. Surviving babies, once adult, demanded some sort of

---

66 T. Hartlief, 'De meerwaarde van het aansprakelijkheidsrecht' in T. Hartlief and S. Klosse (eds), *Einde van het aansprakelijkheidsrecht?* (Boom Juridische Uitgevers 2003), p. 25; P.S. Atiyah, *The Damages Lottery* (Hart Publishing 1997), pp. 143–154.

67 Belgian Common Guarantee Fund: wetsontwerp betreffende de verplichte aansprakelijkheidsverzekering in zake motorrijtuigen, *Parl. St.* Kamer 1955–1956, nr. 351/004, 2–3; Victim Compensation Fund: wetsontwerp (M. Barzin) houdende fiscale en andere bepalingen (arts 25 to 43 and 93). Verslag namens de commissie voor de justitie, *Parl. St.* Kamer 1984–1985, nr. 1281/016, 5; Asbestos Compensation Fund: wetsvoorstel (M. Gerkens et al) tot oprichting van een Schadeloosstellingsfonds voor asbestslachtoffers, *Parl. St.* Kamer 2005–2006, nr. 2602/001, 3; Fund for Medical Accidents: Wetsontwerp betreffende de vergoeding van schade als gevolg van gezondheidszorg (I), *Parl. St.* Kamer 2009–2010, nr. 2240/006, 4; Fund for Technological Accidents: wetsvoorstel (M.-C. Marghem) betreffende de schadeloosstelling van lichamelijke en geestelijke letsels ingevolge een technologisch ongeval. Verslag., *Parl. St.* Kamer 2010–2011, nr. 1286/011, 4.

68 Wetsontwerp betreffende de verplichte aansprakelijkheidsverzekering in zake motorrijtuigen, *Parl. St.* Kamer 1955–1956, nr. 351/004, 2–3.

69 See also the current discussions 'il est temps de reconnaître la situation spécifique des victimes du Softenon …', Question de Mme C. Fonck in Integraal Verslag van 1 maart 2018 namiddag, *Parl. St.* Kamer, 2017–2018, plen. 216 [question of Ms C. Fonck in Integral Report of 1 March 2018, afternoon, *Parl. Disc.* Chamber 2017–2018, plen. 216].

compensation from the government. They were promised financial aid, for the purpose of which the government would set up a compensation fund. Due to a change in government, however, this fund was never established. The victims facing this impasse continued their pursuit for compensation in court. In February 2018, the Brussels Court of Appeal ordered the current government to uphold the promise of the former government and present a Bill of law in the Chamber of Representatives in order to create this fund,[70] a rather remarkable decision.[71] This led to the Act of 5 May 2019 granting a one-off compensation for the *Softenon*-babies.[72] This solution is based on direct government payment and does not involve the creation of a genuine compensation fund.

4.3. 'HISTORICAL RESPONSIBILITY'

Sometimes disasters and accidents are (additionally) the result of a lack of intervention by the State. This is the case with asbestos-related diseases. As explained above, the legislature only fully banned asbestos in 2001. Earlier legal measures in 1978, 1986 and 1998 came too late to avoid the harmful effects that had already entered into effect years before. As a way to apologise for this late intervention,[73] the government created a damage fund. It literally refers to its own historical responsibility for the damage.[74] The Bill of law on the Fund for Technological Accidents makes a reference to historical responsibility as well. Indeed, it is the government that allows factories and other dangerous infrastructures to be exploited by granting owners permission.[75] In the author's opinion,

70 Court of Appeal of Brussels 22 February 2018, unpublished, *De Juristenkrant* 28 March 2018, nr. 366, 1 and 6 (reproduction C. Borucki, F. Auvray, P. Gillaerts and I. Samoy).

71 C. Borucki, F. Auvray, P. Gillaerts and I. Samoy, 'Softenon: (eenzijdige) regeringsbelofte maakt schuld', *De Juristenkrant* 28 March 2018, nr. 366, 1 and 6 (annot. Court of Appeal Brussels 22 February 2018).

72 Wet van 5 mei 2019 betreffende de toekenning van een forfaitaire bedrag ana de personen die lijden aan aangeboren misvormingen die het gevolg zijn van het innemen van geneesmiddelen met thalidomide door de moeder tijdens de zwangerschap, *BS* 16 mei 2019 [Act of 5 May 2019 granting a one-off compensation to people suffering from congenital misformations caused by pregnant mothers ingesting medication containing thalidomide, *OB* 16 May 2019].

73 However, without admitting responsibility.

74 Wetsvoorstel tot oprichting van een Fonds voor de asbestslachtoffers, *Parl. St.* Kamer 2003–2004, nr. 1244/001, 4 en 11; wetsvoorstel asbestfonds 2006, 3.

75 Wetsvoorstel (M.-C. Marghem) betreffende de schadeloosstelling van lichamelijke en geestelijke letsels ingevolge een technologisch ongeval. Verslag., *Parl. St.* Kamer 2010–2011, nr. 1286/011, 5.

the same reasoning can be applied to the Fund for Environment and Nature when it compensates damage caused by protected animals, even though this is not expressly mentioned in the preparatory works. Since citizens are not free to eliminate these animals themselves, they cannot avoid the damage they cause, owing to the government's (Belgian and European) decision to protect these animals.[76]

4.4. PRESSURE FROM PUBLIC OPINION

Unfortunately, in some cases a less thoughtful reason lies behind the creation of funds. Mostly, this happens when a disaster has stirred up a popular proclamation that the legislature should take action in favour of the victims. A clear example is the Asbestos Compensation Fund. An action group (ABEVA, *Belgische Vereniging voor Asbestslachtoffers*, Belgian Association for Asbestos Victims) has most likely exerted its pressure to convince the legislature to create the said fund.[77] The same can be said regarding the Fund for Technological Accidents that was created after the gas explosion in Gellingen. This case-by-case approach leads to an incoherent approach as illustrated below.

4.5. EUROPEAN AND INTERNATIONAL INFLUENCES

Lastly and equally important, European and international legislation have instigated the creation of certain funds. Namely the Workmen's Occupational Diseases Fund,[78] the Belgian Common Guarantee Fund[79] and the Victim Compensation Fund[80] have their roots in European

[76] Voorstel van Jachtdecreet. Verslag namens de Commissie voor Leefmilieu en Natuurbehoud (M. Capoen), *Parl. St.* Vl. Parl. 1990–1991, nr. 481/10, 36.

[77] See <http://www.kanker.be/pati-ntenhulp/pati-ntenorganisaties/asbest>.

[78] General Conference of the International Labour Organisation, Convention nr. 18 of 10 June 1925 concerning Workmen's Compensation for Occupational Diseases, <https://www.ilo.org/dyn/normlex/en/f?p=NORMLEXPUB:12100:0::NO::P12100_ILO_CODE:C018>.

[79] Article 1, fourth section second Council Directive 84/5/EEC of 30 December 1983 on the approximation of the laws of the Member States relating to insurance against civil liability in respect of the use of motor vehicles, *Pb.L.* 11 January 1984, afl.8, 17.

[80] European Convention of 24 November 1983 on the Compensation of Victims of Violent Crimes, <http://www.coe.int/en/web/conventions/full-list/-/conventions/rms/0900001680079751>.

and international organisations. This is an interesting fact: will the international and European level, especially the EU, advance on this course? Some authors suggest so as they point at European activity in this field.[81] Indeed, the EU harbours a compensation fund of its own, the EU Solidarity Fund. This fund shares its main features with the Belgian Disaster Fund: Member States that have suffered from major (natural) disasters can apply for compensation.[82]

5. KEY FEATURES OF BELGIAN COMPENSATION FUNDS

In this chapter the main features of Belgian compensation funds are set out. Compensation funds show many variations, yet they can be classified in relation to certain characteristics that they share.

5.1. NATURE OF INTERVENTION

'Nature of intervention' refers to the relation of funds to liability law and other compensation sources. Some funds take precedence over other compensation sources and are thus dominant. Other funds are rather subordinate to the classic compensation sources. Funds can intervene in four possible ways.

The first group of funds are *subsidiary*. Typically, these are the guarantee funds, for they only intervene when liability (insurance) fails its compensation objective. In other words, a victim should first try to address the liability insurer of the wrongdoer. If successful, the compensation fund will not come into play.

Representatives of this group are the Belgian Common Guarantee Fund, the Fund for Medical Accidents and *Fedris* (as Workmen's Occupational Accidents Fund). This list is not confined to guarantee funds as two damage funds also make the list. These are the

81 L. Lacroix, 'Installations dangereuses, catastrophes technologiques et indemnisation: un comparatif franco-belge (prétexte pour un plaidoyer européen)' [2013] Riseo nr. 1, 41.

82 Council Regulation (EC) No 2012/2002 of 11 November 2002 establishing the European Union Solidarity Fund, Pb.L. 311, 14 November 2002, 3; European Commission, 'EU disaster support to be faster and simpler', panorama inforegio 2013, nr. 47, 4–5; <https://eur-lex.europa.eu/legal-content/EN/TXT/?uri=celex%3A32002R2012>.

Victim Compensation Fund and the Flemish Disaster Fund. The Victim Compensation Fund only redresses a victim when no other compensation source is available. These sources must be interpreted broadly and contain court action, insurance and social security payments as well as other payment schemes. For example, when possible, victims are required to bring a personal action before court as civil plaintiff.[83] The Flemish Disaster Fund is a subsidiary fund because victims should first try to get compensation from their fire insurer. When the victim fails to take out an insurance policy the Flemish Fund does not even intervene.[84]

Second are the funds that act as a *safety net* in so far that they will help victims when normally no other compensation source is available and especially in the absence of liability. The Fund for Medical Accidents and the Fund for Environment and Nature are part of this group. The Fund for Medical Accidents falls under this category when it compensates the so-called 'moza', the medical accident without liability. One of the conditions to receive compensation is indeed absence of liability.[85] Yet victims can access the fund at any time, also when their healthcare practitioner is liable. Whenever the Fund supposes that liability is in play, it takes a mediating role. Together with the supposedly liable person and his insurer, the fund will draft a compensation proposal.[86] In other words, from the moment that the fund has determined liability, the fund procedure does not end. In case of liability a victim can choose between the fund method or the court method. Victims can even change course during the handling of the claim.[87] This double option system is called the 'double-trail system' in literature.[88]

83 Article 31*bis* of the Wet Slachtofferfonds [Victim Compensation Fund Act]; N. Estienne, 'L'aide financière aux victimes d'infractions pénales en Belgique: le Fonds spécial d'aide aux victimes d'actes intentionnels de violence' in GRERCA (ed.), *La socialisation de la réparation: fonds d'indemnisation et assurance*, above n. 17, p. 84; Andre-Dumont, Becue, De Voet, De Laminne De Bex, Hullebroeck, Junion, Schildermans, Sollie and Vandergeten (eds), *Kluwer's verzekeringshandboek*, above n. 14, p. 152.

84 Faure, 'Vergoeding voor natuurrampen in Frankrijk, Nederland en België', above n. 47, p. 345.

85 Article 4 of the Wet Medische Ongevallen [Medical Accidents Act].

86 Article 8, §1, 1° and 4° of the Wet Medische Ongevallen [Medical Accidents Act].

87 I. Boone, 'De verhouding tussen het aansprakelijkheidsrecht en de vergoeding door het fonds voor medische ongevallen' in Boone and Lierman (eds), *Vergoeding van slachtoffers van medische ongevallen*, above n. 33, pp. 68–69.

88 Vansweevelt, 'De wet medische ongevallen: de krachtlijnen, de filosofie en het toepassingsgebied', above n. 33, p. 13.

Regarding the nature of intervention of the Fund for Environment and Nature, the law is not so clear. For damage caused both by game and by protected animal species, the fund will only intervene in the absence of liability, although this is not expressly mentioned. Damage caused by an animal that was not hunted after in the year of the damage, animals that live in a sanctuary[89] and protected animals that no one is allowed to shoot or eliminate otherwise, are all examples of faultless damage for which the holder of the hunting right is not accountable. From this list one deduces that the fund only intervenes in case of absence of liability.

Other compensation funds go a step further and offer a genuine *alternative* for liability law. The Asbestos Compensation Fund is a good example of this type of funds. Irrespective of the cause of the asbestos-related disease (responsibility or not) and irrespective of whether he or she can appoint the liable person or not, the victim can access the fund. Even in case of liability, a victim can still choose between suing that person before the court or applying for fund compensation (in contrast to subsidiary funds that give priority to other compensation sources). Yet victims should beware of one major restriction: when they choose the fund procedure first, they are no longer allowed to go to court (e.g. for additional compensation). Conversely, they are allowed to go to court first and ask for (complementary) compensation at the fund afterwards.[90] The exclusion of the court procedure is typical for Belgium and must be understood in the context of the so-called 'historical compromise' lasting from the early twentieth century. It has its origins in the Workmen's Occupational Diseases Fund Act.[91] A 'compromise' between employers and workmen was concluded which consisted of strict liability of the employer towards his employees. In return, employees refrain from suing their employer and the latter is granted legal immunity.[92] The National Trade Board deemed it necessary that the Asbestos Compensation Fund inserted a similar immunity rule.

89 Article 25 of the Jachtdecreet 1991 [Hunting Decree 1991].

90 Article 25; §1 of the Programmawet (I) van 27 december 2006, *BS* 28 december 2006 [art. 118 of the Finance Act (I) of 27 December 2006, *OB* 28 December 2006]; de Kezel, *Asbest, gezondheid en veiligheid*, above n. 6, pp. 531–532; I. Boone, *Verhaal van derde-betalers op de aansprakelijke* (Intersentia 2009), pp. 160–161.

91 Wetsvoorstel asbestfonds 2006, 11–13; J. Van Langendonck, *Handboek socialezekerheidsrecht* (Intersentia 2011), p. 316.

92 Article 46 of the Arbeidsongevallenwet [Occupational Accidents Act]; Van Langendonck, *Handboek socialezekerheidsrecht*, above n. 91, pp. 316 and 360.

The Fund for Technological Accidents is also an alternative to liability law: victims can choose between compensation from the fund or try their luck at court.[93]

The fourth category of funds sets aside the access to court (almost) completely. These are typically funds that have close connections with social security. In Belgium, the sole representative of this group is *Fedris* in its role as Workmen's Occupational Diseases Fund. It comes closest to a no-fault compensation scheme as victims have no choice but to go to the fund for compensation. Only in specific cases, e.g. when the employer or his or her agent has intentionally caused the accident and in case of on-the-way-to-work accidents, access to court is open.[94]

5.2. AMOUNT OF COMPENSATION

What victims are interested in the most is, of course, the amount of compensation they receive in the end. Funds tend to be quite diverse on this point.

While most funds provide only a limited level of compensation, the calculation varies from fund to fund. The Asbestos Compensation Fund offers a fixed and normative sum, the amount of which depends on the kind of disease. Victims of asbestosis receive a monthly amount of €15 times the percentage of bodily incapacity. In case of death, the spouse receives one sum of €15,000. Mesothelioma victims are eligible for €1,500 per month, the spouse (in case of death) for €30,000.[95]

The Flemish Disaster Fund uses a scale that determines the percentage of compensation that can be paid out by the fund. The amount is thus normative and fixed as well.[96] In contrast to the Asbestos Compensation Fund, the Flemish Disaster Fund applies a franchise of €500.[97]

---

93 Article 3, §2 of the Wet Technologisch Ongeval; K. Bernauw, 'De vergoeding van schade door technologische rampen' [2013] T. Verz. 146.

94 Article 46 of the Wet Arbeidsongevallen.

95 Article 10–14 of the koninklijk besluit van 11 mei 2007 ter uitvoering van hoofdstuk VI, van titel IV, van de programmawet (I) van 27 december 2006 tot oprichting van een Schadeloosstellingfonds voor asbestslachtoffers, *BS* 29 mei 2007.

96 Article 9, A, 2° *io.* 11 of the wet van 12 juli 1976; Durant, 'Belgium', above n. 47, pp. 61–62 and 64–65.

97 Article 24 of the Besluit van de Vlaamse Regering van 23 december 2016 tot uitvoering van het decreet van 3 juni 2016 betreffende de tegemoetkoming voor schade, aangericht door algemene rampen in het Vlaamse Gewest, *BS* 13 februari 2017 [Resolution of the Flemish Government of 23 December 2016 on the execution of the Decree

The Fund for Nature and Environment only compensates 'important damage',[98] whereas the Fund for Technological Accidents only compensates physical damage[99] and *Fedris* offers a limited compensation based on the percentage of incapacity and the income of the victim.[100]

On the other side are funds that offer full compensation, namely the Fund for Medical Accidents[101] and the Belgian Common Guarantee Fund.[102]

Lastly, the Victim Compensation Fund has a particular way of calculating compensation. It offers no compensation in the strict sense. Indeed, the goal of the sum it grants is not compensating damage (fully or partially) in the strict sense of the word. Rather, it aims to redress the difficult financial situation of victims and to soften the pain victims have suffered due to the crime. In theory, the aid does not have to be in relation to the actual damage but in reality the fund calculates the damages using the 'Indicative Table' (a guideline on damage and damages) which is also used by the common courts. For moral damage the fund tends to give higher damages[103] but will generally not pay more than the court assigned to the victim (in case the victim did go to court but the wrongdoer was insolvent). Other compensation that the victim has already received such as insurance pay out, money from social security and so on is taken into account.[104] The total amount that the Fund can

of 3 June 2016 on the compensation of damage caused by general disasters in the Flemish Region, *OB* 13 February 2017].

98 Article 24 of the Jachtdecreet en art. 4, §1 of the Soortschadebesluit.

99 Article 9, §1 of the Wet Technologische Ongevallen [Technological Accidents Act]; E. Verjans, 'Nieuwe wettelijke regeling voor de vergoeding van slachtoffers van grote technologische rampen' [2013] RW 1076.

100 *Partim* Workmen's Occupational Accidents Fund: arts 10–39 of the wet van 10 april 1971 betreffende de arbeidsongevallen, *BS* 24 april 1971. *Partim* Workmen's Occupational Diseases Fund: arts 32–41*ter* of the Wetten van 3 juni 1970 betreffende de preventie van beroepsziekten en de vergoeding van de schade die uit die ziekten voortvloeit, gecoördineerd op 3 juni 1970, *BS* 27 August 1970.

101 Boone, 'De verhouding tussen het aansprakelijkheidsrecht en de vergoeding door het fonds voor medische ongevallen', above n. 87, p. 70.

102 Notwithstanding a few exceptions: see art. 19*bis*-13, §3 of the WAM-wet [*WAM*-Act]; S. Vereecken, 'Kettingbotsing tussen het Gemeenschappelijk Motorwaarborgfonds en WAM-verzekeraars in artikel 19bis-11 WAM' in Boone, Claeys and Lavrysen (eds), *Liber amicorum Hubert Bocken. Dare la luce*, above n. 47, p. 258.

103 P. Verhoeven and L. Vulsteke, *Het Fonds voor financiële hulp aan slachtoffers van opzettelijke gewelddaden en aan occasionele redders* (Larcier 2011), p. 141.

104 Article 33 of Wet van 1 augustus 1985 and Andre-Dumont, Becue, De Voet, De Laminne De Bex, Hullebroeck, Junion, Schildermans, Sollie and Vandergeten (eds), *Kluwer's verzekeringshandboek*, above n. 14, s. II.7.9, p. 3.

pay is €125,000.[105] Moreover, the Fund can only compensate certain heads of damage.[106]

5.3. ACCUMULATION WITH OTHER COMPENSATION SOURCES

Accumulation of resources is one of the hardest aspects of compensation law but at the same time one of the most important, from a practical point of view. It concerns the question of whether or not a victim who is eligible for different compensation sources can combine these damages. Knowledge of the accumulation rules can save victims from needless procedures.

For a better understanding, two situations are handled separately: accumulation with damages from tort procedure on the one hand and accumulation with compensation from health insurance on the other hand.

5.3.1. Accumulation with Liability Law

As a golden rule in liability law, a victim cannot be compensated twice for the same damage (principle of integral compensation).[107] So, accumulation is only possible to the extent of full compensation.

Guarantee funds follow this golden rule per definition as they will only intervene when a tort action is impossible and thus no damages can be received elsewhere. The Flemish Disaster Fund follows this general rule too.[108] The Fund for Medical Accidents should not face accumulation

---

105 Article 33, §2 of Wet Slachtofferfonds [Victim Compensation Fund Act].

106 Article 32 of Wet Slachtofferfonds [Victim Compensation Fund Act].

107 Cass. 17 januari 1929, *Pas.* 1929, I, 63; Cour de Cassation belge 2012, 225; B. Dubuisson, N. Estienne and D. de Callataÿ, [Droit belge] in P. Pierre and F. Leduc (eds), *La réparation intégrale en Europe* (Larcier 2012), p. 171.

108 Article 4, derde lid of the Decreet van 3 juni 2016 betreffende de tegemoetkoming voor schade, aangericht door algemene rampen in het Vlaamse Gewest, *BS* 23 juni 2016 [Decree of 3 June 2016 on the compensation of damage caused by general disasters in the Flemish Region, *OB* 23 June 2016] and art. 23, tweede lid of the Besluit van de Vlaamse Regering van 23 december 2016 tot uitvoering van het decreet van 3 juni 2016 betreffende de tegemoetkoming voor schade, aangericht door algemene rampen in het Vlaamse Gewest, *BS* 13 februari 2017 [Resolution of the Flemish Government of 23 December 2016 on the execution of the Decree of 3 June 2016 on the compensation of damage caused by general disasters in the Flemish Region, *OB* 13 February 2017]; Durant, 'Belgium', above n. 47, pp. 59–60.

issues because it acts either as a guarantee fund, or when no liability comes into play at all (and thus no damages will be received). Yet the law on this fund contains several articles on accumulation. This stems from the double trail system and the victim's choice between court and fund correspondingly. Suppose a victim sued the wrongdoer and simultaneously started a procedure at the fund and both the court and the fund found reasons to compensate the victim. In that case double compensation would become reality. To avoid this, the law contains several rules such as the victim's duty to inform the fund when he pursues a court procedure.[109]

Accumulation is usually speaking not problematic for *Fedris* since it excludes liability (employer's immunity).[110] Only in the event that the immunity of the employer is breached does accumulation come into play. *Fedris* allows accumulation of non-physical damage for occupational accidents[111] but does not allow any accumulation for occupational diseases.[112]

Some funds do not comply with the general rule of integral compensation. For example, the Victim Compensation Fund gives an equitable compensation which can be more or less than a full compensation. Although not excluded, it is rather seldom that compensation is higher than what a common court judge would allow based on the general compensation rules.

The Asbestos Compensation Fund does not comply with the general rule either. Victims of mesothelioma can combine compensation from any source (Belgian or foreign) with the Fund's damages for 100%. Victims of asbestosis however can 'only' combine with compensation from liability law, from health insurance and for invalidity and this is for 50%. In any way, accumulation above the full compensation limit is allowed.[113] This is rather astonishing, for no sufficient explanation is given as to why these victims deserve more protection than others, e.g. victims of car accidents.[114] This shows that the lawmaker intended

109 Article 12, §5 of the Wet Medische Ongevallen [Medical Accidents Act].

110 Article 51 of the Beroepsziektenwet [Occupational Diseases Act] and art. 46, §2 of the Arbeidsongevallenwet [Occupational Accidents Act].

111 Article 46, §2 of the Arbeidsongevallenwet [Occupational Accidents Act].

112 Article 51, §2of the Beroepsziektenwet [Occupational Diseases Act].

113 Article 121, of the Programmawet (I) van 27 december 2006, *BS* 28 december 2006 [art. 118 of the Finance Act (I) of 27 December 2006, *OB* 28 December 2006]. An exception is made for the cost of healthcare, which can be cumulated fully. See Boone, *Verhaal van derde-betalers op de aansprakelijke*, above n. 90, pp. 160–161.

114 Boone, *Verhaal van derde-betalers op de aansprakelijke*, above n. 90, p. 161.

not only to compensate the victims yet also admitted that he was not able to avoid this damage, as explained above.[115] Yet the victim cannot combine its fund compensation with damages received according to common liability law when he first went to the fund.[116]

The law on the Fund for Environment and Nature is not very clear on this point. In the absence of any divergent rule, the general rule (prohibition of double compensation) should be applicable in the author's opinion.

5.3.2. *Accumulation with Health Insurance*

The health insurance act has a very specific rule for accumulation issues.[117] Health insurance will not pay out to an insured person when other compensation sources have already paid out to said insured.[118] Only when the benefits of the other source are lower than the sum that the insurance would pay out will health insurance will top up the difference.[119] Less clear is the question of whether the same rule applies when the other compensation source is merely available to the victim but the latter does not address this source (e.g. a compensation fund). Like Boone, the author of this chapter believes this is not the case. Indeed, the goal of the rule is to avoid double compensation. When the victim has no intention of pursuing his compensation elsewhere, there is no risk of double compensation.[120]

This rule has two exceptions. First, the law on the Fund of Medical Accidents says that it will deduct from its compensation the amount the insurers pay.[121] Thus, health insurers cannot call upon the general rule to escape their duty to compensate the victim. A similar exception can be found at the Belgian Common Guarantee Fund. Health insurers are obliged to pay the insured victim. This victim can only receive compensation

---

115 Ibid.

116 See section 5.1.

117 Gecoördineerde wet van 14 juli 1994 betreffende de verplichte verzekering voor geneeskundige verzorging en uitkeringen, *BS* 27 augustus 1994, *err. BS* 13 december 1994 [Coordinated Act of 14 July 1994 on compulsory insurance for medical care and payments] (further: ZIV-wet [*ZIV*-Act]).

118 Article 136 §2 of the ZIV-wet [*ZIV*-Act].

119 Ibid.

120 Boone, *Verhaal van derde-betalers op de aansprakelijke*, above n. 90, pp. 119–120.

121 Article 25, §4 of the Wet Medische Ongevallen; Boone, 'De verhouding tussen het aansprakelijkheidsrecht en de vergoeding door het fonds voor medische ongevallen', above n. 87, p. 71.

from this fund to the extent that the health insurer did not cover all the damage.[122]

5.4. FUNDING

The financial sources of funds are as diverse as the funds themselves. Not one of them is funded in the same way as the other.

Most funds receive public funding and are financed by government expenditure and/or expenses from social security, supplemented with contributions by certain groups of the population, e.g. contributions of employers to social security.

For example, *Fedris* is supplied by social security, contributions from the 'voluntarily insured' (i.e. the self-employed) from local and provincial governments and from gifts and legacies.[123] The Asbestos Compensation Fund on the other hand is funded by direct government expenditure,[124] contributions from employers in relation to the number of employers that have received compensation from the Fund, a share from the social security of the self-employed and via gifts and legacies.[125] The Fund for Medical Accidents is financed via the administration cost of the RIZIV (*Rijksdienst Ziekte en Invaliditeit*), the health department of social security.[126] The Flemish Disaster Fund receives money from government expenditure (via the Flemish Redemption Fund).[127] The Fund for

122 Article 20 of KB van 11 juli 2003 houdende de vaststelling van de toelatingsvoorwaarden en de werking van het Belgisch Bureau en het Gemeenschappelijk Waarborgfonds, 17 oktober 2003, 50547.

123 Article 56 of the Beroepsziektenwet [Occupational Diseases Act] and arts 58*ter*-59*bis* of the Arbeidsongevallenwet [Occupational Accidents Act].

124 Due to a recent amendment, government expenditure will only be granted to the fund when it has used all its back-up. Since the fund has a fairly large excess amount of savings, this will not occur soon. See Wetsontwerp van 8 mei 2017 met betrekking tot de financiering van het Asbestfonds, *Parl.St.* Kamer 2016–2017, nr. 2369/003 [Bill of 8 May 2017 on the financing of the Asbestos Compensation Fund, *Parl.Disc.* Chamber 2016–2017, no. 2369/003].

125 Article 116 of the Programmawet (I) van 27 december 2006, *BS* 28 december 2006 [art. 118 of the Finance Act (I) of 27 December 2006, *OB* 28 December 2006].

126 Article 137*sexies* of the ZIV-Wet [*ZIV*-Act].

127 Article 1, §2, 2° of the besluit Vl. Reg. van 24 mei 1995 houdende vaststelling van de regelen betreffende de werking en het beheer van het Vlaams Fonds voor de Lastendelging, *BS* 2 september 1995 *io.* art. 53, §4 decreet Vl. Parl.van 21 december 1994 houdende bepalingen tot begeleiding van de begroting van 1995, *BS* 31 december 1994 [art. 1, §2, 2° of the Fl. Gov. Decree of 24 May 1995 on the constitution of the regulations on the functioning and the administration of the Flemish Redemption

Environment and Nature receives a share of the environmental taxes and fines.[128]

The Victim Compensation Fund is financed in a wholly different way that shows its close connection to criminal court cases. Any time a judge convicts an accused person for a crime or a misdemeanour (the two highest categories of criminal offences), he will additionally charge him an amount of €25 that will be deposited on the account of the fund.[129]

The only fund that receives funding via the private way is the Belgian Common Guarantee Fund. This stems from its nature: it is a 'mutual insurance association': the fund itself consists of different insurance companies.[130] So the financial resources come directly from the insurance companies' incomes.[131]

5.5. ORGANISATION

When one takes a closer look at the internal organisation of funds, a few remarkable aspects catch the eye. Firstly, it seems to be a trend to deny legal personality to newly created funds. Instead, funds become either a part of a branch of social security or they merge together. For example, the 2010 Fund for Medical Accidents is a part of the RIZIV,[132]

Fund, *OB* 2 September 1995 *io* art. 53, §4 of the Fl. Parl. Decree of 21 December 1994 on the provisions accompanying the budget of 1995, *OB* 31 December 1994].

128 Article 3 of the decreet van 23 januari 1991 tot oprichting van het Fonds voor preventie en sanering inzake leefmilieu en natuur als gewestdienst met afzonderlijk beheer, *BS* 22 februari 1991 [Decree of 23 January 1991 on the establishment of a Fund for prevention and restructuring of the natural environment and nature as a Regional service with separate administration, *OB* 2 February 1991].

129 Article 29 of the Wet Slachtofferfonds [Victim Compensation Fund Act].

130 Andre-Dumont, Becue, De Voet, DDe Laminne De Bex, Hullebroeck, Junion, Schildermans, Sollie and Vandergeten (eds), *Kluwer's verzekeringshandboek*, above n. 14, s. II.6.12, p. 1; A. De Graeve, 'De onderlinge verzekeringsvereniging: een vreemde eend in de bijt' (note under Kh. Hasselt 25 februari 2003) [2004] TBH 77–81.

131 Article 19*bis*-4 of the WAM-wet [*WAM*-Act].

132 Wet van 19 maart 2013 houdende diverse bepalingen inzake gezondheid (I), *BS* 29 maart 2013 (tweede ed.) [Act of 19 March 2013 on different aspects of health care (I), *OB* 29 March 2013 (2nd ed.)]; Vansweevelt and Dewallens (eds), *Handboek gezondheidsrecht. Volume I. Zorgverleners: statuut en aansprakelijkheid*, above n. 35, p. 1632; W. Buelens, 'Abnormale schade in de Wet Medische Ongevallen: een eerste commentaar bij een advies van het Fonds voor Medische Ongevallen' [2015] T. Gez. 66.

whereas the Asbestos Compensation Fund was part of the Workmen's Occupational Diseases Fund from the beginning.[133] This seems to be a persisting trend. In 2017, both the Workmen's Occupational Accidents Fund and Workmen's Occupational Diseases Fund were merged together into *Fedris*.[134] The purpose is to allow for better visibility and greater efficiency.[135] Maybe this is a step towards the creation of a bigger idea: one super fund?

Another point of interest is the constitution of the administration of each fund. Two main categories can be discerned. Some funds consist of experts in the domain of the fund. Others have an administration that equally represents certain interest groups and/or the government. An example of both types is the Fund for Medical Accidents. The administration consists of representatives of the government, the employers, the self-employed, the employees, the insurance sector, care institutions, medical practitioners and patients. Beside these representatives, two professors specialised in medical law also join the management.[136] The Asbestos Compensation Fund and *Fedris* are good examples of funds whose management only consists of representatives of the social sector (representatives of the government and/or the employers and employees).[137]

---

133 Article 114 of the Programmawet (I) van 27 december 2006, *BS* 28 december 2006 [art. 118 of the Finance Act (I) of 27 December 2006, *OB* 28 December 2006]; AFA, *Het Asbestfonds, 5-jarig bestaan (2007–2012)*, <http://www.afa.fgov.be/pdf/Verslag%205%20jaar%20AFA.pdf>, p. 5.

134 De redactie.be, 'Fusie tussen Fonds voor Beroepsziekten en Fonds voor Arbeidsongevallen', <http://deredactie.be/cm/vrtnieuws/binnenland/1.2365490>, 12 June 2015.

135 S. Delafortrie and C. Springael, 'Fusie van het Fonds voor de beroepsziekten en van het Fonds voor Arbeidsongevallen', *FOD Kanselarij van de Eerste Minister – Algemene Directie Externe Communicatie*, <http://www.presscenter.org/nl/print/83614> and Fonds Voor Arbeidsongevallen, *Fusie tussen het FBZ en het FAO*, <http://www.fao.fgov.be/nl/news-archives>.

136 Article 137*quater*, §2 of the ZIV-Wet [*ZIV*-Act]; D. Verhoeven, 'Verslag Studieavond Medische Ongevallen' in I. Boone and S. Lierman (eds), *Vergoeding van slachtoffers van medische ongevallen*, above n. 33, p. 113.

137 Article 5, §2 of the wet van 16 augustus 2016 met betrekking tot de fusie van het fonds voor arbeidsongevallen en het fonds voor de beroepsziekten, *BS* 5 september 2009 [art. 5, §2 of the act of 16 August 2016 on the fusion of the Workmen's Occupational Accidents Fund and the Workmen's Occupational Diseases Fund, OB 5 September 2016]; AFA, *Het Asbestfonds, 5-jarig bestaan (2007–2012)*, <http://www.afa.fgov.be/pdf/Verslag%205%20jaar%20AFA.pdf>, p. 9.

6. ASSETS AND DRAWBACKS OF FUNDS

6.1. POSITIVE ASPECTS

6.1.1. *Victim Friendly*

Funds do have several advantages, compared to other compensation systems. Firstly, funds are, by nature, victim oriented. Their purpose is to compensate victims who, in other circumstances, would be left out and receive no or a lesser compensation. They are especially appropriate when it comes to compensating serial damage and hidden damage, e.g. asbestos-related damage. The reason is that the general prescription rules do not apply to them.[138] Yet other problems with liability law, e.g. difficulties in finding evidence of fault and causal link can also be avoided to a certain extent. Of course, the causality issue is persistent: even when applying for damages at a fund, a minimal causal link has to be proven.[139] For example, victims of medical accidents are still obliged to prove that the damage was caused due to an accident in the medical sector and thus there must be a link between the damage and the medical act.[140]

Funds such as the Asbestos Compensation Fund and *Fedris* can also strengthen the awareness of certain diseases they cover. On their respective websites a lot of information can be found on these diseases.[141]

6.1.2. *Solution for Uninsurable Risks*

Insurance companies often express their fear that large-scale risks could surpass their financial capacities.[142] Funds can provide a solution for these uninsurable risks. Provided that funds are well maintained, they could offer a buffer, a safety net, in the event of failure of the insurance sector to cope with the disaster.

---

138 B. Dubuisson, 'Les dommages en série – responsabilité, assurance et indemnisation' [2015] RGAR nr. 15182, p. 8.

139 P. Cane, *Atiyah's Accidents, Compensation and the Law* (Cambridge University Press 2006), p. 470.

140 Article 44 of the Wet Medische Ongevallen.

141 Asbestos Compensation Fund: <www.fedris.be/afa/afa_nl.html>; Fedris: <http://fedris.be/fr/home>.

142 Hartlief, *Anno 2010. Beschouwingen over aansprakelijkheid en verzekering* (deLex 2009), p. 96; J. Rogge, 'Assurance de la responsabilité civile et nouveaux risques', in J. Rogge (ed.), *Liber Amicorum Jean-Luc Fagnart*, above n. 65, pp. 257–258.

6.1.3. *Structural Solidarity*

The growth in number of compensation funds shows that solidarity with victims of disasters and accidents is increasing. A fund can offer a solid and lasting structure to express compassion, compared to, e.g. one-off charity actions. Citizens are certain that, in the event of an accident or disaster in the near future, the compensation fund will still be there to help.

6.1.4. *Procedural Assets*

Suing an opponent can be morally and financially exhausting and is time-consuming. In contrast, a compensation fund application takes place in a more amicable setting without the adversarial attitude parties show before the court. The Fund for Medical Accidents will, for example, mediate among parties.[143] Moreover, a fund procedure is more confidential than the (generally speaking) public court procedure. Last but not least, victims do not have to pay any entry fee in order to get access to a fund, in contrast to court proceedings, where enrolment fees have to be paid.[144] The speed of a fund procedure is however debatable. For example, the slowness of the Disaster Fund is notorious[145] and the Fund for Medical Accidents has to cope with delays as well.[146] The cost-free character of the latter fund should be nuanced as the fund does not refund the lawyers' fees.[147]

Beside the abovementioned advantages, some funds have specialised members on their team. Their expertise means that they are better placed than judges to assess specific damage. However, as said before, this is not always the case.

143 Article 8 §1, 5° and 6° of the Wet Medische Ongevallen [Medical Accidents Act].

144 B. Dubuisson, 'Les dommages en série – responsabilité, assurance et indemnisation' [2015] RGAR nr. 15182,11. The Constitutional Court annulled the 2015 act on entry fees. Hence, the fees prior to the 2015 act prevail until the new bill (of 27 June 2017) is passed. See: GwH 9 februari 2017, nr. 13/2017, <www.const-court.be>, *Juristenkrant* 22 februari 2017, 1 (weergave E. Brewaeys) and *VAV* 2017, 52; Wetsontwerp van 27 juni 2017 tot wijziging van het Wetboek der registratie-, hypotheek- en griffierechten teneinde de griffierechten te hervormen, *Parl.St.* Kamer 2016–2017, nr. 2569/001. and N. Luyten, 'Rolrechten en toegang tot de rechter: dansen op een slappe koord' [2017] *Juristenkrant* 13 September 2017, 1.

145 Cfr. Newspaper articles like: 'Rampenfonds loopt jaren achter', <http://www.knack.be/nieuws/belgie/rampenfonds-loopt-jaren-achter/article-normal-47748.html>.

146 RIZIV, *Activiteitenverslag van het Fonds voor de medische ongevallen – 2014*, <http://www.fmo.fgov.be/nl/about-us/annual-reports/pdf/jaarverslag_fmo_2014.pdf>, p. 3.

147 W. Buelens, *Het medisch ongeval zonder aansprakelijkheid* (Universitas Cursusdienst 2018), p. 404.

6.2. DOWNSIDES

Funds undergo a lot of criticism and there are indeed some major disadvantages in the fund system. The most important negative points are enumerated below.

6.2.1. *Funds and Prevention*

Funds and prevention are said not to go hand in hand. A distinction must be made between prevention towards the wrongdoer and towards the victim.

Indeed, when it comes to preventing the tortfeasor from repeating his wrongful actions, funds seem at first sight not as adequate as a regular court proceeding insofar as the wrongdoer (if any) cannot be condemned by the fund.[148] At most he can be addressed by the fund in an action of recourse. This is why some authors cling to the 'the-polluter-pays' principle.[149] For instance, for asbestos damage they suggest that every (formerly) asbestos-producing factory should pay a contribution to the fund. Yet, a Scandinavian research on the behaviour of medical practitioners after the entry into force of a no-fault-based compensation scheme ascertained that the behaviour of medics is not influenced by the absence of court proceedings.[150] Yet it seems fairer, especially from the taxpayers' point of view, to insert the polluter-pays principle.[151]

However, funds do have their own ways of dealing with prevention. Some funds can make recommendations as to how to prevent accidents from happening or conduct investigations into the causes of diseases.[152]

---

148 B. Dubuisson, 'Les dommages en série – responsabilité, assurance et indemnisation' [2015] RGAR nr. 15182, p. 11; Hartlief, *Anno 2010. Beschouwingen over aansprakelijkheid en verzekering*, above n. 64, pp. 99–100.

149 M.G Faure and T. Hartlief, 'Een schadefonds als alternatief voor aansprakelijkheid en verzekering?' [1998] Rm Themis 215; de Kezel, *Asbest, gezondheid en veiligheid*, above n. 6, p. 533.

150 J. Dute, 'A Comparison of No-Fault Compensation Schemes' in M. Faure et al (eds), *No-fault compensation in health care sector* (Springer 2004), p. 471.

151 S. Klosse, 'Meerwaarde van alternatieve (vergoedings)systemen' in Hartlief and Klosse (eds), *Einde van het aansprakelijkheidsrecht?*, above n. 66, pp. 121–122; Faure and Hartlief, 'Een schadefonds als alternatief voor aansprakelijkheid en verzekering?', above n. 149, 218; de Kezel, *Asbest, gezondheid en veiligheid*, above n. 6, p. 533; V. Bruggeman, *Compensating Catastrophe Victims. A Comparative Law and Economics Approach* (Kluwer Law International 2015), pp. 220, 225 and 504.

152 E.g. the Workmen's Occupational Accidents Fund: art. 58, §1, 1° and 11° of the Arbeidsongevallenwet; for the Medical Accidents Fund: art. 8 §2 of the Wet Medische Ongevallen.

For victims, prevention can be necessary as well, albeit on a different level. Some authors suggest that the presence of a compensation fund would make citizens hesitate to take out an insurance policy and instead take advantage of the fund compensation.[153] This comment must be nuanced, nonetheless. Most funds offer only a limited compensation. A first party insurance could top up the rest. Moreover, funds only intervene in very specific circumstances. In other words, funds do not cover every kind of damage, rather to the contrary. Stating that the presence of a fund would influence one's insurance behaviour, in that one will deliberately not take out a private party insurance and consequently declining additional compensation, thus seems a little too farfetched. Above all, victims are not always aware of the presence of a fund.

6.2.2. Funds and Discrimination

One of the most accurate comments on funds is that they (potentially) discriminate against certain victims. This is intrinsic to the nature of funds. Indeed, they are created for damage caused by one or more very specific circumstances. Hence only a limited group of victims falls under the scope of application.[154] Take for example the Asbestos Compensation Fund: only victims of asbestosis and mesothelioma can apply for compensation. Victims of lung cancer, equally caused by asbestos dust are denied access to the fund.[155] And what about victims of environment-related diseases, or from chemical products? They are not covered by a fund, yet their situation could be as pitiful as others.

Numerous examples could be given.[156] A rational and satisfying justification for this different treatment is absent. Often the lawmaker yields for pressure from interest groups and the media.[157] The same goes for the conditions of the Fund for Technological Accidents.[158]

---

153 Bruggeman, *Compensating Catastrophe Victims. A Comparative Law and Economics Approach*, above n. 151, p. 204.

154 Klosse, 'Meerwaarde van alternatieve (vergoedings)systemen', above n. 151, pp. 127–128; Cane, *Atiyah's Accidents, Compensation and the Law*, above n. 139, pp. 476–474.

155 E. de Kezel, 'Asbestfonds "immuniseert" voormalige asbestwerkgevers' [2007] 5 December 2007 *De Juristenkrant* 8.

156 E. de Kezel, 'Asbest, softenon, Pukkelpop: de vragen die we nog moeten stellen' [2011] 9 November 2011 *De Juristenkrant* 10.

157 J.L. Fagnart, 'Recherches sur le droit de la réparation' in J.L. Fagnart (ed.), *Mélanges Roger O. Dalcq* (Larcier 1994), p. 142.

158 K. Bernauw, 'De vergoeding van schade door technologische rampen' [2013] T. Verz. 136–137.

This inequality between victims compromises the funds' legitimacy. Ironically, funds are created in order to redress the inequality of liability law.[159] More importantly, this could create a situation that cannot withstand the non-discrimination test of the Constitution and of European and international treaties.[160] The sole sustainable solutions seems to broaden the scope of application of several funds. In particular, the Asbestos Compensation Fund, the Fund for Technological Accidents and the Fund for Medical Accidents might need to enlarge their scope. More research is required to make correct amendments in that respect. The legislature seems to be aware of this issue, as indicated by statements in relation to a potential large fund for victims of any chemical product and the upcoming broadening of the scope.[161]

6.2.3. *Limited Compensation*

An often-heard remark is that funds 'only' offer limited compensation.[162] While most funds do indeed compensate damage partially, this comment is often misplaced. Indeed, without the fund compensation, victims would end up empty handed.[163] This remark can be relevant however in regard to funds such as the Asbestos Compensation Fund that forbid any access to court and make it impossible for the victim to sue the wrongdoer for the remainder.

6.2.4. *Financial Sustainability*

Intrinsically linked with the amount of compensation is the issue of financial sustainability for the State, for most funds are financed via the State. Fund expenses are thus a burden.[164] Yet, without thorough research of the accountancy of each fund, it is nearly impossible to make proper statements. One should keep in mind that funds do

---

159 Atiyah, *The Damages Lottery*, above n. 66, pp. 143–150.

160 Fagnart, 'Recherches sur le droit de la réparation', above n. 157, p.142; Faure and Hartlief, 'Een schadefonds als alternatief voor aansprakelijkheid en verzekering?' above n. 149, 220.

161 See n. 26. Wetsvoorstel tot oprichting van een Fonds voor de asbestslachtoffers *Parl. St.* Kamer 2003–2004, nr. 1244/001, p. 11.

162 Durant, 'Belgium', above n. 47, pp. 65–66; Cane, *Atiyah's Accidents, Compensation and the Law*, above n. 139, pp. 474–477.

163 Klosse, 'Meerwaarde van alternatieve (vergoedings)systemen', above n. 151, p. 127.

164 H. Arbousset, 'Les financements de risques collectifs: l'exemple des fonds d'indemnisation et de garantie' (2010) 1 *Riseo* 28–29.

receive more than government spending alone and are often partially self-sustainable.

Another important question concerns the person of the fundraiser. Who is better placed to finance these funds: the public or the private (insurance) sector, or rather a specific sector in society?[165] This needs further investigation as well.

6.2.5. *Access to Court and Other Procedural Rights*

Article 6 of the European Convention of Human Rights (ECHR) contains the right of access to justice. Funds such as the Asbestos Compensation Fund and *Fedris partim* Workmen's Occupational Diseases Fund exclude this access (in certain circumstances). Whether or not this is a breach of art. 6 is an interesting question that certainly needs to be explored.

Article 6 ECHR contains other procedural rights, e.g. impartiality and independence of the judge. It is debatable to what extent funds can be considered as 'judge'. Nonetheless, this author believes it remains important that funds can guarantee certain procedural rights such as impartiality. As Knetsch rightly points out, the independence of a fund can be compromised if representatives of the victims have a seat in the fund.[166] This is the case for, e.g. the Fund for Medical Accidents.[167] Likewise, the independence of a compensation fund is threatened if the wrongdoer is represented. But when both parties are equally present at a fund's decisive organ, interests are more balanced. A better way still to ensure independence could be to add independent members to the management, e.g. professors, doctors, chemists, etc.

6.2.6. *Awareness and Expectations*

Compensation funds can only fulfil their goals if they can reach their target group. Given the high number of claims before certain funds, it seems that they do indeed reach the victims they were created for. However, one should keep in mind that there might be a 'silent minority' of people that are not aware of the funds' existence due to

---

165 Cane, *Atiyah's Accidents, Compensation and the Law*, above n. 139, p. 478.

166 J. Knetsch, *Le droit de la responsabilité et les fonds d'indemnisation* (Lextenso éditions 2013), pp. 311–316.

167 Article 137*quater* of the ZIV-wet [*ZIV*-Act].

lesser availability of communication sources, education, etc. Although compensation funds are doing their best by making themselves visible via a website, finding that site and understanding the procedure is not evident for a legal layman.

At the other end of the spectrum are those citizens that are well aware of the funds' existence but hold too high expectations. They sometimes have the unrealistic perception that claiming before a fund automatically leads to compensation whereas in fact certain burdens still remain. This is especially apparent in relation to the Fund for Medical Accidents.

7. CONCLUDING REMARKS

In this chapter it has become clear that compensation funds are well established in Belgium. In different domains of life and law (transportation, healthcare, work, etc.) compensation funds are present. Their increasing number is proof of a shift in perspective from liability towards compensation. Indeed, the main objective of compensation funds is supporting victims. Blaming the wrongdoer and holding him responsible for his acts plays a lesser role and often is absent. Funds offer more than compensation, however. Most funds also play an important role in assessing and preventing accidents. Funds such as the Asbestos Compensation Fund and *Fedris* also create awareness of diseases they compensate. Neither liability law nor insurance are equally suited for such tasks.

Notwithstanding the advantages of funds, one cannot lose sight of the chaos into which the fund landscape has developed. Not much coherence can be found between these funds. For victims seeking compensation, this is not an ideal situation. For each damaging event they have to walk the serpentine roads of compensation law and figure out whether they have access to a compensation fund and if so, how much compensation they could receive, and whether or not they can cumulate fund compensation with other payments and so on. It is a complex patchwork that often stems from *ad hoc* policy.[168] Not only is this bothersome for victims, it also potentially infringes discrimination law.

---

[168] J.-F. Leclercq and D. De Roy, 'Quelques observations sur l'intervention de l'etat dans la reparation de certains prejudices' in Rogge (ed.), *Liber Amicorum Jean-Luc Fagnart*, above n. 65, p. 594.

It seems to be better to harmonise funds where this is possible. The Fund for Medical Accidents could figure as a possible role model. Its so-called double trail system enables victims to choose between court and fund procedures. Consequently, victims are not denied access to court. Moreover, it offers full compensation and the composition of its management is balanced.

One question still remains: does one super fund need to evolve as already exists in New Zealand?[169] This could solve the problem of discrimination.[170] The legislature has mentioned the creation of one large fund for victims of chemical products, which can be seen as a step in that direction.[171] Whether a super fund would be reasonable and payable for the State is yet unclear. This would require very thorough research. But even without having to install a super fund, more coherence is possible by creating a 'single window' (*guichet unique* or *eenheidsloket*) that would direct victims towards the available compensation source.[172]

One thing is for sure: in Belgium, compensation funds are no stranger in our midst. To the contrary, more evolution in the field can be expected, probably towards the merging of funds. Perhaps one can already speak of 'fund law' as a distinct fourth branch of compensation law.

---

169 Klosse, 'Meerwaarde van alternatieve (vergoedings)systemen', above n. 151, p. 137.

170 Fagnart, 'Recherches sur le droit de la réparation', above n. 157, p. 142.

171 Wetsvoorstel tot oprichting van een Fonds voor de asbestslachtoffers, *Parl. St.* Kamer 2003–2004, nr. 1244/001, 11.

172 For more information see: Knetsch, *Le droit de la responsabilité et les fonds d'indemnisation*, above n. 166, pp. 471–472.

COMPENSATION FUNDS IN FRANCE AND GERMANY

Jonas KNETSCH*

1. INTRODUCTION

For decades, accident compensation in France and Germany has not only been a matter of tort law, but also of other legal mechanisms. Like in many other European countries, both private insurance and social security have led to a certain socialisation or collectivisation of the settlement of compensation claims.[1] More recently, this 'decline of individual liability',[2] well documented in the legal literature, has been accentuated by the appearance of compensation funds.

* The author can be contacted at jonas.knetsch@univ-st-etienne.fr.

1 See only René Savatier, 'Vers la socialisation de la responsabilité et des risques individuels?' [1931] *Recueil hebdomadaire Dalloz* chr 9; Karl Sieg, 'Überlagerung der bürgerlich-rechtlichen Haftung durch kollektive Ausgleichssysteme' [1980] *Zeitschrift für Versicherungsrecht* (VersR) 1085.

2 See Geneviève Viney, *Le déclin de la responsabilité individuelle* (L.G.D.J. 1965).

Despite their increasing number, compensation funds are still a Cinderella issue for many tort lawyers. Some French or German textbooks on tort law mention alternative compensation schemes in the sections on medical malpractice or in the chapter on traffic accidents, barely touching the technicalities of the subject. Others simply recognise the existence of compensation funds as a complement to the traditional tort law, designed to occasionally fill the gaps in the ordinary civil liability system.[3]

Either one of these two approaches might have been adequate 20 years ago, when compensation funds played only a limited role. In recent years, the situation has become completely different because compensation funds have undergone a kind of 'emancipatory movement'. Since the beginning of the twenty-first century, they have been considered more and more to be an autonomous legal compensatory instrument, halfway between private insurance and social security.

The following lines are intended to provide a brief overview of the situation of compensation funds under French and German law. It is obvious that this chapter cannot address *all* of the issues that arise during comprehensive research on compensation funds. First, those issues are far too numerous, and the author would like to refer the reader to more detailed studies.[4] Second, it is not an easy task to organise the questions relating to compensation funds, because they touch on many legal areas, such as public budgetary law, social protection law and the law of proceedings.

With these caveats in mind, this chapter will concentrate on four sets of fundamental issues that may be divided into a dogmatic (Section 3),

---

3 See for example, Geneviève Viney, *Introduction à la responsabilité*, 4th edn (L.G.D.J. 2019), para. 31; Gert Brüggemeier, *Haftungsrecht: Struktur, Prinzipien, Schutzbereich* (Springer 2006), p. 638. This is particularly true for German textbooks on 'legal obligations', which include tort law. See for example, Manfred Wandt, *Gesetzliche Schuldverhältnisse*, 9th edn (Vahlen 2019), p. 271.

4 See Gerhard Hohloch, *Entschädigungsfonds auf dem Gebiet des Umwelthaftungsrechts* (Umweltbundesamt 1994); Philippe Casson, *Les fonds de garantie – Accidents de la circulation et de chasse, infractions pénales, actes de terrorisme et contamination par le VIH* (L.G.D.J. 1999); André Favre Rochex and Guy Courtieu, *Fonds d'indemnisation et de garantie* (L.G.D.J. 2003); Alexis Frank, *Le droit de la responsabilité administrative à l'épreuve des fonds d'indemnisation* (L'Harmattan 2008). See also Jonas Knetsch, *Le droit de la responsabilité et les fonds d'indemnisation* (L.G.D.J. 2013) and *Haftungsrecht und Entschädigungsfonds* (Mohr Siebeck 2012). Both books contain further references and a detailed bibliography. To provide non-Francophone or non-German speaking readers easier access to the relevant legal sources, the references mentioned hereinafter are – if possible – English-language literature.

a practical (Section 4), a procedural (Section 5) and an organisational part (Section 6). To lay the groundwork for this overview, it is essential, however, to start by providing a survey of the diversity of compensation funds in both countries (Section 2).

2. DIVERSITY OF COMPENSATION FUNDS IN FRANCE AND GERMANY

There are more than 25 different compensation funds in France and Germany, which can be divided into four groups.

The first group of compensation funds includes those that cover traffic accident and crime victims.[5] If you look at the history of no-fault compensation schemes, gaps in tort law were first identified in these two areas. The legislature established specific compensation schemes in order to help victims who cannot claim damages, either because the tortfeasor failed to stop at the scene of the road accident (Germans call those cases *Fahrerfluchtfälle*; in French, *délit de fuite*) and could not be identified, or in cases of criminal offences, because the tortfeasor cannot pay compensation.

For this to happen, a Motor Guarantee Fund (*Fonds de garantie automobile*) was created in France in 1951, mainly funded by insurance companies through an insurance premium supplement.[6] Over the years, the scope of application of this fund has been widened. Today, the fund is called *Fonds de garantie des assurances obligatoires de dommages*, because hunting accidents and road accidents involving animals have been added to the initial field of application.[7] In Germany, a motor guarantee fund was established in 1965, but compensation files have to be referred to

5 For a comparative survey, see European Commission, *Compensation of Victims of Cross-Border Road Traffic Accidents in the EU* (MARKT/2001/11/D, 2008) and Oxera (ed.), *Insurance Guarantee Schemes in the EU* (Oxera 2007), p. 199.

6 Suzanne Tunc, 'France: Establishment of "Fonds de garantie" to Compensate Victims of Motor Vehicle Accidents' (1953) 2 *American Journal of Comparative Law* 232. See also the comparative work of Burchard Bott, *Der Schutz des Unfallgeschädigten durch die Kraftfahrzeug-Pflichtversicherung* (VVW 1964), p. 113.

7 Code des assurances, art. L 421-1. For an actual presentation of the legal background, see Bureau central français (ed.), *French Law on Compensation for Road Traffic Accidents* (BCT 2008) and Ruth Redmond-Cooper, 'No Fault Liability on the French Roads' [1995] *Journal of Personal Injury Litigation* 291, 302. See also the information available in English on the FGAO's website <https://www.fondsdegarantie.fr/en/home-2/>.

and are dealt with by an association under private law called *Verein Verkehrsopferhilfe*.[8]

As for the compensation of crime victims,[9] only the French legislature has created a special compensation fund. The Guarantee Fund for Victims of Terrorism and Other Offences (*Fonds de garantie des victimes d'actes de terrorisme et d'autres infractions*) has its origin in an Act of 1977, and its range of action was significantly strengthened during the 1980s when France faced a wave of terrorist attacks.[10] Surprisingly, the situation in Germany is quite different, because the compensation of victims of crime and terrorism does not fall under the authority of a compensation fund, but under the Federal Law of war pensions, paid by regional authorities.[11]

The second and probably most important group of compensation funds addresses victims of medical accidents and health-related serial damages. In both France and Germany, there have been public-health disasters requiring a legislative response for the concerned victims. In 1970, a fund was set up for the victims of thalidomide, a drug which was widely marketed in West Germany to counteract the effects of pregnancy-related morning sickness and which caused severe malformations of unborn children.[12] Other *ad hoc* funds have been established over the years for victims of HIV-contaminated blood

---

8 Pflichtversicherungsgesetz, §§12–13. See Werner Pfennigstorf, 'Unification of the Protection of Traffic Victims in Europe' (1966–1967) 15 *American Journal of Comparative Law* 436, 453 and the English website <http://www.verkehrsopferhilfe.de/en/>.

9 David Miers, 'State Compensation for Victims of Violent Crime' in Inge Vanfraechem, Antony Pemberton and Felix Mukwiza Ndahinda (eds), *Justice for Victims: Perspectives on Rights, Transition and Reconciliation* (Routledge 2014).

10 Code des assurances, art. L 422-1. Olivier Moréteau and Fabien Lafay, 'Liability for Acts of Terrorism under French Law' in Bernhard A. Koch (ed.), *Terrorism, Tort Law and Insurance. A Comparative Survey* (Springer 2004). See, for a general comparative overview, Marshall S. Shapo, *Compensation for Victims of Terrorism* (Oxford University Press 2005); Rianne Letschert and Karin Ammerlaan, 'Compensation and Reparation for Victims of Terrorism' in Rianne Letschert, Ines Staiger and Anthony Pemberton (eds), *Assisting Victims of Terrorism: Towards a European Standard of Justice* (Springer 2010).

11 Opferentschädigungsgesetz, §1. See Ulrich Magnus, 'Liability for Acts of Terrorism under German Law' in Koch, *Terrorism, Tort Law and Insurance. A Comparative Survey*, above n. 10; Yasemin Kürtek, 'Crime Victim Compensation in Germany – an Overview' NKU Papers on Social Science 5/2009. See also the English website of the Federal Ministry of Labour and Social Affairs <https://www.bmas.de/EN/Our-Topics/Social-Security/compensation-and-assistance-for-victims-of-violent-crime.html>.

12 Conterganstiftung für behinderte Menschen. See Marc S. Stauch, 'Medical Malpractice and Compensation in Germany' (2011) 86 *Chicago Kent Law Review* 1139, 1146; Christiane Wendehorst, 'Compensation in the German Health Care Sector' in

products[13] and for former East German athletes who suffered from the State-supported doping programme in the German Democratic Republic.[14]

In France, the infected blood scandal also led to the implementation of a specific compensation scheme run by the *Fonds d'indemnisation des transfusés et hémophiles*, which was set up in 1991.[15] But, unlike in Germany, the French legislature later established a compensation fund with a much broader scope, the *Office national d'indemnisation des accidents médicaux* (ONIAM).[16] Indeed, the Patients' Rights Act of 2002 organised the compensation of medical injuries that cannot be attributed to any misconduct (*aléa médical*).[17] Besides those medical hazards, the 2002 Act also addressed victims of hospital-acquired infections by allowing them to seek compensation from the French compensation office.[18] Eventually, in 2004, the HIV-dedicated compensation fund created in 1991 was merged into the ONIAM.

Since the establishment of the ONIAM in 2002, the legislature added several other, more specific grounds for compensation: Hepatitis C infections through blood transfusions, infections resulting from mandatory vaccinations, injuries resulting from growth hormone therapy and victims of a drug called *Mediator*, which was widely prescribed as a weight-loss drug for overweight diabetics, but killed and injured thousands of people due to cardiovascular complications.[19] All in all, the ONIAM deals with more than 6,000 claims a year, all types of injury taken together.

Jos Dute, Michael G. Faure and Helmut Koziol (eds), *No-Fault Compensation in the Health Care Sector* (Springer 2004), p. 270.

13 See Stauch, 'Medical Malpractice and Compensation in Germany', above n. 12, p. 1147; Wendehorst, 'Compensation in the German Health Care Sector', above n. 12, p. 272.

14 In 2002, a first compensation fund was established, but only 194 former athletes could receive compensation due to short application deadlines. In June 2016, a second compensation scheme was implemented (Giselher Spitzer, 'Zweites Dopingopfer-Hilfegesetz: Antragsfrist verlängert bis 31. Dezember 2019' (2018) *Neue Justiz*, 504).

15 Code de la santé publique, art. L 3122-1. See Eric A. Feldman, 'Blood Justice: Courts, Conflict, and Compensation in Japan, France, and the United States' (2000) 34 *Law & Society Review* 651, 683; Monika Steffen, 'The Nation's Blood: Medicine, Justice, and the State in France' in Eric A. Feldman and Ronald Bayer (eds), *Blood Feuds: AIDS, Blood, and the Politics of Medical Disaster* (Oxford University Press 1999).

16 On the actual legal background, see Geneviève Helleringer, 'Medical Malpractice and Compensation in France. Part II: Compensation Based on National Solidarity' (2011) 86 *Chicago Kent Law Review* 1125 and Simon Taylor, *Medical Accident Liability and Redress in English and French Law* (Cambridge University Press 2015), p. 53.

17 Code de la santé publique, art. L 1142-1 II.

18 Ibid, art. L 1142-1-1.

19 As a result, ONIAM is now responsible for the compensation of six different kinds of medical accidents (medical hazard, vaccination damages, HIV blood transfusion

The third fund group contains the compensation schemes laid out for the victims of environmental harm.[20] France and Germany signed the 1971 International Convention on the Establishment of an International Fund for Compensation for Oil Pollution (IOPC) and the follow-up 1992 Convention.[21] The IOPC provides compensation for maritime oil pollution damages in both countries. Both countries have also established specific national compensation schemes for sewage sludge-related harm[22] and agricultural damages caused by wild animals.[23] The French legislature has gone very far in environmental compensation law by creating a compensation fund for asbestos victims.[24] In Germany, a compensation fund for mining damages should also be mentioned.[25]

---

cases, Hepatitis B and C blood transfusion cases, Benfluorex damages and health emergency-related damages). ONIAM is also in charge of the compensation in medical malpractice cases, if the health professional was not insured, if the insurance guarantee is not sufficient or if the insurer refuses to offer compensation. See Dominique Thouvenin, 'French Medical Malpractice Compensation since the Act of March 4, 2002: Liability Rules Combined with Indemnification Rules and Correlated with Several Kinds of Proceedings' (2011) 4 *Drexel Law Review* 165, 188.

20 See Hubert Bocken, 'Alternatives to Liability and Liability Insurance for the Compensation of Pollution Damages' [1987] *Tijdschrift voor milieu aansprakelijkheid* 83; Michael Faure and Ton Hartlief, 'Compensation Funds versus Liability and Insurance for Remedying Environmental Damage' (1996) 5 *RECIEL* 321.

21 For a recent overview, see for example, Jingjing Xu, 'The International Legal Framework Governing Liability and Compensation for Ship-Source Oil Pollution Damage' in *Selected Issues in Maritime Law and Policy: Liber Amicorum Proshanto K. Mukherjee* (Nova Science Publishers 2015), p. 105.

22 Klärschlamm-Entschädigungsfonds (Germany) and Fonds de garantie des risques liés à l'épandage agricole des boues d'épuration urbaines ou industrielles (France). On this issue, see European Commission, *Disposal and recycling routes for sewage sludge. Part 1: Sludge use acceptance report* (Office of Official Publications of the European Communities 2001).

23 Wildschadensausgleichkasse (Germany) and Fonds d'indemnisation des dégâts de sangliers (French region of Alsace-Moselle).

24 Act no. 2000-1257 of 20 December 2000, art. 53. See Annie Thébaud-Mony, 'Justice for Asbestos Victims and the Politics of Compensation: The French Experience' (2003) 9 *International Journal of Occupational and Environmental Health* 280; Cécile Manaouil, Marie Graser and Olivier Jarde, 'Compensation of Asbestos Victims in France' (2006) 25 *Medicine and Law* 435; Gakuto Takamura, 'The French Indemnification Fund for Asbestos Victims: Features and Formative Historical Factors: Preliminary Observations for a Comparative Analysis of Asbestos Relief Frameworks' in Kenichi Miyamoto, Kenji Morinaga and Hiroyuki Mori (eds), *Asbestos Disaster. Lessons from Japan's Experience* (Springer 2011). For a recent comparative work on this topic, see Andrea Boggio, *Compensating Asbestos Victims: Law and the Dark Side of Industrialization* (Routledge 2016).

25 Bergschadensausfallkasse (Berggesetz, §122). See Gunther Kühne, 'Abandonment and Reclamation of Energy Sites and Facilities. Germany' (1992) 10 *Journal of Energy & Natural Resources Law* 4, 18.

The fourth and last group of compensation funds intervenes in the field of financial services. Different compensation schemes have been created to protect individuals from the consequences of the failure of a bank or an insurance company.[26] In Germany, a fund has been implemented by the notarial chambers to reimburse clients in case of notary fraud.[27]

All of the aforementioned funds present not only fundamental differences in the broadness of their scope of application, but also variations in the compensation mechanisms. Those variations may be used as a starting point for drawing up a rough classification. The existing compensation schemes can be grouped depending on whether or not the claimant retains a right of action under the traditional law of torts. Using the German terminology, one might distinguish between funds *replacing* civil liability (*haftungsersetzend*) and those *completing* civil liability (*haftungsergänzend*). The vast majority of the compensation acts in France and Germany did not rule out the possibility of seeking damages in court. But it is noteworthy that the legislative debates regularly mention the perspective of replacing tort law by alternative compensation schemes, as is the case in work-related accidents.[28]

Another criterion for distinction could be the existence of a subsidiarity rule as a prerequisite of compensation by a fund. There are several compensation schemes which require the claimant to have tried unsuccessfully to obtain damages from the tortfeasor or his insurer. If comprehensive compensation is not available under tort law, funds offering subsidiary compensation will remedy the tortfeasor's insolvency or his/her non-insurance, or in case the amount of damages exceeds liability limitations, will offer additional damages. At the other end,

---

26 Einlagensicherungsfonds (Germany) and Fonds de garantie des assurés/Fonds de garantie des dépôts (France). For a recent comparative overview, see Eric Laeven, 'Deposit Insurance in the European Union' in Charles Enoch and others (eds), *From Fragmentation to Financial Integration in Europe* (International Monetary Fund 2014); Asli Demirgüç-Kunta, Edward Kaneb and Luc Laeven, 'Deposit Insurance Around the World: A Comprehensive Analysis and Database' (2015) 20 *Journal of Financial Stability* 155.

27 Notarversicherungsfonds (Bundesnotarordnung, §67). See Christoph U. Schmid, 'The Dutch and German Notarial Systems Compared' in Christine Godt (ed.), *Cross Border Research and Transnational Teaching under the Treaty of Lisbon* (Wolf Legal Publications 2013).

28 This is particularly true in Germany, where compensation funds, designed as a substitute for tort law, have been discussed for damages caused by pharmaceutical products and for environmental damages. See Knetsch, *Haftungsrecht und Entschädigungsfonds*, above n. 4, pp. 38 and 41 with further references.

authorities frequently establish funds offering compensation without subsidiarity to provide fast and unbureaucratic compensation, even if this means imposing a financial burden on the fund.[29]

A last approach to establishing a typology of compensation funds would be to assess the political context of their establishment. There is a quite subtle distinction between what may be called *prospective* and *retrospective* compensation schemes.[30] Indeed, some of the regimes are intended to be a long-term response to obvious gaps in the civil liability system and address therefore an undetermined number of claimants.[31] Others have been designed to respond to a public health or environmental catastrophe whose causes lay in the past and which concerns a specific number of victims. The thalidomide fund in Germany or the HIV-blood fund in France are the most obvious examples.

The characteristics of those retrospective funds are directly related to the context in which the compensation law has been enacted. Very often, public authorities tend to divert a potentially massive litigation away from the courts and find fund-based compensation schemes to be a very convenient means to deal with those claims more quickly and more quietly.[32]

It is obvious that these classification proposals are merely for ease of presentation and do not resolve more important issues that arise from the multiplication of compensation funds and their coexistence with traditional civil liability.

3. DOCTRINAL ISSUES: WHAT EXACTLY IS A COMPENSATION FUND?

There are only a few comprehensive studies on the general phenomenon of compensation funds. Instead of discussing the general role of those compensation schemes in the legal systems of France and Germany, legal

29 The damages advanced by the fund will be difficult or impossible to recover from the tortfeasor.

30 On the shortcomings of this criterion, see Knetsch, *Haftungsrecht und Entschädigungsfonds*, above n. 4, p. 123.

31 This is the case of the Motor Guarantee Fund or the compensation of medical injuries without medical malpractice by French ONIAM.

32 It seems that one of the objectives of the compensation fund established after the infected blood scandal in France was indeed to avoid trials against the State, and consequently, a public debate about the liability of public bodies.

scholars tend to give more attention to the advantages and shortcomings of each specific regime.

This relative discretion of the legal literature could be due to discomfort in addressing the legal nature of compensation funds and the distinction with other compensatory instruments. Sometimes, specific compensation regimes are analysed together with private insurance; some experts go so far as to speak of 'insurance funds'.[33] Sometimes, compensation funds are also presented as a part of French or German social security systems.

The proximity between compensation funds and insurance may be illustrated by the French compensation regime available to victims of terrorism.[34] The Guarantee Fund for Victims of Terrorism and Other Offences (FGTI) pays full compensation for personal injuries and their physical and material consequences. In cases of death, the fund also pays damages to the family members of the deceased. Due to the 2015 and 2016 terrorist attacks, the Guarantee Fund has handled over 10,000 requests from victims and their families, i.e. more than twice the number of requests the fund has dealt with between its establishment in 1990 and the *Charlie Hebdo* attack.[35]

To understand the link between private insurance and compensation funds, one has to examine the FGTI's funding regulations. In fact, until recently,[36] the Guarantee Fund did not receive any subsidy from the State budget; its resources only came from an additional charge on property insurance policies (€5.90) paid by the policyholders.[37] Considering that a house insurance scheme (*assurance-habitation*) is compulsory for both tenants and flat owners, and that property insurance policies also include compulsory motor insurance, it is obvious that almost every household, if not resident, in France takes part in the Guarantee Fund's financing.[38]

---

33 Peter Landau, 'Sonderopfer des technischen Fortschritts' in Konrad Duden and others, *Gerechtigkeit in der Industriegesellschaft* (C.F. Müller 1972), p. 121. See also Jean-Luc de Boissieu, *Introduction à l'assurance* (L'Argus de l'assurance 2005), p. 117.

34 See references above n. 10.

35 See Daniel Psenny, 'Attentat de Nice: l'État promet d'indemniser rapidement les victimes', *Le Monde* 20 July 2016.

36 In 2017, the French state and the Guarantee Fund signed an agreement providing for a tax-funded reinsurance scheme in case a massive terrorist attack leads to cash flow vulnerabilities <https://www.fondsdegarantie.fr/wp-content/uploads/2017/06/Convention_cadre_Etat-FGTI.pdf>.

37 Governmental order, 30 October 2015, art. 1. See, on the legal nature of this additional charge, Francis Quérol, 'L'indemnisation des victimes d'actes de terrorisme. Le financement du fonds de garantie' [1988] *Revue française de droit administratif* 106.

38 See Thierry Renoux, *L'indemnisation publique des victimes d'attentats* (Economica/PUAM 1988), para. 254 and Yvonne Lambert-Faivre, 'Le sinistre en assurance de

Keeping this in mind, it is not absurd to consider that the FGTI compensation regime is nothing more than a government-imposed first-party insurance for personal injuries due to terrorist attacks. The additional charges on said insurance policies may be seen as a form of insurance premium providing coverage for all potential victims of terrorism. The compensation scheme can thus be analysed as an insurance contract 'for whom it may concern' (*Versicherung für wen es angeht* or *assurance pour le compte de qui il appartiendra*) because every contributor finances not only his or her right to compensation, but also the compensation of others, in case they are hit by a terrorist attack.[39]

Yet, despite a number of obvious similarities, the proximity between both legal instruments does not mean that compensation funds are a specific kind of private insurance, mainly for two reasons.

First of all, the legal relationship between the contributors and the compensation fund is not a contractual one, but one that arises by operation of law (*kraft Gesetzes* or *par l'effet de la loi*). One could assert that this argument is not relevant because there are several compulsory insurance contracts under French and German law, but the mere obligation to contract does not establish *ipso facto* a legal bond between an insurer and the insured person. The obligation to subscribe an insurance contract leaves the freedom to conclude a contract with the insurer of one's choice, which is not the case in the field of compensation funds.

The second key difference between compensation funds and private insurance concerns the rules for determining the fund contributions. Unlike in insurance law, there is no individual premium calculation using actuarial methods. The contributions to fund budgets are fixed by public authorities, regardless of any individual risk coefficient or exposure level of the individual contributors.[40]

This brings us to the second comparison intended to provide greater clarity on the legal nature of compensation funds. Since the legal relationship between a compensation fund, its contributors and its

responsabilité et la garantie de l'indemnisation des victimes' [1987] *Revue générale des assurances terrestres* 193, 222.

39 See, on this type of insurance contract, Jürgen Basedow and others (eds), *Principles of European Insurance Contract Law (PEICL)* (Sellier 2009), p. 265 and in French, Véronique Nicolas, *Essai d'une nouvelle analyse du contrat d'assurance* (L.G.D.J. 1996), para. 541.

40 See Hans Möller, 'Moderne Theorien zum Begriff der Versicherung und des Versicherungsvertrages' [1962] *Zeitschrift für die gesamte Versicherungswissenschaft* 269, 273; Horst Baumann, *Leistungspflicht und Regreß des Entschädigungsfonds für Schäden aus Kraftfahrzeugunfällen* (VVW 1969), p. 98.

beneficiaries is the result of statutory law and not contract, one might assume that fund-based compensation schemes are nothing more than a new branch of social security (*protection sociale* or *Sozialversicherung*).[41]

This view is supported by the analogy between the goals of social security and those of compensation funds. In both cases, benefits are granted in order to provide protection for individuals against the main risks in life: illness and disability.[42]

Looking, though, at the theoretical bases and the implementation of social security and compensation funds, there are significant differences between both legal instruments. First, the allowances granted by the compensation funds go beyond the scope of social security benefits, because the beneficiaries are awarded damages for non-pecuniary loss (*préjudice moral*) or for harm to property (*atteinte aux biens*). Compensation funds operate thus more like a supplement to social security than like an autonomous branch of social protection.[43] Second, there is no need to attest financial needs to be entitled to compensation by a fund, nor is the claimant requested to prove that he or she has paid a financial contribution to the fund. Third and finally, the claimant must establish that the harm has occurred under specific circumstances, for example, in a terrorist act, whereas under social security law, the cause of the injury does not matter. Briefly, it could be said that the law of compensation funds is governed by a 'causal principle', while social security benefits are awarded in accordance with a 'final principle', because the starting point is the actual situation of the insured person.[44]

---

41 Both schemes are implemented by law and provide supra-individual protection against social risks. See, on the concept of social risk, Jef van Langendonck (ed.), *The New Social Risks* (Kluwer Law 1997); Constanzo Ranci (ed.), *Social Vulnerability in Europe: The New Configuration of Social Risks* (Palgrave Macmillan 2010).

42 There is congruency between the tort law-based concept of personal injury and the concepts of illness and professional incapacity, specific to social security. See for example, Maximilian Fuchs, *Zivilrecht und Sozialrecht – Recht und Dogmatik materieller Existenzsicherung in der modernen Gesellschaft* (C.H. Beck 1992), p. 157; Eberhard Eichenhofer, *Sozialrecht*, 11th edn (Mohr Siebeck 2019), para. 243.

43 At most, compensation funds could be qualified as a subcategory of 'social compensation' (*soziale Entschädigung*), a branch of social protection law in Germany. See Bertram Schulin, *Soziale Entschädigung als Teilsystem kollektiven Schadensausgleich* (Heymanns 1981); Ulrich Becker, *Soziales Entschädigungsrecht: Bestand, Grundsätze und Neuordnung* (Nomos 2018); in English, Danny Pieters, *Social Security: An Introduction to Basic Principles*, 2nd edn (Kluwer Law 2006), p. 6.

44 On these two terms, see Helmar Bley, 'Alternative Elementarprinzipien des Sozialleistungsrechts' [1978] *Zeitschrift für Sozialreform* 1; Helmar Bley, Ralf Kreikebohm and Andreas Marschner, *Sozialrecht*, 9th edn (Vahlen 2007), para. 96.

The comparison with private insurance and social security showed that it is difficult to find an adequate category for compensation funds in the existing legal system. They fall between those two legal instruments and seem to be a category apart, whose only point in common is the grant of partial or full compensation for injuries suffered under circumstances outlined by law.

4. PROCEDURAL ISSUES: WHAT IS THE DIFFERENCE BETWEEN A CIVIL LIABILITY ACTION AND COMPENSATION BY A FUND?

In order to know whether fund regimes provide a genuine alternative to civil liability, it is important to assess the relevant compensation procedures and to compare them to a court action. In fact, instead of turning to the courts, a fund beneficiary brings his or her claim before the competent body of the compensation fund, which often is a multidisciplinary committee in charge of investigating the claim, and when appropriate, ordering compensation payments.

The extrajudicial nature of this compensation procedure is generally presented as an asset, both in terms of timeliness and simplicity. Almost every fund regime has its own website where victims can download standard application forms and information about the conditions for compensation and the description of the procedure.[45] There is no need for a lawyer, nor for a costly investigation about the applicable law and court jurisdiction. Providing comprehensive support and information, fund administrations are deemed to be exemplary in matters of assistance to victims and families. One could speak of a 'quasi-administrative' procedure, without the burden of bureaucracy.

Although at first glance, the compensation procedures under a fund regime seem to be above all criticism, this positive evaluation should not preclude a critical assessment. How could you otherwise explain that the French asbestos compensation fund FIVA is challenged before the courts in more than 500 new cases every year?[46]

---

45 See for example, the very comprehensive website of the French FGTI and FGAO <http://www.fondsdegarantie.fr>. See also the German equivalent <http://www.verkehrsopferhilfe.de>. Both websites allow eligible victims to file a compensation claim very easily.

46 See Fonds d'indemnisation des victimes de l'amiante, *Rapport d'activité 2018* (FIVA 2019), p. 24.

Apart from the issue of the extent of compensation (which will be addressed hereafter), it seems that the reason for this regrettable statistic lies in the procedural weaknesses of the compensation procedure under the fund regimes, which has been criticised for not offering the same guarantees as a court action.

Two major elements seem to contribute to the lack of acceptance of special compensation regimes and to explain the amount of litigation related to fund decisions challenged by victims.

First, victims compensated by funds often regret the administrative character of the procedure, insisting on a more active role in the process. Victimological studies show, in fact, that claimants often want to tell their side of the story and to express their emotional needs. If a third party has caused the injury, an official condemnation of the act and the resulting recognition of the claimants' victim status are the best remedy against what is known as 'secondary victimisation'.[47]

It is obvious that compensation funds cannot offer both a simple and swift procedure and the satisfaction of all of the claimants' needs. Nevertheless, the example of the French Compensation Office of Medical Accidents proves that there is a way in between, and that it is possible to find a balance between an efficient procedure and responsiveness to the victims.

Indeed, the Patients' Rights Act of 2002[48] introduced so-called Commissions of conciliation and compensation (*commissions régionales de conciliation et d'indemnisation* [CRCI]) in each region, responsible for dealing with compensation claims.[49] Those commissions are chaired by a magistrate and composed of 20 persons, divided into six major categories of members representing patients, health professionals, hospital practitioners, health institutions and facilities, the Compensation Office, and insurers.[50] The procedure guarantees that the claimants will have comprehensive participation rights and entitles

47 On this question, see Uli Orth, 'Secondary Victimization of Crime Victims by Criminal Proceedings' (2002) 15 *Social Justice Research* 313; Hans Joachim Schneider (ed.), *Internationales Handbuch der Kriminologie* (de Gruyter, 2007), vol. 1, p. 409.

48 See the references made above nn. 16 and 19 and Florence G'sell-Macrez, 'Medical Malpractice and Compensation in France: Part I: the French Rules of Medical Liability since the Patients' Rights Law of March 4, 2002' (2011) 86 *Chicago Kent Law Review* 1093.

49 On this procedure, see especially Thouvenin, 'French Medical Malpractice Compensation since the Act of March 4, 2002: Liability Rules Combined with Indemnification Rules and Correlated with Several Kinds of Proceedings', above n. 19.

50 Code de la santé publique, art. R 1142-5.

them, in particular, to request a hearing. The statistics published by the Compensation Office are very promising, and one might suppose that the low number of challenged CRCI decisions is not unrelated to these procedural characteristics.[51]

Second, it is important that the compensation acts provide for specific procedural guarantees ensuring the claimant's right to a fair hearing. It may seem surprising to insist on the importance of the principle of fair trial in this context, given that one of the main objectives of these acts is to prevent victims from going to court to obtain compensation. Are the simplification of the procedures and the resulting deactivation of some procedural guarantees not the natural counterpart of timeliness and simplicity?

Despite the advantages offered by fund regimes, an increasing number of claimants feel that their request for compensation is not treated with all the objectivity required. The *ad hoc* compensation schemes implemented after an environmental or public health disaster are especially concerned by such criticism, which is mainly based on an allegedly unbalanced composition of the fund committees.[52]

The experiences with the asbestos fund in France and the thalidomide fund in Germany show that it is of great importance that the body responsible for dealing with the compensation claims affords basic procedural guarantees, such as independence and impartiality, to prevent failed claimants from going systemically to court in order to challenge the denial or, even worse, from filing a claim based on the same facts. To ensure procedural economies, and more broadly, the success of fund-based compensation regimes, there is also a need to strengthen the role of lawyers during the procedure. Claimants are not always aware of their lack of understanding of the legal conditions and the scope of their right to compensation.[53]

If these conditions are met, the compensation procedures implemented by fund regimes may be a real alternative to civil liability actions. But what about the substantive outcome of the compensation process?

---

51 See, most recently, ONIAM, *Rapport d'activité 2018* (ONIAM 2019), p. 21.

52 See, on the composition of the thalidomide foundation's board, Dietrich Böhm, *Die Entschädigung der Contergan-Kinder* (D. Böhm Verlag 1973), p. 157. In France, see especially Anne Guégan-Lécuyer, *Dommages de masse et responsabilité civile* (L.G.D.J. 2006), para. 184 and Christophe Guettier, 'Le fonds d'indemnisation des victimes de l'amiante' [2002] *Responsabilité civile et assurances* 2002, chr no. 19.

53 On this aspect, see Knetsch, *Haftungsrecht und Entschädigungsfonds*, above n. 4, p. 171.

Can all compensation funds offer full compensation as is the case under tort law, or is reduced compensation the necessary downside of a rapid and simple procedure?

5. PRACTICAL ISSUES: ARE FUND BENEFITS EQUAL TO FULL COMPENSATION UNDER TORT LAW?

In France, compensation funds have been subject to growing criticism because of the amount of damages paid to the victims. One cannot deny that the level of compensation varies greatly from one scheme to another, and even within the same compensation fund.[54] Some of the regimes offer full compensation in accordance with the principle of *réparation integrale*, whereas others only award partial compensation or a mere lump-sum.

The existing differences, which are one of the trademarks of compensation funds, seem to break a basic rule of civil liability and can be seen as a source of discrimination among victims. Yet those inequalities have to be put in perspective.

Indeed, some of the compensation funds are established to fill compensation gaps in cases where no third party can be held liable for damages. The French agricultural disaster fund or the compensation schemes for victims of motor vehicle accidents caused by unidentified drivers may be cited in this regard. In those cases, victims have no choice but to claim compensation from a fund, because there is no other remedy available. So, in the absence of a frame of reference, fund benefits cannot be adequately compared to full compensation.[55]

In general, physical injuries receive a more favourable treatment than damages to property, which often are only partially compensated, as they are seen to be less disastrous. Other distortions might be explained by policy choices, as illustrated by the existing differences between victims of terrorism and those of other offences.

---

54 This is the case before the French *Fonds de garantie des victimes d'actes de terrorisme et d'autres infractions* (FGTI). Whereas the principle of full reparations applies to victims of terrorist acts, those of ordinary crimes are subject to a deductible or a maximum compensation account. See Jean Favard and Jean-Michel Guth, 'La marche vers l'uniformisation ? La quatrième réforme du droit à indemnisation des victimes d'infractions' [1990] *La Semaine Juridique Édition générale* (JCP G) I no. 3466.

55 See Knetsch, *Haftungsrecht und Entschädigungsfonds*, above n. 4, p. 181.

Under French law, the principle of full compensation only applies fully to victims of terrorist acts, whereas individuals affected by ordinary criminality have to meet additional conditions, such as a certain seriousness of the offence or a certain level of income. This discrimination is not only related to budgetary reasons,[56] but also reflects the specific accountability of the state for acts of crime, directed against the society or its government.[57]

However, the criticism goes well beyond that. Compensation funds are also accused of applying a minimalist view of the concept of full reparation (*réparation intégrale*) and of granting compensation which is less comprehensive than the damages that a court would award in a similar case. Such an analysis may come as a surprise to foreign lawyers, because it is hard to see how a *full* reparation, for example, of a personal injury, can be 'more or less full'.

This issue needs to be looked at, because of the peculiar place of non-pecuniary damages under French law.[58] Over the last decades, civil courts have given increasing weight to the compensation of *préjudice moral*. Although French tort law has always had a very liberal approach towards damages, a significant increase in the number of different types of non-pecuniary damages can be observed in the case law. Non-pecuniary damages may not only include pain and suffering (*souffrances endurées*), but may also give rise to separate amounts for the loss of amenity (*préjudice d'agrément*), sexual impairment (*préjudice sexuel*) or aesthetic harm (*préjudice esthétique*).[59]

Until recently, every single type of non-pecuniary damages was assessed rather arbitrarily by a judge because there were no official rules on how the amounts should be calculated. Thus, it was not surprising that the court practice revealed significant regional disparities. The pain of

---

56 On this aspect, see Marie-Ève Roujou de Boubée, *Essai sur la notion de réparation* (L.G.D.J. 1974), p. 405; Geneviève Viney and Patrice Jourdain, *Les effets de la responsabilité*, 2nd edn (L.G.D.J. 2001), para. 309.

57 For a detailed assessment of the link between the level of collective responsibility and the scope of compensation, see Knetsch, *Haftungsrecht und Entschädigungsfonds*, above n. 4, p. 149.

58 See Jean-Sébastien Borghetti, 'Non-pecuniary Damages in France' (2015) 3 *Chinese Journal of Comparative Law* 268.

59 Under French law, non-pecuniary damages are divided into several distinct heads of damages. See Jonas Knetsch, 'La désintégration du préjudice moral' [2015] *Recueil Dalloz* 443. For a comparative analysis, see Gerhard Wagner, 'Ersatz immaterieller Schäden: Bestandsaufnahme und europäische Perspektiven' [2004] *Juristenzeitung* 319, 322.

a broken leg was evaluated in the same way if the claimant had been a victim of a car accident in Brittany as it was in Provence.[60]

Some of the compensation funds, such as the National Compensation Office for Medical Accidents ONIAM, have developed so-called compensation guidelines (*référentiel d'indemnisation*) based on a statistical survey of damages awarded by judicial and administrative courts.[61] The benchmarks closely follow the average amounts allocated by the courts, so that some victims are awarded lower damages than those they could have been offered before the competent court.

To address this issue, the French Ministry of Justice published a draft version of a reform act of the civil liability law in February 2017,[62] and at the same time, announced the enactment of unique compensation guidelines, which shall apply not only to court actions, but also to transactions with insurance companies and compensation funds.[63] Meanwhile, the existing discrepancies in the assessment of non-pecuniary damages encourage claimants not just to accept the benefits awarded by a fund, but to ask for judicial review and for additional compensation in order to meet the standards of the most generous jurisdictions.[64]

This very complex issue leads directly to the last point regarding the interplay between tort law and compensation funds, and in general, the place of fund-based compensation schemes within a legal system.

---

60 See Martine Quenillet-Bourrié, 'L'évaluation monétaire du préjudice corporel: pratique judiciaire et données transactionnelles' [1995] *La Semaine Juridique Édition générale* (JCP G) I no. 3818; Pierre Bailly, 'Indemnisation et aléa judiciaire' [1992] *Recueil Dalloz* chr 202.

61 <http://www.oniam.fr/procedure-indemnisation/bareme-indemnisation>. See Dominique Martin, Philippe Tréguier and Olivier Saumon, 'La réparation des accidents médicaux: un engagement fort de la solidarité nationale' [2005] *Gazette du Palais* 1651, 1656.

62 <www.textes.justice.gouv.fr/art_pix/avpjl-responsabilite-civile.pdf>. See on the 2016 preliminary draft, Geneviève Viney, 'L'espoir d'une recodification du droit de la responsabilité civile' [2016] *Recueil Dalloz* 1378; Jean-Sébastien Borghetti, 'Vue d'ensemble de l'avant-projet de réforme' [2016] *Recueil Dalloz* 1386. See also supplement to no. 30-35 of [2016] *La Semaine Juridique Édition générale* (JCP G). See also Jean-Sébastien Borghetti and Simon Whittaker, *French Civil Liability in Comparative Perspective* (Hart Publishing 2019).

63 Draft Reform Act art. 1271(1) ('Un décret en Conseil d'État fixe les postes de préjudices extrapatrimoniaux qui peuvent être évalués selon un référentiel indicatif d'indemnisation, dont il détermine les modalités d'élaboration et de publication. Ce référentiel est réévalué tous les trois ans en fonction de l'évolution de la moyenne des indemnités accordées par les juridictions.')

64 The issue of the admissibility of those actions has arisen particularly in France, where legal scholars have qualified this question as one of '*cumul d'indemnités*', i.e. of the accumulation of damages.

6. ORGANISATIONAL ISSUES: HOW SHOULD COMPENSATION FUNDS BE COORDINATED WITH TORT LAW?

Should victims be allowed to file a claim against an alleged tortfeasor even after they have received 'full compensation' from a compensation fund? On a wider scale, the question of *cumul d'indemnités* raises the issue of the interplay between civil or administrative liability and the compensation funds.

The answer given by some French courts is quite curious, because the administrative courts, and above all, the Council of State (*Conseil d'État*) decided in the 1990s to satisfy the requests of victims of the HIV blood scandal for additional compensation.[65] The reason for this astonishing decision was that, in the mind of the legislature, the assessment of non-pecuniary damages by the compensation fund did not preclude any further compensation for the same types of damage. In other words, the right to compensation was not extinguished by the acceptance of the compensation offer made by the fund. Compensation funds, on the one hand, and civil and administrative liability, on the other hand, were seen by the Council of State as two separate systems, and nothing should prevent the claimant from taking advantage of the existing discrepancies between the relevant assessment methods.

After several years of hesitation, particularly due to the opposite view of the Court of Cassation regarding civil liability actions,[66] the issue has been resolved by the legislature. Every compensation act now lays down a provision that prohibits an accumulation of fund benefits and additional damages in court. In accepting the offer of compensation made by the fund, the claimant is deemed to drop any pending lawsuit and to renounce any future lawsuit against the alleged tortfeasors. In some compensation acts, the legislature even qualifies the acceptance of a compensation offer by the victim as an out-of-court settlement (*transaction*).[67]

Apart from the problem of the accumulation of damages (*cumul d'indemnités*), which now has found a satisfactory solution under French

---

65 CE (avis) 15 October 1993, RFD adm 1994, 553 and CE 16 June 1997, D 1997, inf rap 177.

66 Cass civ (2) 26 January 1994, Gaz Pal 1994, jur 525; 14 January 1998, Resp civ assur 1998, comm 157.

67 See for example, Code de la santé publique, art. L 3122-3 (4) ('L'acceptation de l'offre de l'office par la victime vaut transaction au sens de l'article 2044 du code civil.').

law, the issue of coordination between compensation funds and tort law also raises the question of consolidating the existing fund regimes. Would it not be more appropriate to bring together every specific compensation scheme under the roof of a so-called 'super-fund'?

The German legal literature says little about this issue, possibly because of the small number of compensation funds, although some authors suggested the establishment of a comprehensive fund for environmental damages in the 1980s.[68] In contrast, the idea of a 'super-fund' received resounding support among French legal scholars.

Indeed, the French legal literature of the 1990s and early 2000s provides for a wide range of suggestions varying from the replacement of tort law with a comprehensive compensation scheme for personal injuries, comparable to the New Zealand Accident Compensation Corporation, to the establishment of a general subsidiary compensation fund designed to cover all of the existing gaps in civil and administrative liability.[69]

As interesting as it may seem, the idea of clustering existing compensation funds or creating a 'super-fund' of whatever kind seems to be neither a realistic nor an opportune option.

It is not realistic because the establishment of a unique compensation scheme for all personal injuries would amount to a 'legal revolution' because tort law remedies would largely be replaced with a no-fault compensation scheme administered by a fund or another state-related organisation. Obviously, this would significantly affect the interests of both insurance companies and lawyers, because they would find themselves completely marginalised. The New Zealand reform could only succeed because of exceptional political circumstances: a disorganised national bar association and a weakened insurance lobby.[70] History shows that

---

68 See Reinhard Ganten, 'Entschädigungsleistung durch Fonds – Gedanken über eine Sozialisierung der Schadensersatzpflicht bei Umweltschäden' in Rainer Lagoni and Marian Paschke (eds), *Seehandelsrecht und Seerecht. Festschrift für Rolf Herber zum 70. Geburtstag* (LIT Verlag 1999); Gerhard Hohloch, *Entschädigungsfonds auf dem Gebiet des Umwelthaftungsrechts* (Umweltbundesamt 1994).

69 See Philippe le Tourneau, *Droit de la responsabilité et des contrats* (Dalloz 2014), para. 90; Julien Bourdoiseau, *L'influence perturbatrice du dommage corporel* (L.G.D.J. 2010), para. 350; Christophe Radé, 'Plaidoyer en faveur d'une réforme de la responsabilité civile' [2003] *Recueil Dalloz* 2247; Louis Mélennec, *L'indemnisation du handicap* (Desclée De Brouwer 1997), p. 177. See also André Tunc, 'Evolution du concept juridique de responsabilité' (1996) 31 *Droit et cultures* 19, 27.

70 See Richard Gaskins, 'Regulating Private Law: Socio-legal Perspectives on the New Zealand Accident Compensation Scheme' (2009) 17 *Torts Law Journal* 24;

other jurisdictions that have been attracted to the New Zealand no-fault compensation scheme failed to enact such a radical change.[71]

An attempt to merge the existing compensation funds would also not be opportune. Fund-based regimes are a highly flexible legislative device to address the consequences of public health or environmental disasters.[72] The diversity of the conditions and the extent of fund benefits not only reflect the inability of the legislature to build a coherent compensation system, but also – and perhaps most importantly – the need for an instrument which is malleable enough to deal with different kinds of shortcomings in tort law. The strength of a fund-based compensation regime is that everyone can see something different in it, and that you can discretely avoid the word 'liability'.

An acceptable alternative solution might be for the legislature to create a 'single-window' for individuals whose claims fall in the scope of one or more compensation funds.[73] The idea would be to regroup administratively existing compensation funds, while maintaining the different schemes with specific conditions and compensation levels in order to facilitate access to compensation funds. This strategy has already been taken up by the French legislature.[74]

The legislature should not give up a differentiating system of fund-based compensation regimes whose specifics are the result of policy choices, budgetary considerations and the pressure of public opinion. It would impoverish the law of compensation, whose apparent complexity is only the reflection of the complex reality of our society.

Geoffrey Palmer, 'Big Change, Exciting Adventures: Accident Compensation' in Geoffrey Palmer (ed.), *Reform: A Memoir* (Victoria University Press 2013). See also Peter McKenzie, 'The Compensation Scheme No One Asked for: The Origins of ACC in New Zealand' (2003) 31 *Victoria University of Wellington Law Review* 193.

71 See Geoffrey Palmer, *Compensation for Incapacity: A Study of Law and Social Change in New Zealand and Australia* (Oxford University Press 1979), p. 174; Mark Robinson, *Accident Compensation in Australia: No-Fault Schemes* (Legal Books 1987), p. 17.

72 Knetsch, *Haftungsrecht und Entschädigungsfonds*, above n. 4, p. 213.

73 The idea of a single entry point for different administrative procedures originates from the field of international trade. See United Nations, *Establishing a Legal Framework for an International Trade Single Window* (ECE/TRADE/401, 2013). See also Maria A. Wimmer, 'A European Perspective Towards Online One-stop Government: The eGOV Project' (2002) 1 *Electronic Commerce Research and Applications* 92.

74 This is especially relevant in the field of healthcare-related injuries (ONIAM) and accidents covered by compulsory insurance (FGAO). See Knetsch, *Le droit de la responsabilité administrative à l'épreuve des fonds d'indemnisation*, above n. 4, para. 639.

7. CONCLUSION

This chapter deliberately did not get into the details of each compensation scheme, but tried to show instead that, over the last 25 years, fund-based regimes have become an integral part of the law governing compensation in both countries, and that they raise a great number of difficult issues.

Not all of them could be mentioned within the limits of this contribution. Further research should be undertaken to overcome the remaining uncertainties related to compensation funds. For example, the exact legal nature of the funds' contribution is still unclear.[75] Another question that needs examination is whether funds established to redress historical injustices[76] should be regarded as *compensation* funds.[77]

The aforementioned issues and those which need to be addressed in further research show that compensation funds are a 'confounder' within the traditional tort law system. Neither a subcategory of private insurance nor a branch of social security, they may be located somewhere in between, which is what makes their assessment through the lens of traditional categories so difficult. The future will tell us if the success story of compensation funds in France and, to a lesser extent, in Germany can continue in other legal systems. In the meantime, it is worthwhile to explore further such a fine academic subject.[78]

---

75 Can we qualify them as taxes or other public levies? If so, must the legislature comply with the rules of public budgetary law? See, for example, the decision of unconstitutionality BVerfG, 18 May 2004, BVerfGE 110, 370 (dissolution of the German solidarity fund for the return of waste [*Solidarfonds Abfallrückführung*]). On this aspect, see Knetsch, *Le droit de la responsabilité administrative à l'épreuve des fonds d'indemnisation*, above n. 4, para. 362.

76 For example, the foundation for the victims of Nazi forced labour (*Stiftung 'Erinnerung, Verantwortung und Zukunft'*) or the funds created for mistreated children who received their education under residential care in both West and East Germany (*Fonds Heimerziehung in der Bundesrepublik Deutschland, Fonds Heimerziehung in der DDR* and *Stiftung 'Anerkennung und Hilfe'*). See on this issue from a French standpoint Kelly Picard, *La responsabilité de l'État du fait du préjudice historique* (Institut Francophone pour la Justice et la Démocratie 2019).

77 Often, those regimes only pay a symbolic sum to the victims or their families.

78 The author of this contribution is very much looking forward to the outcome of two ongoing PhD projects on this subject at the Antwerp Faculty of Law.

COMPENSATION FUNDS IN THE NETHERLANDS

Michael FAURE, Ton HARTLIEF and Gerrit VAN MAANEN*

1. COMPENSATION FUNDS IN GENERAL

1.1. WHY ARE COMPENSATION FUNDS NEEDED?

In recent decades the Netherlands have been confronted with various types of catastrophes. In some cases, this concerned natural disasters, particularly an earthquake in Southern Limburg, flooding in south-east Netherlands and heavy rains. There were also man-made disasters that led to a lot of attention in the media. In particular, the explosion of a fireworks

* This chapter elaborates on earlier publications by the first two authors: M. Faure and T. Hartlief (eds), 'The Netherlands' in *Financial Compensation for Victims of Catastrophes: A Comparative Legal Approach* (Springer 2006), pp. 195–226; T. Hartlief, 'Schadefondsen en de rol van de overheid' in *Kring van aansprakelijken bij massaschade* (Sdu Uitgevers 2002), pp. 61 et seq.

factory in Enschede,[1] the large fire in a cafe in Volendam,[2] a legionella epidemic in Bovenkarspel,[3] Q fever in the south of the Netherlands,[4] the shooting in Alphen aan de Rijn[5] and the crash of the MH17 on 17 July 2014 in the Ukraine killing all 283 passengers and 15 crew on board,[6] were incidents that hit many victims. In all of these cases the question arose as to what legal instruments could be used to provide compensation.

Dutch legal writers have often pointed to the difficulties that victims will encounter in their attempts to obtain compensation for the financial consequences of catastrophes through normal methods. For instance, the possibility to apply tort law in cases of natural disasters (such as flooding or earthquake) will often be difficult for the simple fact that a liable injurer may often be lacking.[7]

This issue has thus given rise to various occasions when the Dutch government has indeed intervened with a public budget to provide *ad hoc* compensation to the victims, albeit that the legal arrangements in that

---

1 The Enschede fireworks disaster (known in the Netherlands as the *Vuurwerkramp* meaning 'fireworks disaster') was a catastrophic fireworks explosion occurring at the SE Fireworks depot on 13 May 2000 at 13.00 GMT, in the eastern Dutch city of Enschede.

2 The Volendam New Year's fire was a cafe fire in the Dutch town of Volendam on the 2000–2001 New Year's night. The fire began early on New Year's Day 2001 and caused the death of 14 young people. In all, there were 241 people admitted to hospital, 200 of whom suffered serious burns.

3 The Bovenkarspel legionellosis outbreak (Dutch: *Legionellaramp*; Legionella disaster) began on 25 February 1999 in Bovenkarspel, the Netherlands, and was one of the largest outbreaks of legionellosis in history. With at least 32 dead and 206 severe infections it was the deadliest legionellosis outbreak since the original 1976 outbreak in Philadelphia, USA.

4 Since 2007 the Netherlands has been faced with the largest outbreak of Q fever ever reported. Over 4,000 cases have been reported.

5 On 9 April 2011, six people were killed by a gunman who entered the Ridderhof mall in Alphen aan den Rijn, the Netherlands, a town approximately 33 km south-west of Amsterdam. Using a rifle, 24-year-old Tristan van der Vlis shot several people and then killed himself, reportedly with a different firearm. There were seven deaths, including the killer, and 17 wounded, making it the deadliest assault attack in the Netherlands since the 2009 attack on the Dutch Royal Family in Apeldoorn.

6 The Boeing 777-200ER airliner lost contact about 50 km from the Ukraine–Russia border and crashed near Torez in Donetsk Oblast, Ukraine, 40 km from the border. The crash occurred during the battle in Shakhtarsk Raion, part of the ongoing war in Donbass, in an area controlled by the Donbass People's Militia. According to American and German intelligence sources, the plane was mistakenly shot down by pro-Russian insurgents using a Buk surface-to-air missile (SA-11) fired from the territory which they controlled.

7 See T. Hartlief, 'Schadefondsen en de rol van de overheid', in: *Kring van aansprakelijken bij massaschade* (2002), pp. 61 et seq.

respect are not unified and that the arrangements have been the subject of criticism. As will be highlighted below, a specific Act (*Wet Tegemoetkoming Schade bij Rampen*,[8] 'WTS') was created with the aim of providing a – more or less – general tool for compensation to the victims of catastrophes.

Another main argument can be found in the shortcomings of tort law in specific situations. Sometimes it is felt that it is not fair or too harsh for the victim to prove wrongful behaviour of the tortfeasor. For example, in cases of an unmotorised victim in a traffic accident with a car. In most legal jurisdictions tort law has been modified in order to give the unmotorised victim a more favourable position. The French Law on Traffic liability, the so-called Loi Badintair of 1985, introduces an almost absolute liability for all traffic victims – with the exception of the driver – and even eliminates the normal requirement of a causal link and replaces that with the simple requirement that a motor vehicle must have been involved.

1.1.1. A General Fund: WTS 1998

During the 1990s an intense debate took place in the Netherlands concerning compensation for victims of catastrophes, of flooding in particular. The debate also concerned the so-called binding decisions of the insurers not to cover natural disasters. Remarkably, the Dutch government first contemplated introducing the French model of a compulsory additional coverage for natural disasters. Originally the government argued against the French solution since it was feared that free consumer choice would be limited and that this compulsory system would lead to increased costs for the citizen.[9] Later the government apparently considered these problems as less important since it introduced a draft largely similar to the French solution: a fund would be installed financed through a tax on housing insurances. All insured (bad or good risks) would have to pay the tax. However, the Dutch Council of State formulated a negative advice concerning this draft. The Council argued that it would be more likely to allow the government to finance this risk. Moreover, the Council of State held that it would be likely that the risk of flooding could be insured.[10]

---

8 Until 2010, known as *Wet Tegemoetkoming Schade bij Rampen en Zware Ongevallen*.

9 See *Kamerstukken II* 1993–1994, 23 400 VII, no. 34, 2 and for a further discussion of this parliamentary debate see M. Faure and T. Hartlief (eds), 'The Netherlands' in *Financial Compensation for Victims of Catastrophes: A Comparative Legal Approach* (Springer 2006), pp. 185–186.

10 *Kamerstukken II* 1995–1996, 26 640, no. 1, 2–3.

The criticism of the Council of State was considered to be so serious that the government decided to withdraw the draft.

In the next phase the Belgian example of the catastrophes fund of 1976 suddenly seemed appealing and this act became the model for the so-called WTS, an Act concerning compensation of damage in case of catastrophes and large accidents. The goal of the WTS was to offer a more structural solution to the compensation of victims of catastrophes instead of the applicable system of *ad hoc* solutions as used at the time. The WTS provides a right to compensation of damage and lays down the main principles of compensation.[11] The WTS is applicable in case of flooding as a result of fresh water, or earthquakes that are considered a catastrophe or large accident in the sense of the WTS. In addition, art. 3 of the WTS provides that the WTS can be declared applicable through a Royal Decree, which can only be the case if the government considers the incident to be a catastrophe or large accident mentioned in art. 1 of the *Wet veiligheidsregio's* (Act on Security Regions).[12] The parliamentary proceedings make clear that such an accident at least requires that many governmental organisations and services of various disciplines must have intervened in a coordinated way and that the accident has endangered the health of many persons and moreover caused substantial damage.[13]

The WTS clearly has a *subsidiary* character which is made clear in the Act itself. Article 4 for instance provides that the victim will receive compensation for particular heads of damage, like damage to a dwelling, commercial loss and property damage. Also, other heads of damage can be declared to fall under the scope of the WTS, but pure economic loss will not be compensated since this is considered to be a normal business risk.[14] Importantly, art. 4.3 of the WTS stipulates that the victim is not entitled to compensation under the WTS when the damage was reasonably insurable or when the victim was able to obtain compensation from another source. The parliamentary proceeding made clear that damage is considered as reasonably insurable when it is not generally excluded from coverage and that it is generally insurable without limiting conditions or excessively

---

11 For details see F.J. de Vries, 'Vergoeding van Rampschade' [1998] NJB 1908–1913, Faure and Hartlief (eds), 'The Netherlands', above n. 9, pp. 149–172 and J.F. de Groot, 'Na de ramp. Een beschouwing over de toepassing van de WTS' [2004] *Overheid en Aansprakelijkheid* (O&A) 141–152.

12 Act of 11 February 2010, on fire prevention, prevention of catastrophes, crises management and medical assistance.

13 *Kamerstukken II* 1996–1997, 25 159, no. 3, 4–5.

14 See *Kamerstukken II* 1996–1997, 25 159, no. 5, 25–26.

high costs. It is therefore explicitly mentioned that, for instance, damage to motor vehicles will not be compensated through the WTS, since that type of damage is insurable.[15] If, however, insurance could theoretically be possible, but victims would *de facto* not have used this possibility since the premium charged would not be proportional to the coverage provided, the WTS may be applicable again.[16]

The subsidiary nature of the WTS also has consequences for the relationship to liability law. Indeed, a consequence of art. 4.3 is that the damage should not be recoverable from another source. Practice has shown that as a result the WTS may not be applicable in all cases of man-made disaster, when in principle the damage can be claimed from a liable injurer. During the parliamentary proceedings the question was asked whether the WTS could be applied in case of damage caused by an airplane crash; immediately the government indicated that in such a case liability law would apply, so the WTS would not be applicable.[17] The WTS therefore can only be applicable in case of damage as a consequence of natural disasters.[18] The subsidiary nature of the WTS can arise from two circumstances: either the WTS is applicable, but certain heads of damage are recoverable from another source and therefore not covered under the WTS, or the WTS is not applicable at all, given the claim possibilities in tort law. The events in Enschede, Volendam, Alphen aan de Rijn and the MH17 crash make painfully clear how limited in fact the impact of the WTS is for catastrophes that are not natural disasters. In some of these cases the government has financially intervened in a very generous way, but not through the WTS. This may show that the legislature has not succeeded in its (at least implicit) attempt to create an exclusive arrangement for government contributions in case of catastrophes with the WTS.

Indeed, overviews show that the WTS mainly applies to damage caused as a result of heavy rain.[19] In a paper published in October 2004, De Groot claimed that in its six years of existence the WTS had only been applied four times.[20] The first times it applied it also concerned cases of heavy

15 See *Kamerstukken II* 1996–1997, 25 159, no. 3, 15.
16 *Kamerstukken II* 1996–1997, 25 159, no. 5, 7.
17 *Kamerstukken II* 1996–1997, 25 159, no. 5, 3.
18 See in this sense also M. Faure and T. Hartlief, 'Schade als gevolg van natuurverschijnelen: de betekenis van de WTS', [2001] MenR, 241 et seq.
19 E. van der Schans, 'Regen als ramp. Wateroverlast en de WTS' [2000] *Tijdschrift voor Milieuaansprakelijkheid* (TMA) 13 et seq.
20 de Groot, 'Na de ramp. Een beschouwing over de toepassing van de WTS', above n. 11, p. 152.

rain. Since in both cases the heavy rain did not concern a formal flood in the sense of art. 1 of the WTS, the WTS needed to be declared applicable by Royal Decree. It is a remarkable result that this statutory arrangement that was specifically created by the legislature to compensate victims of catastrophes has in fact merely been applied in case of damage caused by heavy rainfall (thus usually mainly touching the agricultural sector) but not in case of serious man-made disasters with heavy personal injuries like in the cases of Volendam and Enschede. It is therefore not surprising that the WTS has been the subject of criticism in the literature and is most likely the subject of a serious revision in the near future.

1.1.2. Examples of Specific Compensation Funds

Also in the Netherlands, a debate has taken place on the function of compensation funds. In the literature, some have advanced the idea of increasing the use of compensation funds, arguing that funds would be able to provide a remedy for all the shortcomings of liability law.[21] Others have been far more critical.[22] This call in legal doctrine for an increasing use of compensation funds has various sources. In some cases, one argues that the compensation fund should intervene when the damage cannot be insured (more particularly in case of flooding and earthquakes). In other cases the fund should intervene to solve problems of tort liability (like lacking proof of a causal link or latency problems) and in some cases the fund should remedy insolvency problems. In some cases, the funds have an *ad hoc* character, whereas in other cases the compensation funds are more or less structural.

Examples of all these cases can be found in Dutch law. For instance, *ad hoc* compensation took place after a flooding in 1995 in Limburg, with the background as the fact that insurance for flooding was not available at the time. A more or less structural arrangement took place for victims of mesothelioma to deal with the problems of latency and insolvency of an employer. The structural fund to compensate victims of violent crime has a similar background: it aims at providing compensation in case of

---

21 See for instance L. Dommering-Van Rongen, *Schade vergoeden door fondsvorming* (Wolters Kluwer 1996), L. Dommering-Van Rongen, 'Een schadefonds voor asbestslachtoffers' [1996] TMA 97–101 and E. Bauw, 'Tussen traditie en efficiëntie; na een wettelijke regeling voor de afwikkeling van massaschade' [1995] NJB 622–630.

22 See inter alia M. Faure and T. Hartlief, 'Een schadefonds als alternatief voor aansprakelijkheid en verzekering?' [1998] *Rechtsgeleerd Magazijn Themis* (RM Themis), 211–228.

an unidentifiable or insolvent injurer. The compensation fund for damage caused by air pollution on the other hand primarily aims at solving problems in tort liability, like causation problems. Compensation after the catastrophes in Enschede and Volendam did not directly take place via a normal fund, but through the so-called national catastrophes fund, which in fact is a private initiative, although the government provided substantial funds as well. Again, it is remarkable that most of these arrangements took place outside of the scope of the earlier-mentioned WTS 1998, even though this arrangement was created precisely to provide a structural arrangement for the victims of catastrophes.

These pre-existing compensation funds[23] may be of help to victims of some catastrophes, but most of them were not created with the particular goal of assisting victims of catastrophes. This is the case for instance for the compensation fund for victims of violent crime (*Schadefonds Geweldsmisdrijven*),[24] which provides compensation for personal injury damage caused by an intentional violent crime which caused serious personal injury to the victim. This is a subsidiary fund (social security and private insurance have priority over the fund) that provides some compensation to the victim based on equity. The maximum for property and for non-pecuniary losses since 2014 is one amount of €35,000. The fund is financed through the general public budget. Only between 4,000–5,000 victims apply to this fund on a yearly basis, whereas the potential group of victims that could use the fund would be between 20,000 and 30,000.[25] In recent years there has been an increasing number of demands and compensations. This is partially due to the fact that insurers exclude all damage from coverage that has been caused intentionally.[26] The fund can of course be used by some victims of crimes that could qualify as 'catastrophes' although the conditions are rather restrictive: the fact that the damage must have been the result of an intentional violent crime may not apply to all man-made disasters (except perhaps the case of terrorism).

---

23 Moreover, in the literature there is discussion of introducing compensation funds for other types of damage as well. This is particularly the case for environmental damage, where the introduction of a compensation fund has also been suggested.

24 For an analysis of this fund, see M.S. Groenhuijsen, 'Schadefondsen in Nederland en in het buitenland: supra nationale normen, rechtsvergelijkende en empirische beschouwingen' [2001] *Delikt en Delinkwent* (DD), 930–947.

25 See *Kamerstukken II* 2000–01, 27400 VI, no. 59, 1–3.

26 See on these highly debated insurance issues J.H. Wansink, 'De aansprakelijkheidsverzekering en opzettelijk veroorzaakte schade: Een Januskop in beweging' [2000] AV&S 14–17 and J.H. Wansink, 'Assurance oblige: de maatschappelijk verantwoord handelende verzekeraar in de 21^{e} eeuw' [2003] AV&S 50.

In 2016, the government proposed to extend the scope of the compensation fund for victims of violent crime (*Schadefonds Geweldsmisdrijven*) to claims of bereavement of the descendants of victims of violent crimes. Descendants can now claim a fixed sum of €5,000 for bereavement due to the loss of loved ones.[27]

The same is probably the case for the fund for the compensation of air pollution damage. This fund is also subsidiary in the sense that it only compensates when the victim cannot claim compensation from another source (insurance or tort law). The fund is again financed through the public budget. An assessment of the functioning of this fund[28] shows that:

- most of the compensations relate to the agricultural sector and concern damage to crops;
- personal injury damage is almost never compensated (given the availability of social security and insurances) and ecological damage is not compensated either since the fund requires that the damage must have been caused by a sudden polluting act;
- although the fund formally provides compensation based on equity, *de facto* the full loss of the successful claimant is often compensated.

On average this fund did not pay more than approximately €100,000 on a yearly basis, which means that the importance of this fund compared to the real impact of air pollution damage can be considered as rather small. Again, this fund probably pays no significant role at all for damage caused by disasters.

Like in most European jurisdictions, in the Netherlands there is a Compensation Fund for Traffic Victims (*Waarborgfonds Motorverkeer*) for situations when standard tort law fails. So, for example, in situations of hit-and-run casualties, theft, joy-riding and uninsured drivers, traffic victims can obtain damages from this fund. As with most funds, it has a subsidiary character and there is a threshold of €250. The fund is financed by the insurance industry and the public budget. In 2014, some 45,000 claims were made. 23,000 claims for damage to parked cars and 15,000 claims for damage to objects on the road like crash barriers. For personal injuries there were some 5,000 claims. On average half of the claims were awarded. In total some €51,000,000 was paid to the claimants.

---

27 See R. Rijnhout, 'Heeft de uitbreiding van het Schadefonds Geweldsmisdrijven de weg geplaveid voor vergoeding van affectieschade?' (2016) 2 *Letsel en Schade* 3–5.

28 See T. Hartlief and M. Hertoghs, 'Evaluatie van het fonds luchtverontreiniging' [2000] MenR 64–69.

Many *ad hoc* compensation funds could be mentioned as well. For instance, after a catastrophic air crash with an El Al plane that flew into an apartment building in the Amsterdam neighbourhood of Bijlmer,[29] the government created the Stichting Hulpfonds Gedupeerden Bijlmer ramp (Foundation Compensation Fund to Victims of the Bijlmer Catastrophe). This fund was created as a result of a demand by the parliament to provide help to those victims who still suffered financial and psycho-social problems after several years as result of the catastrophe. Victims receive a lump sum payment of 4,000 Guilders (approximately €2,000) if it could be proven that he/she suffered psycho-social problems as a result of the catastrophe. After it appeared that the damage caused by the so-called legionella epidemic in Bovenkarspel (North Holland) could not be recovered through liability law, the Dutch government created a fund that was compatible to the Bijlmer catastrophes fund. The government made an amount of 2,000,000 Guilders (approximately €1,000,000) available to a foundation that provided compensation to victims: they received a lump sum payment of 4,000, Guilders (€2,000) and descendants of the deceased received an amount of 10,000 Guilders (€5,000).

Whereas these are examples of *ad hoc* compensation funds related to particular incidents, a more structural arrangement has been created for the victims of mesothelioma. For the particular case of victims of asbestos, a specific structural arrangement was brought to life. A victim can receive (again financed through the public budget) a lump sum payment of €15,882 under the following conditions:

- he/she had to be alive on 6 June 1997;[30]
- that he/she incurred so-called malign mesothelioma as a result of exposure to asbestos during work;
- no financial compensation from an employer was obtained; and

[29] On 4 October 1992, El Al Flight 1862, a Boeing 747 cargo aircraft of the State-owned Israeli airline El Al, crashed into the Groeneveen and Klein-Kruitberg flats in the Bijlmermeer (colloquially 'Bijlmer' neighbourhood (part of Amsterdam-Zuidoost) of Amsterdam, the Netherlands. Due to the location of the crash in the Bijlmermeer, it is known in Dutch as the Bijlmerramp (Bijlmer disaster). A total of 43 people were officially reported killed, including the aircraft's three crew members, a non-revenue passenger in a jump seat, and 39 people on the ground. Many more were injured. The exact number of people killed on the ground is in dispute, as the building had a high concentration of illegal immigrants.

[30] This was simply the date that the government took the decision to install the compensation arrangement.

- no possibilities of a claim on the employer exist either because the employer cannot be identified, thus does not exist any longer, is insolvent or because the statute of limitations has passed.[31]

If one summarised certain trends when addressing all of these various compensation funds one could argue that most of them have in principle a subsidiary nature, meaning that only the damage will be compensated that in principle cannot be compensated from any other source (social security, private insurance or tort law). However, one could also notice that the social/legal basis for creating a compensation fund for this particular type of victim is different in every case. In general, one could notice that the government usually simply wants to make a gesture towards the victim as an expression of the solidarity of the community towards the victims. Only the compensation fund for air pollution damage is subject to lots of criticism, since apparently only the agricultural sector benefits from this fund, whereas one can equally doubt whether the types of damage that are compensated today through this fund are truly uninsurable. Thus, it has been suggested in the literature that this fund should probably not be abrogated and replaced by an arrangement whereby the agricultural industry itself would finance its compensation.[32]

Finally, it should be mentioned that in the literature many critical voices have been formulated as far as the existence of compensation funds is concerned. The crucial question that is always asked in this literature is why the government would install a particular compensation fund for the particular type of victims. This, so it is held, always means that a certain category of victims will receive preferential treatment, for which the legal basis seems to be doubtful. Of course, it is argued that the compensation fund will never provide the 'luxury of tort law', being full compensation, but only a gesture of solidarity. The government cannot provide a full guarantee of the individual wealth of all of its citizens.[33] As long as a victim cannot successfully call on tort law one can of course defend an intervention from

---

31 See on these arrangements M. Faure and T. Hartlief, 'Een asbestfonds als alternatief voor aansprakelijkheid van de werkgever?' [1996] *Sociaal Recht* (SR) 37 et seq. and J.P. Hustinx and C.J.J.M. Stolker, 'Massaschade en fondsvorming' [1997] *Verzekeringsarchief* (VA), 58–66 as well as A.E. Dek, 'Asbestontwikkelingen. Oprechte tegemoetkomingen of doekjes voor het bloeden?' [1999] TMA 61–62.

32 See E.H. Hulst, 'Actualiteiten milieuaansprakelijkheid. Schadelijk water en schadefonds, pleidooi voor adequate oplossingen!' [1999] TMA 33.

33 See J.A.J. Peeters, 'Rampschade' [1980] NJB 503–504. See also J.A.J. Peeters, 'Rampschade' in M.J.P. Verburgh, A.R. Bloembergen and G.J. de Groot et al. (eds), *Schade lijden en schade dragen* (Wolters Kluwer 1980), pp. 59–84.

the public budget based on a feeling of national solidarity (although the choice in this respect will always depend upon political will and thus be arbitrary). A consequence is, however, that even when a compensation fund exists, in most cases the victim will still have to carry part of the damage itself.[34]

1.2. GENERAL SCOPE OF THE COMPENSATION

The general structure of the compensation system in the Netherlands is relatively compatible to solutions in other legal systems. Usually a combination of legal instruments will be used, whereby largely a distinction can be made between personal injury on the one hand and property damage on the other hand, and the case of the natural disasters on the one hand and the case of man-made disasters on the other hand. As far as personal injury is concerned victims will primarily be able to rely on the social security system that will provide them with a basic guarantee against income losses as a result of disability; moreover social security will also take care of the medical bills and healthcare expenses (depending on whether one has private insurance or not, this coverage will be very generous or a bit less). However, social security usually only covers part of the damage. For instance, the top of one's income will usually not be compensated under social security, nor will there be compensation for the non-pecuniary losses. In that respect the victim will just have to look for additional compensation mechanisms whereby tort and insurance are the primarily indicated systems.[35]

Tort can obviously only be used when a liable injurer can be found. In that respect a distinction can generally be made between the natural disasters and the man-made disasters. In case of natural disasters, it will usually not be the case that a liable injurer can be found (except the case of liability of public authorities), whereas with most man-made disasters an injurer can usually be identified.[36] If the injurer can be held liable and is solvent (or has liability insurance to cover his obligations) the victim

34 See Faure and Hartlief, 'Een schadefonds als alternatief voor aansprakelijkheid en verzekering?', above n. 22, p. 228.

35 In that respect it is sometimes argued that social security provides an *Existenzsicherung*, whereas tort law provides the 'luxury' of full coverage. See M. Faure and T. Hartlief, 'Economic perspectives' in U. Magnus (ed.), *The impact of social security law on tort law* (Springer 2003), pp. 228–229.

36 Again with some exceptions, for instance when pollution caused personal injury damage and the source cannot be identified.

can receive coverage through tort law. If this is not the case the victim can in some cases call on a personal accident insurance that might provide compensation for personal injury. Most of these accident insurances provide for lump sum payments (and sometimes additional coverage of lost income for the part not covered under social security) to cover the damage resulting from personal injury. However, those personal accident insurances are not mandatory and the scope of coverage therefore very much depends upon the policy conditions. Note that with these personal accident insurances, coverage will usually take place for personal injury damage irrespective of the source of the damage. As far as personal injury is concerned these insurances may thus cover both in case of natural as well as in case of man-made disasters.

If there is no liable injurer and no first-party insurance covering the damage the victim might call on specific compensation regimes if these apply to his particular situation. For instance, if he is a victim of crime the victim may call on the crime compensation fund. In other cases, he may call on specific *ad hoc* compensation mechanisms if the government (for political reasons) decided that for that particular risk compensation needed to be made available.

A similar structure governed the situation of the victim of property damage although there are a few important differences. A victim of property damage will not be able to call on social security. He will thus have a larger need to use alternative compensation mechanisms like tort or private insurance. As far as tort law is concerned the same possibilities and limits apply as with personal injury damage: there may be possibilities in case of man-made disaster (provided that a solvent liable injurer can be found), but less so in case of natural disasters. An additional difficulty is that in case of property damage insurance coverage may be particularly difficult and, until recently, to a large extent not even available.

Dutch insurers indeed considered the damage caused by natural disasters as uninsurable and as a result of that they had excluded damage resulting from risks such as earthquake, flooding or heavy rain from coverage. This *de facto* led to the situation that those victims suffering property damage as a result of natural disasters could only call on *ad hoc* solutions through government (or other) aid to hope to obtain compensation of their damage. Some victims, in particular farmers or owners of greenhouses suffering crop damage as a result of heavy rainfall, were relatively successful. Indeed, they sometimes succeeded in convincing the government to apply the specific statutory solution (WTS) that provides additional indemnification for specific victims of natural disasters.

1.2.1. *Liability in Tort*

As has already been indicated, tort law will play only a modest role in the compensation of victims of catastrophes for the simple reason that, particularly with natural disasters, a liable injurer often cannot be identified. The only cases where liability law could thus play a role are either the man-made disasters or the natural disasters where there could be liability of public authorities. At the time of several floods at the start of the 1990s, the possibilities of liability of public authorities have been examined.[37] In that respect, various shortcomings of public authorities were mentioned, in particular:

- lacking maintenance of rivers, canals and mechanisms to prevent flooding;
- late warning for flooding;
- issuing licenses to build in flood-prone areas;
- failure to act whereas there was reason to take measures based on previous floods.

Case law will judge the liability of the water board on the basis of various criteria.[38] Elements that play to the advantage of the public authorities are generally the fact that the authority has discretionary power to act and usually only limited means at its disposition. This may lead the judge to a restrictive application of liability of public authorities, but that is far from certain.[39]

---

37 See more particularly, T. Hartlief, 'Vergoeding van watersnoodschade' [1995] NJB 311 et seq. and T. Hartlief, 'Vergoeding van watersnoodschade' in M. Faure and F. Stroink (eds), *Recht in het water. De juridische aspecten van watersnood* (Maklu Uitgevers 1995), pp. 131–142 as well as M. Hertoghs, 'Hoogwater in Den Haag: de rol van de Rijksoverheid' in Faure and Stroink (eds), *Recht in het water. De juridische aspecten van watersnood*, above, pp. 35–62.

38 As determined by the *Hoge Raad der Nederlanden* (Dutch Supreme Court, HR) in HR 9 October 1981, [1982] *Nederlandse Jurisprudentie* (NJ), 332 with case note by C.J.H. Brunner, HR 8 January 1999, [1999] NJ, 319 with case note by A.R. Bloembergen.

39 On 26 August 2003, at 2.00 am, a dike broke in Wilnis and washed away the rural lower parts of the dike. Around 2,000 people were evacuated but could come back later that evening. The dike was mainly built out of bog which has the tendency to act like a sponge and hold water in wet periods, but the warm and dry summer evaporated the water completely causing the soil to become too light for the rainfall in August and caused a 60-metre long part of the dike to collapse. The Dutch Supreme Court denied liability of public authorities (As determined by the *Hoge Raad der Nederlanden* (Dutch Supreme Court, HR) in HR 17 December 2010, [2012] *Nederlandse Jurisprudentie* (NJ), 155 with case note by T. Hartlief).

Liability of public authorities may not just play a role in case of failure to prevent natural disasters. In addition, in case of man-made disasters (in the introduction to this chapter, it was indicated that the Netherlands has in recent years been confronted with many), the question has been asked whether shortcomings of public authorities have contributed to the risk of accidents. For instance, at the time of some of the recent disasters the following shortcomings were mentioned:

- as far as the legionella infection in Bovenkarspel was concerned the question was raised whether the authorities could be made liable for a lack of adequate regulation and/or lacking enforcement of existing regulation;
- at the time of the catastrophic New Year's Eve fire in the cafe in Volendam the question was again asked whether the regulations concerning the prevention of fires had been sufficiently enforced;
- at the time of the explosion of the fireworks factory in Enschede various shortcomings of different authorities may have contributed to the risk. For instance, the central government was blind to the fact that nothing had been done with the information acquired on the occasion of a previous explosion of a fireworks factory a few years before in Culemborg. But blame was equally addressed to local authorities for lacking control of regulations and permit conditions;
- the shooting in Alphen aan de Rijn was the subject of civil proceedings in the Court of Appeal in 2016. Compensation has been awarded to the victims of personal injury, however the shopkeepers were not compensated for financial damage. The case was decided by the Dutch Supreme Court on the 20 September 2019.[40]

In all those cases liability of public authorities is theoretically possible. However, it will of course depend on the assessment by the courts whether this liability will effectively be accepted or not.[41] For instance as far as a liability for lacking control and enforcement is concerned, until recently legal doctrine held that there is no formal duty of public authorities to enforce legislation, so that it is highly questionable whether a lacking

---

40 *Hoge Raad der Nederlanden* (Dutch Supreme Court, HR) in HR 20 September 2019, ECLI:NL:HR:2019:1409 [2019]; JB 2019/187 with case note by R.J.B Schutgens.

41 See W. van Boom and I. Giesen, 'Civielrechtelijke overheidsaansprakelijkheid voor het niet voorkomen van gezondheidsschade door rampen' [2001] NJB 1676.

enforcement can indeed give rise to liability. Moreover, the victim may also be confronted with causation problems since the question can of course be asked in what respect a shortcoming of public authorities can be considered the cause of the victim's loss.

The reason victims often seek (or at least discuss) the possibilities of public authorities are of course linked to the fact that victims of catastrophes may often not be compensated through the liable injurer or through first-party insurances. Indeed, the problem with a liability claim on direct injurers have already been mentioned. In case of natural disasters there simply may not be a liable injurer; in case of man-made disasters, this may be the case, but lacking (or limited) liability insurance and limited solvency of the injurer may make a liability claim on the direct injurer not very effective. This explains why victims increasingly seek recovery through liability of public authorities although it is still doubtful that the case law in the Netherlands will also award those claims. However, the call on public authorities giving the lack of compensation through other instruments is a reality and some have therefore held that in case of catastrophes authorities may well be inclined to organise *ad hoc* compensation for victims also to reduce the likelihood of liability claims.

1.2.2. Social Security

As indicated earlier social security will play a primary role in the compensation of damage suffered as a result of personal injury, but less so as far as property damage is concerned. Without going into detail, it should be mentioned that (although there have been important changes in recent years) the scope of protection of social security law in the Netherlands is still relatively broad, at least as far as personal injury damage is concerned.[42] For instance a national insurance in principle covers all citizens against the loss of maintenance caused by the death of a breadwinner. However, strict income thresholds apply and the number of beneficiaries is reduced. The effects of personal injury on an employee's income are covered through a variety of complicated arrangements. Indeed, the employees generally receive a higher protection than other groups of the population (like self-employed individuals).

42 For details see C.E. du Perron and W.H. van Boom, 'The Netherlands' in Magnus (ed.), *The impact of social security law on tort law*, above n. 35, pp. 153–155.

Generally, it is important to remember that – also in the Netherlands – social security thus provides relatively easy (although with more stringency in recent years) coverage, but the amount of compensation is limited. The easy character of the compensation lies in the fact that the victim usually only has to prove a certain illness or other condition that satisfies the statute, but the cause of the event is generally irrelevant and the contributory negligence of the victim is not considered in social security systems.[43] However, as a result of these low thresholds the compensation provided as a result of social security will necessarily be limited. It therefore plays a role in compensating (part of) healthcare expenses and income losses, but it does not provide compensation for non-pecuniary losses, not for the (luxury of) compensating the top of one's income, nor for property damage. For those heads of damage, the victim will therefore have to rely on other systems like tort or private insurance.

Note that the other compensation systems, the various compensation funds and the WTS 1998 in particular, clearly declared to have a subsidiary character. In those cases, one will therefore first principally examine whether the victim could obtain compensation via insurance or tort law from the injurer. The WTS even goes a step further by *excluding* all damage that was 'reasonably insurable' (even if insurance may *de facto* not be available). These additional systems only intervene after the primary systems (social security, tort and insurance) have been exercised.

In addition, it should briefly be mentioned that the legal basis and possibilities of exercising the abovementioned rights of subrogation provide a rather complicated picture, since every specific social security act has (in some cases different) subrogation arrangements whereby some limitations also apply. It would lead too far to discuss these complicated arrangements in detail within the scope of this chapter; it will therefore be limited to some general notions.[44]

---

43 There are, however, some exceptions as a result of which contributory negligence may equally limit the victim's right on compensation in social security. See S. Klosse, 'Vergoeding als noodverband?' [2003] *Aansprakelijkheid Verzekering en Schade*, (AV&S), 25–33 and W.H. van Boom, 'Waarheen leidt de weg … van werknemersschade?' [2003] AV&S 33–40.

44 For a more detailed analysis see G.E. van Maanen and P. Römers, *De tijdelijke regeling verhaalsrechten, verhaalsmogelijkheden voor verzekeraars en uitkeringsinstanties* (Ars Aequi 1994), S.P. de Haas and T. Hartlief, *Collectivering en institutionalisering van regres* (Verbond van verzekeraars 1996) and especially the dissertation of E. Engelhard, *Regres. Een onderzoek naar het regresrecht van particuliere en sociale schadedragers* (Kluwer 2003).

1.2.3. *Criticism*

The Netherlands has, as the previous section showed, been hit by many disasters during the last decades. In some cases, this concerned natural disasters, but the most striking recent events were man-made. In all of the cases just discussed one could notice that there was a large number of victims and that hence the total amount of the damage was enormous. In all of these cases the question arose what legal instruments could be used to pay compensation to the victim. Initially attention was always given to tort law, but given the inherent limits of this system, to other compensation systems as well.

One can notice that as a result of various calls for intervention on the Dutch government different *ad hoc* compensation funds were created. Sometimes these funds needed to solve problems of liability law, like in the case of natural disasters; in other cases, the fund only needed to provide a 'gesture' as a sign of solidarity with the victims like in the cases of Enschede, Volendam and Bovenkarspel. The major criticism on all of this of course concerns the fact that the attempt of the government to provide a *structural* compensation arrangement for victims, being the WTS 1998, largely failed since this instrument was not applicable to the major disasters that had hit the Netherlands in recent years. Therefore, the entire system of compensation of victims of catastrophes has been seriously criticised in the literature from various perspectives.[45]

There is *first* of all criticism on the fact that the government on an *ad hoc* basis intervenes with specific funding for victims of catastrophes. This preference for victims of catastrophes (compared to victims of other accidents) has been criticised from the angle of the equality principle.[46] *Second*, legal doctrine also held that, if specific compensation needs to be provided for victims of catastrophes, it would be more desirable to have a structural solution instead of the current *ad hoc* solutions. In that respect the WTS 1998, which apparently did not serve that goal, would have to be revised. *Third* it is also stressed that there might be reasons to increase duties on potential tortfeasors to guarantee their solvency. Both in Volendam and in Enschede large damage was caused by activities for

---

45 For a summary of this criticism see T. Hartlief, above n. 9, pp. 61–103.

46 See already A.R. Bloembergen, 'Een schadefonds geweldsmisdrijven?' in *Bloembergens werk* (Kluwer 1992), pp. 51 et seq. and J.M. Polak, 'Schade en schadevergoeding bij incidentele calamiteiten. Een vervolg' [1997] NJB 1093–1094.

which no compulsory insurance applied. Hence it was argued that a duty to seek insurance coverage might be introduced on a larger scale or, where it exists, the amounts should be increased.[47] *Fourth*, it seems logical to also increase the possibilities of first-party insurance. Now that the prohibited cartel agreements do not cover the consequences of natural disasters where withdrawn, it seems logical that insurance policies covering those risks would be brought onto the market. This is apparently, as described above, now the case for agricultural damage caused by heavy rainfall.

1.2.4. Reform

It should first of all be mentioned that at the time of both the fireworks disaster in Enschede and the fire in Volendam specific committees were instituted to examine both the causes and the compensation arrangements. In some of the conclusions of these committees some opinions were also formulated concerning an optimal compensation of the victims. However, these usually applied to the specific cases of these particular disasters. But, for instance, the commission instituted at the time of the fireworks explosion in Deventer (*Commissie Oosting*) had also formulated proposals to come to a more structural financial arrangement for victims of catastrophes.[48] However, the government did not follow that proposal since it considered that the Netherlands already had a structural arrangement in the WTS 1998. Moreover, the central government had provided generous support to both the *Nationale Rampenfonds* (a private initiative) and the *Stichting Financiële Hulpverlening Vuurwerkramp*, so that the government felt that it had satisfied its duty to provide a gesture of national solidarity towards the victims.[49]

Nevertheless, the government has installed a committee with the specific task of providing an assessment of the WTS 1998. Indeed, a so-called *Commissie Tegemoetkoming bij Rampen en Calamiteiten* – CTRC (*Commission for the Compensation in Cases of Catastrophes and Incidents*) was asked to provide advice to the government on the optimal compensation in case of catastrophes.[50] The committee first of all had to

---

47 Compare in this respect W.H. van Boom, 'De strategische verzekeringsplicht' [2001] AV&S, 165 and J.H. Wansink, 'De verzekering van rampschade' in A.J. Akkermans and E.H.P. Brans (eds), *Aansprakelijkheid en schadeverhaal bij rampen* (Ars Aequi 2002), pp. 131 et seq.

48 See *Kamerstukken II* 2000–2001, 27 157, no. 20, 59.

49 *Kamerstukken II* 2000–2001, 27 157, no. 20, 60.

50 *Kamerstukken II* 2001–2002, 27 157, no. 44, 4.

examine what the existing possibilities of compensation were, but second also to formulate proposals for additional compensation that should probably be made available.[51] The final version of the report of the CTRC was presented in The Hague in December 2004 and, inter alia based on experiences abroad (more particularly in France, Belgium, Germany and Sweden) the commission formulated several interesting suggestions:

- tort law needs to be amended in order to manage mass torts more easily and to reduce the trials; alternative dispute resolution should be stimulated;
- insolvency guarantees for injurers need to be introduced or increased;
- for catastrophes where no liable injurer can be identified the commission suggests an increasing use of first-party insurances. The proposal is not to make the purchase of disaster coverage mandatory (like in France), but to facilitate the insurability of risks on the one hand by letting the State act as reinsurer (if necessary) and by pursuing an active information policy;
- change the WTS into a national solidarity fund that would, on the basis of clear rules and structures provide various types of compensation, inter alia for the case of uninsurable damage.

Until now these proposals have not been accepted at the political level. One can say that most of these proposals of the committee are in line with what has been suggested in the legal doctrine as far as the revision of the compensation of victims of catastrophes is concerned. It is however unlikely that this revision will be implemented in the WTS in the near future.

1.2.5. A Superfund?

A national solidarity fund such as suggested by the Commission for the Compensation in Cases of Catastrophes and Incidents in 2004 has not led to great enthusiasm in official circles. But, considering the above, would this be a good idea? Of course, a national solidarity fund can have a smaller or a wider scope. But how broad the scope of such a compensation fund may be, at the end of the day someone has to pick up the cheque. The big question

51 The Commission has been installed by formal decision of the Secretary of State of Internal Affairs of 3 April 2003, which also specifies its formal task (see [7 April 2003] Stcrt. no. 68, 9).

is whether compensation by means of a fund is preferable to compensation by traditional forms of compensation as discussed in the above: tort law, social security and private insurance (mandatory or voluntary). A national solidarity (super)fund will never be able to provide for full compensation comparable to the tort system. Thresholds will be inevitable. And every threshold will create inequalities and disappointment. So certain categories of victims will receive preferential treatment. Is that fair?

1.2.6. *Alternatives*

The shortcomings of the traditional tort system could be reduced by adapting tort law regimes to the specific needs and by creating specific regimes for mass tort claims for situations where many victims are involved. One might think of strict liability, adaptation of the causality requirement and a reversal of the burden of proof.

A good example of a useful adaptation of the tort system is the French legislation on traffic accidents, the so-called Loi Badintair of 1985. What is seen there is in fact a system of automatic compensation that functions like a system of social security. The fault requirement is almost completely removed from the system as well as the requirement of a causal link. The only thing the victim has to prove is 'implication', that is involvement of a motor vehicle.

An alternative for the problem of insolvency of the tortfeasor could be compulsory third-party insurance for professionals in order to diminish the risk of insolvency.

Social security will play a primary role in the compensation of damage suffered as a result of personal injury, but less so as far as property damage is concerned. The scope of protection of social security law in the Netherlands is still relatively broad, at least as far as personal injury damage is concerned. For instance, a national insurance covers in principle all citizens against the loss of maintenance caused by the death of a breadwinner. However, strict income thresholds apply and the number of beneficiaries is reduced. The French example of an insurance for all kinds of accidents – the so-called '*garantie des accidents de la vie*' – could be considered as an alternative as well.

In 2014 a proposal was made to extend the possibilities for claiming damage for mass torts.[52] It will then be possible to claim financial

52 See H.N. Schelhaas, 'Collectieve acties. Verslag jaarvergadering Vereniging voor Burgerlijk Recht' [2016] NTBR 127–130.

compensation on the basis of art. 3:105a and b of BW. The legislative proposal was approved by the House of Representatives on 29 January 2019 and by the Senate on 19 March 2019. Once enacted, the legislative proposal will be known as the Act on the Resolution of Mass Claims in Collective Action (*Wet Afwikkeling Massaschade in Collectieve Actie*) (WAMCA). The date of entry into force of the WAMCA is still to be announced, but is expected to be January 2020. The WAMCA will apply to collective actions for damages initiated on or after the date of its entry into force that relate to 'events' that occurred on or after 15 November 2016.[53]

These kinds of legal instruments extend the possibilities of traditional tort law which is in essence a tool for individual situations concerning one victim and one tortfeasor. By introducing specific tools for combining actions for multiple victims and arrangements for settlements for such situations tort law is better adapted to serve its role as a compensation instrument in situations where there are many victims of a single event.

2. CONCLUSION

It is clear that compensation funds can have some big advantages over traditional tort law regimes. They can compensate for the shortcomings of tort law. In certain situations when it is too harsh for the victim to ask him to prove that the person responsible for his damage acted wrongfully or to prove the causal link. One can think of traffic accidents where unmotorised victims are involved or victims of asbestos exposure who have been working for different employers and are so unable to prove which employer is responsible for the asbestos particle that caused the mesothelioma. Funds can also give compensation in situations where it is impossible to obtain first-party insurance or in situations of insolvent tortfeasors.

Compensation funds will remain a necessary instrument for specific types of situations where tort law fails. But compensation funds are not a panacea to all the existing problems of tort law.

---

53 See M.W.F. Bosters, 'Voorontwerp afwikkeling massaschade in een collectieve actie' [2015] NJB 1584; J. Kortmann, 'Wetsvoorstel afwikkeling massaschade in collectieve actie (34608). Aanzienlijk verbeterd, maar het moet nog beter!' [2018] NJB 555–561 and Kortmann <https://www.stibbe.com/en/news/2019/june/overview-of-legislative-proposal-on-collective-action-nl--update-june-2019>.

NEW ZEALAND'S UNIVERSAL NO-FAULT PERSONAL INJURY COMPENSATION FUND

Kim Watts

1. INTRODUCTION

New Zealand is renowned for being the only major jurisdiction that operates a universal and comprehensive no-fault compensation fund for injury. It provides coverage for every person in New Zealand (including tourists) if they are injured in an accident, no matter their age, social security status or occupation.[1] Individuals forego the right to sue for compensatory damages for injury under the common law, in exchange for this comprehensive cover and compensation. The fund also has a mirror injury prevention and rehabilitation focus.

The intended audience of this chapter is a European legal reader that does not already have detailed familiarity with the New Zealand jurisdiction or its no-fault compensation fund. This chapter does not aim to provide a detailed description of every minute development of the New Zealand scheme over its history. Rather, the reader will hopefully gain a philosophical and practical comparative law understanding of the New Zealand scheme as a compensation fund, and how and why it was created within the context of the New Zealand jurisdiction. This chapter will highlight some 'tricky issues' and recent developments which

1 Accident Compensation Corporation, 'What We Do' <https://www.acc.co.nz/about-us/who-we-are/what-we-do/>. This chapter contains a detailed analysis of the ACC Scheme and the ACC body itself, but a useful plain English overview can be found at Accident Compensation Corporation, 'Our History' <https://www.acc.co.nz/about-us/who-we-are/our-history/>.

showcase the limits of the scheme and reveal legal and policy challenges for the fund's sustainable development.[2]

For ease of referencing, the term 'ACC Scheme' will be used throughout this chapter to refer generally to New Zealand's no-fault personal injury compensation fund – in other words, the relevant rights and obligations enacted by primary and secondary legislation and their fulfilment by its administrative body, the Accident Compensation Corporation, on a daily basis. This is because the term 'compensation fund' would not be the kind of term used in New Zealand itself to describe the ACC Scheme. The ACC Scheme has always given complementary weighting to compensation, rehabilitation, administrative efficiency and community responsibility. The universal and compulsory nature of the ACC Scheme forces it to straddle the fields of personal injury compensation, social insurance and private insurance cover. The ACC Scheme is indeed a compensation fund, in the sense that it has funds available (and invested) to pay for the cost of eligible personal injuries occurring anywhere in New Zealand. But another purpose of the invested funds is to reduce the incidence and severity of injuries (through safety initiatives), as well as covering the lifetime cost of existing claims.[3] The ACC Scheme has a wider and more entrenched purpose in New Zealand than the narrowly targeted compensation funds that exist in other jurisdictions.

Half a century has passed since the publication of the ground-breaking 'Woodhouse Report', the Royal Commission report that recommended the creation of New Zealand's comprehensive no-fault accident compensation fund. This is a suitable milestone to consider the operation and effect of the scheme to date, and to anticipate how the fund will develop in the future.

2. SCHEME OVERVIEW

The ACC Scheme is currently governed by the Accident Compensation Act 2001 ('the Accident Compensation Act') and managed by the Accident

---

2 A jurisdiction which has effectively 'stepped out' of tort law in the area of personal injury has developed its own quirks which are not convenient to summarise in a general comparative law chapter such as this. Interested readers will find more detailed analysis of New Zealand tort law and the ACC Scheme in the following texts which are leading commentary and practical handbooks for New Zealand lawyers: Stephen Todd (ed.), *The Law of Torts in New Zealand*, 8th edn (Thomson Reuters 2019); Doug Tennent, *Accident Compensation Law* (LexisNexis New Zealand 2013).

3 'Your ACC' in Accident Compensation Corporation, 'Annual Report 2017' (2017) <https://www.parliament.nz/resource/en-NZ/PAP_75085/cd5473578a0a648b7c15d0d819d2f36d8ba477c2>.

Compensation Corporation ('ACC'). Earlier legislation still governs any claims that occurred before the current Accident Compensation Act came into force (claims that are still subject to ongoing claims or payments by the ACC). The purpose of the Accident Compensation Act is to 'enhance the public good and reinforce [a] social contract' by providing for a fair and sustainable scheme for managing personal injury, with the twin goals of minimising the incidence of injury and the impact (economic, social and personal) of injury in the community.[4] Compensation is defined as weekly compensation or lump sums where appropriate for permanent impairment.[5]

Personal injury is generally defined to mean:[6]

- death;
- physical injuries (like a strain or a sprain);
- mental injury caused by a physical injury;
- mental injury suffered by victims of some types of sexual criminal offences;
- some types of work-related mental injury; and
- damage to dentures or prostheses (other than by wear or tear).

Personal injury generally does *not* include:

- injury caused wholly or substantially by a gradual process, disease or infection *unless* it is work related;[7]
- a heart attack or a stroke;[8] and
- injury caused wholly or substantially by the ageing process (this includes damage to teeth or dentures through normal use).[9]

Case law has explored the limits of these various definitions of injury. Injury as a result of medical treatment (called 'treatment injury') is also covered in some circumstances under the ACC Scheme, but it is *not* considered an accident.[10]

---

4 Accident Compensation Act 2001 s. 3; Accident Compensation Corporation, 'Briefing to the Incoming Minister' (2017), p. 6 <https://www.acc.co.nz/assets/corporate-documents/minister-briefing-2017.pdf>.
5 Accident Compensation Act 2001 s. 3(d).
6 Ibid, s. 26.
7 Ibid, s. 20(2).
8 Ibid, s. 28(3).
9 Ibid, s. 26(4).
10 Ibid, s. 25(2).

2.1. THE LEGISLATIVE HISTORY

New Zealand is a small and highly stable common law jurisdiction, with a British Westminster system of government.[11] New Zealand has had a unicameral legislature since 1951 and has a strong history of centralised government.[12]

The ACC Scheme's legislative beginnings were a Royal Commission established in 1966; it was charged with surveying and reporting on the existing law relating to compensation and claims for damages for incapacity or death arising out of workplace accidents (including diseases).[13] In 1967 the Royal Commission published its findings, commonly known as the Woodhouse Report (named after its author and Commission chairman Sir Owen Woodhouse, at that time a judge). A White Paper and a Select Committee report immediately followed the Woodhouse Report.[14] The Accident Compensation Act 1972 was the original legislation that enacted the ACC Scheme in New Zealand. There have been five major versions of the relevant legislation, and a number of amendments between and after legislative rewrites. It is useful to briefly describe the five major legislative milestones, as they give a sense of the overall evolution of the scheme:

1. The original 1972 legislation[15] created comprehensive, compulsory coverage for all victims of accidental personal injury in New Zealand,

---

11 Like the UK, New Zealand has no written constitution. Key differences from the UK are New Zealand's mixed member proportional voting system (introduced in 1996), and the fact that New Zealand has only one legislative house (Parliament). New Zealand is ranked internationally as having strong legal rights across public and private indicators – World Bank, 'Strength of Legal Rights Index (0=weak to 12=strong) | Data' <https://data.worldbank.org/indicator/IC.LGL.CRED.XQ?locations=NZ>.

12 Geoffrey Palmer, *Compensation for Incapacity: A Study of Law and Social Change in New Zealand and Australia* (Oxford University Press 1979), p. 63.

13 Royal Commission to Inquire into and Report upon Workers Compensation, *Compensation for Personal Injury in New Zealand* (Government Printing Office 1967), p. 30.

14 New Zealand Parliament, *Personal Injury: A Commentary on the Report of the Royal Commission of Inquiry into Compensation for Personal Injury in New Zealand* (Government Printer 1969); Select Committee on Compensation for Personal Injury in New Zealand and George F. Gair, *Report of Select Committee on Compensation for Personal Injury in New Zealand* (Government Printer 1970).

15 Accident Compensation Act 1972. Following a change in government, the ACC Scheme's coverage was extended by legislative amendments before it came into force to cover all types personal injury victims, including the unemployed and tourists. A Committee established in 1975 to investigate extending the scheme to sickness was curtailed by another change in government.

in exchange for a bar on the right to sue or claim workers' compensation. The new ACC Scheme took effect in April 1974. 'Personal injury by accident' was not fully defined in the statute, allowing the concept to be defined further by decision-making bodies and processes created by the legislation. A statutory body, called the Accident Compensation Commission, was created to administer the regime. Compensation generally took the form of medical expenses and associated costs and weekly earnings-related payments, with lump sums available in limited circumstances. Funding came from employers and the self-employed, motor vehicle owners and general taxation. The model created by the 1972 legislation was neither social security (as understood in the New Zealand sense, i.e. funded by general taxation with means-tested flat-rate payments) nor commercial insurance, but rather a unique type of social insurance (funded by compulsory levies with earnings-related compensation and universal entitlement).[16] The 1972 legislation can be seen as largely fulfilling the original spirit of the Woodhouse Report.

2. The 1982 legislation[17] made some significant administrative and funding changes. The Accident Compensation Corporation company entity replaced the Accident Compensation Commission. Funding was changed to a pay-as-you-go model, meaning that levies for the year paid all costs (old and new claims), but did not cover continuing costs of claims in future years. The government then faced (successful) political pressure from employers to reduce levies.[18] This led to funding reserves being depleted during the 1980s (reserves which had been accumulated since 1974 under the prior quasi-full funding model).
3. The 1992 legislation[19] introduced stricter definitions about what constituted accidental personal injury (for the purposes of cover under the legislation) and removed judicial discretion to define the limits of statutory definitions. The 'medical misadventure' definition introduction in the 1992 legislation required consideration of fault-based elements, which a 2003 ACC and Department of Labour review found to be problematic given the no-fault nature of the ACC Scheme. In a cost-cutting move, the legislation abolished lump sum

---

16 Todd (ed.), *The Law of Torts in New Zealand*, above n. 2, p. 26.
17 Accident Compensation Act 1982.
18 Todd (ed.), *The Law of Torts in New Zealand*, above n. 2, p. 27.
19 Accident Rehabilitation and Compensation Insurance Act 1992.

payments and allowed for some unemployed claimants to be moved off the ACC Scheme's books and onto social welfare. Pay-as-you-go funding was retained, but the funding pool was extended to all earners, including employees.[20]

4. The 1998 legislation[21] introduced some privatisation elements and reversed the 1982 legislation funding changes. The new legislation required employers to provide statutory benefits for workplace injury via private insurance companies or a new state-owned insurer (set up to compete with the private insurers). ACC administered the rest of the scheme (i.e. for non-workplace injuries). There was a switch back from pay-as-you-go to full funding. The government's justification for both of these changes was the need for an increased focus on safety and rehabilitation, which it believed could be delivered through competition and a funding scheme that rewarded injury prevention innovation.[22] The privatisation elements of the 1998 legislation were quickly reversed in 2000 following a change in government.[23]
5. The 2001 Act retained the full funding model. It also re-introduced lump sum compensation for some situations. A 2005 amendment changed the medical error and mishap definitions (called 'medical misadventure', introduced by the 1992 legislation) to a broader 'treatment injury' definition. Cover for some types of work-related mental injury was introduced in 2008. A 2008 government proposal to reintroduce privatisation never came to fruition.[24]

2.2. THE ACCIDENT COMPENSATION CORPORATION

ACC is a type of Crown Entity,[25] a government-controlled entity that includes corporations created by statute. ACC is a Crown agent which

---

20 Todd (ed.), *The Law of Torts in New Zealand*, above n. 2, pp. 27–29. The 1992 legislation cannot properly be described without mentioning a related 1988 Law Commission report and some major political and ideological clashes in the 1980s and early 1990s about the ambit and funding of the ACC Scheme. See section 3.3 below for more detailed discussion. See also Bill Birch, *Accident Compensation: A Fairer Scheme* (Office of the Minister of Labour 1991).

21 Accident Insurance Act 1998.

22 Accident Insurance Bill (203-1) 1999.

23 Todd (ed.), *The Law of Torts in New Zealand*, above n. 2, pp. 29–30.

24 Ibid, pp. 31–32.

25 Accident Compensation Act 2001 s. 259(2).

must give effect to government policy when directed by the Government's Minister for ACC.[26] ACC's board is appointed by the Minister,[27] and the board in consultation with the Minister selects ACC's chief executive.[28]

ACC must adhere to a Code of ACC Claimants Rights, which confers rights on claimants and obligations on ACC.[29]

3. WHY WAS THE ACC SCHEME ESTABLISHED?

The establishment of the ACC Scheme was a landmark event in the New Zealand legal landscape. It was established following the comprehensive survey of the existing state of the law by the Woodhouse Report. The Woodhouse Report advocated a comprehensive no-fault compensation scheme covering all accidental personal injury (with a view to later extending the scheme to cover other types of ailments). This was an unusual result because it was far broader than the Royal Commission's own terms of reference (which concerned compensation for workplace injury). The Commission recommended, somewhat radically, that there should be a comprehensive system of accident prevention, rehabilitation and compensation which would avoid the disadvantages of existing processes, meet the requirements of community responsibility, comprehensive entitlement, complete rehabilitation, real compensation and administrative efficiency, and satisfy the requirement of financial affordability.[30]

The Woodhouse Report's recommendations therefore widened the responsibility to compensate victims to encompass the whole community, rather than the classic common law focus on the fault of the defendant(s).[31] Remarkably, there was no pressing reason, crisis or disastrous event in New Zealand that created an overwhelming public policy impetus for the creation of the ACC scheme.[32] The Woodhouse Report's proposals

---

26 Crown Entities Act 2004 s. 7.

27 Accident Compensation Act 2001 s. 267.

28 Ibid, sch. 5, cl. 17.

29 Ibid, ss. 39–47; Code of ACC Claimants' Rights 2002. This code was provided for under the 2001 Act following criticism that ACC behaved in in an unduly adversarial and harsh way towards claimants. See Todd (ed.), *The Law of Torts in New Zealand*, above n. 2, pp. 92–93.

30 Royal Commission to Inquire into and Report upon Workers Compensation, *Compensation for Personal Injury in New Zealand*, above n. 13, p. 39.

31 Todd (ed.), *The Law of Torts in New Zealand*, above n. 2, pp. 23–25.

32 Peter McKenzie, 'The Compensation Scheme No One Asked For: The Origins of ACC in New Zealand' (2003) 34 *Victoria University of Wellington Law Review* 193, 206

were handled generally thoughtfully by the legislature, and both of New Zealand's main political parties came to support the proposed basic principles of an accidental injury compensation scheme.[33]

This section will look at the pre-ACC Scheme history of compensation law in New Zealand, the Woodhouse Report itself, the social and political context of the Woodhouse Report era, and finally the implementation of the ACC Scheme.

3.1. THE HISTORY OF COMPENSATION IN NEW ZEALAND

The background to New Zealand's novel compensation fund approach can be traced back to the start of the twentieth century. In 1900, New Zealand became one of the first countries in the world to create a (limited) worker injury compensation scheme.[34] The New Zealand legislation was modelled on UK legislation passed three years earlier, and the roots of the UK scheme could be found in 1884 German legislation.[35] The 1900 Act granted weekly compensation to injured workers and compensation to the families of fatally injured workers. It was funded by compulsory employer insurance and operated as a gloss over existing common law tort remedies.

By the late 1960s personal injury litigation dominated New Zealand's law of negligence, and was a significant area of activity for lawyers, the courts and the trade unions.[36] The legal landscape offered an injured person the option of seeking compensation via the common law, supplemented with some statutory options (depending on the cause of the injury and the injured person's circumstances):

- An updated worker injury compensation scheme funded by compulsory insurance for employers.[37] This offered a basic level of compensation for work-related accidents.

<https://www.victoria.ac.nz/law/research/publications/vuwlr/prev-issues/vol-34-2/mckenzie.pdf>.

33 Palmer, *Compensation for Incapacity: A Study of Law and Social Change in New Zealand and Australia*, above n. 12, p. 83.

34 Workers' Compensation for Accidents Act 1900.

35 Royal Commission to Inquire into and Report upon Workers Compensation, *Compensation for Personal Injury in New Zealand*, above n. 13, p. 33.

36 McKenzie, 'The Compensation Scheme No One Asked For: The Origins of ACC in New Zealand', above n. 32, p. 195.

37 Workers' Compensation Act 1956.

- Social security legislation which provided subsistence level welfare payments to individuals who met the requirements of a means test.[38]
- Criminal injuries compensation legislation which provided State-funded compensation payments to victims of certain serious crimes.[39] Compensation amounts related to victims' actual expenses, pecuniary loss and extra compensation for pain and suffering, subject to a statutory ceiling.
- Compulsory motor insurance legislation which funded damage payments through a pooled insurance company scheme.[40] This included cases where the defendant/tortfeasor was (illegally) uninsured or could not be found.

3.2. THE WOODHOUSE REPORT

The Woodhouse Report is remarkable to read, 50 years later. It is clearly written, espouses thoroughly contemporary concepts of social justice, and is devoid of much 'legalese'. The Royal Commission, although tasked only to consider workplace injury, had no hesitation in clearly recommending a comprehensive New Zealand-specific social insurance compensation scheme from the outset of its report. The Woodhouse Report noted that personal injury, as a consequence of social progress, required that victims of all kinds 'receive a co-ordinated response from the nation as a whole'.[41] The existing negligence action under the common law was unjust because it was a form of lottery. Existing worker compensation legislation provided some meagre compensation for workplace injuries, social security could assist some who satisfied a means test, but all others were left to fend for themselves. This was declared unsatisfactory. These three existing remedies were declared to be fragmented, gave rise to injustice and perpetuated anomalies such as double compensation. The report said that it was time for a new universal scheme to replace the status quo.[42]

---

38 Social Security Act 1964. The underlying purpose of this legislation has not fundamentally changed in the past 50 years.

39 Criminal Injuries Compensation Act 1963.

40 Transport Act 1962.

41 Royal Commission to Inquire into and Report upon Workers Compensation, *Compensation for Personal Injury in New Zealand*, above n. 13, p. 19. There is mention in particular of the 'grave risks of the road' – the technological advances which led to a greater number of motor vehicles on the road in the mid-twentieth century had opened up new and much greater dimensions of personal injury risk for the community.

42 Ibid, pp. 20, 41.

To illustrate the Woodhouse Report's spirit, it is useful to directly quote the Commission's summarised explanation of its guiding principles for the proposed new scheme:[43]

> First, in the national interest, and as a matter of national obligation, the community must protect all citizens (including the self-employed) and the housewives who sustain them from the burden of sudden individual losses when their ability to contribute to the general welfare by their work has been interrupted by physical incapacity;
>
> Second, all injured persons should receive compensation from any community financed scheme on the same uniform method of assessment, regardless of the causes which gave rise to their injuries;
>
> Third, the scheme must be deliberately organised to urge forward the physical and vocational recovery of these citizens while at the same time providing a real measure of money compensation for their losses;
>
> Fourth, real compensation demands for the whole period of incapacity the provision of income-related benefits for lost income and recognition of the plain fact that any permanent bodily impairment is a loss in itself regardless of its effect on earning capacity;
>
> Fifth, the achievement of the system will be eroded to the extent that its benefits are delayed, or are inconsistently assessed, or the system itself is administered by methods that are economically wasteful.

The Royal Commission noted that it was arbitrary to distinguish accidental personal injury from other kinds of ailments. However, it also recognised that the proposal for a universal accident compensation scheme was already quite radical. The 'issue of drawing a line between injury by accident and sickness or disease is a mixed question of law and medicine' that required further analysis,[44] but the proposals 'put forward for injury leave the way entirely open for sickness to follow whenever the relevant decision is taken'.[45]

3.3. SOCIAL AND POLITICAL CONTEXT

In its critique of the common law system, the Woodhouse Report cited a passage of Professor John G. Fleming's book on Australian tort law that

---

43 Ibid, p. 39.
44 Ibid, pp. 113–114.
45 Ibid, p. 26.

claimed: 'The individualistic fault dogma has been replaced by the mid-twentieth century quest for social security.'[46] The mid-twentieth century was a time of phenomenal change as well as economic growth for many western economies, including New Zealand. There was new scope to consider generous and egalitarian legal frameworks in response to technological change. From colonisation until the mid-twentieth century, New Zealand's economy was centred on commodities (food and raw materials) exported to the UK. International economic pressures (diversification, technology and consumer choice) and the favouring of market-focused economic theories led to the New Zealand economy's major market liberalisation in the second half of the twentieth century.[47]

In terms of politics, the farming sector was New Zealand's dominant political lobby in the early and mid-twentieth century. Other lobby groups and interest groups existed but did not hold the same degree of influence and political leverage as the farming sector.[48] The Woodhouse Report affected the insurance industry, the legal profession and the trade union movement. None of the groups opposed the scheme to an extent that progress could not be made.[49] Geoffrey Palmer gives one possible explanation for the lack of insurance industry clout at the time of the Woodhouse Report's implementation: the industry's low political profile and lack of donations to the private-enterprise focused centre-right National Party who were in Government at the time.[50]

The legal profession was divided on the Woodhouse Report's proposals but ultimately the New Zealand Law Society took a balanced view. New Zealand has a fused legal profession, where the majority of lawyers hold practicing certificates as both barristers and solicitors. In 1971, fewer than 20% of lawyers handled personal injury work (but those who did undertook a significant amount).[51] Lawyers had a number of years' advance warning of the ACC scheme's implementation, and had time to adapt their practices.[52] Trials relating to accidental injury before 1974 continued to play out until 1978. Additionally, in 1969 a comprehensive civil legal aid scheme came into effect, and there was a simultaneous increase in town

46 Ibid, p. 43.

47 B.H. Easton, *In Stormy Seas: The Post-War New Zealand Economy* (University of Otago Press 1997), p. 185.

48 Ibid, p. 213.

49 Palmer, *Compensation for Incapacity: A Study of Law and Social Change in New Zealand and Australia*, above n. 12, p. 115.

50 Ibid, pp. 122–123.

51 Ibid, p. 123.

52 Ibid, p. 128.

planning-related tribunal work. A prosperous legal environment and adequate adjustment time for this small jurisdiction's legal profession may indeed have stifled any significant legal profession opposition to the ACC Scheme.

The relatively non-combative nature of New Zealand's pressure groups certainly made it easier for the government to implement the ACC Scheme. This comes into sharp focus when one compares the New Zealand situation with Australia. In 1973 the newly elected (and eager to reform) Australian Labor Government invited Owen Woodhouse to chair an inquiry on national rehabilitation and compensation for personal injury in Australia.[53] The scope of the inquiry became wider than New Zealand, because it was extended in 1974 to include sickness. The Australian inquiry had greater complexity to consider, given Australia's federal structure, bicameral federal legislature, individual state legislatures and written constitution.

It was Australia's influential and well-organised pressure groups that stifled reform attempts – insurance companies, the legal profession, trade unions and state governments.[54] The insurance companies did not have a united front, but various submissions from insurance companies and associated lobbies highlighted the practical and economic problems of a comprehensive scheme. The Australian legal profession earned more money from the common law and workers' compensation than New Zealand lawyers. The Australian legal representative bodies were well organised with their opposition and raised many practical objections to the system (rather than defending the common law on its merits). The trade union movement had recently achieved 100% of earnings compensation and had an unwavering belief in the strength of the common law. State governments had political and personality differences at play in addition to existing, state-specific compensation frameworks. Together, the political weight and active opposition of all of these groups combined with legislative difficulties to prevent from enacting a similar nationwide comprehensive compensation scheme.

Back in New Zealand, political and parliamentary activity a decade later is relevant to understanding the implementation philosophy of the scheme's early history. A 1988 government-commissioned Law Commission review of the scheme firmly recommended that the ACC Scheme be extended to include sickness and non-accidental incapacity

53 Ibid, pp. 131–173.
54 Ibid, pp. 174–196.

(in line with the original Woodhouse Report vision).[55] The report disagreed with a dominant public and political perception that the ACC Scheme was facing a financial crisis and concluded that an extension of the scheme would not lead to a cost blow-out. However legislative attempts to bring the 1988 Law Commission review's recommendations into legislative reality were curtailed by a change of government. The new centre-right conservative government concluded (following its own policy review) the Scheme was too expensive and took a different policy approach.[56] To this day, the ACC Scheme remains limited to accidental injury and favours a quasi-private insurer approach to funding and compensation by ACC, whilst retaining the social contract of compensatory benefits in exchange for the right to sue. Simon Connell has argued that the duality of community insurance versus compulsory insurance has appeal across the political spectrum and is a reason behind the Scheme's longevity and why it has not expanded further beyond personal injury.[57]

4. HOW DOES IT OPERATE?

Although the coverage provided by the ACC Scheme is a type of social insurance,[58] the rights conferred on injured claimants are done so directly by the general law of the land.[59] This is a notable difference to European jurisdictions where social security and health-related rights are often founded on an insurance basis. There has been some dalliance by New Zealand legislatures over the years between an insurance-based approach and a rights-based approach. A legislative change in 1998 by the centre-right government sought to privatise the provision of accident compensation benefits via employers for workplace-related accidents.

---

55 New Zealand Law Commission, 'Personal Injury: Prevention and Recovery – Report on the Accident Compensation Scheme' (1988), paras 83–102 <http://www.lawcom.govt.nz/sites/default/files/projectAvailableFormats/NZLC R4 part 1.pdf>.

56 Birch, *Accident Compensation: A Fairer Scheme*, above n. 20; Todd (ed.), *The Law of Torts in New Zealand*, above n. 2, pp. 27–28.

57 Simon Connell, 'Community Insurance versus Compulsory Insurance: Competing Paradigms of No-Fault Accident Compensation in New Zealand' [2019] Legal Studies 1 <https://www.cambridge.org/core/product/identifier/S0261387518000508/type/journal_article>.

58 Royal Commission to Inquire into and Report upon Workers Compensation, *Compensation for Personal Injury in New Zealand*, above n. 13, p. 107.

59 New Zealand Law Commission, 'Personal Injury: Prevention and Recovery – Report on the Accident Compensation Scheme', above n. 55.

It has been argued that this was a first step towards evolving the Scheme into a system of universal personal insurance.[60] These privatisation measures were reversed a year later following a change in government. Privatisation of employer accounts was once again mooted ten years ago when a centre-right government returned to power,[61] but this policy did not come to fruition.

4.1. BASICS OF HOW THE ACC SCHEME IS OPERATED AND HOW/WHEN COMPENSATION IS PAID OUT

The ACC's claims assessment process broadly consists of two steps: evaluating whether an injury or condition is covered by the Scheme, and then (if it is covered) deciding what kind of entitlements the claimant should receive.[62] The healthcare provider (doctor, hospital emergency room, etc.) usually makes the initial assessment of whether an individual's injury is covered by the ACC Scheme and submits the necessary documentation to ACC.[63] For a covered accidental injury, ACC will pay most or all of the treatment cost directly to the healthcare provider. Confirmation of coverage is by letter to the injured person.

Generally, weekly compensation of the injured person's earnings is paid by ACC (at an 80% rate) from one week after the injury date. In the case of a work-related personal injury as an employee, the employer must pay the injured person's earnings for the first week (at an 80% rate).[64] This is to incentivise good health and safety practices in the workplace.[65] This means that people injured in non-workplace accidents must bear the first week's loss of earnings themselves.[66] There are various formulae in the statute for calculating the weekly earnings of self-employed people

60 Todd (ed.), *The Law of Torts in New Zealand*, above n. 2, p. 30.

61 Nick Smith, 'Increasing Choice in Workplace Accident Compensation' (2011) <https://www.beehive.govt.nz/speech/increasing-choice-workplace-accident-compensation>.

62 Miriam Dean, 'Independent Review of the Acclaim Otago (Inc) July 2015 Report Into Accident Compensation Dispute Resolution Processes' (2016), p. 8 <http://www.mbie.govt.nz/info-services/employment-skills/legislation-reviews/accident-compensation-dispute-resolution/document-and-images-library/independent-review.pdf>.

63 Accident Compensation Corporation, 'What to Do If You're Injured' (2017) <https://www.acc.co.nz/im-injured/what-to-do/>; Accident Compensation Act 2001 s. 49.

64 Accident Compensation Act 2001 s. 98.

65 Todd (ed.), *The Law of Torts in New Zealand*, above n. 2, pp. 82–83.

66 However, the employee may be entitled to sick leave during this first week under the Holidays Act 2003 and the terms of their employment contract.

and those with irregular or multiple sources of income.[67] The current legislation also allows weekly compensation payments to be stopped after a period of time if a claimant is fit to return to work.[68] Weekly compensation is payable to a surviving spouse/partner and child in the event of a fatal accident.[69]

Lump sum compensation is paid for permanent impairment.[70] A feature of the original 1972 legislation, lump sum payments were abolished under the 1992 legislation. This was controversial and viewed by some as a breach of the social contract underlying the ACC Scheme.[71] The minimum lump sum amount payable for personal impairment is $2,500, and the maximum lump sum amount payable is $100,000.[72] ACC also makes one off payments to the dependants and survivors of a fatal accident victim.[73] What this means, in effect, is that there is little compensation available for pain and suffering under the ACC Scheme.

Rehabilitation is one of the key goals of the ACC Scheme.[74] ACC's key obligation is the identification of a suitable rehabilitation plan to meet

67 Accident Compensation Act 2001 ss. 9, 14, 15, 49 and 100.

68 Ibid, ss. 6, 107, 112. Fitness to return to work is called 'vocational independence' under the legislation. This is defined under s. 6 as meaning the claimant's capacity to engage in work (that he/she is suited to by experience, education and/or training) for 30 hours or more a week. A strict work capacity test had been introduced by the 1992 legislation, but it was found to be unworkable in practice – see Todd (ed.), *The Law of Torts in New Zealand*, above n. 2, p. 82. The 1991 Government report that preceded the 1992 legislative changes noted that rehabilitation 'cannot be forced on an individual, but an insurer must have the right to terminate income maintenance if the injured person refuses to cooperate in rehabilitation.' See Birch, *Accident Compensation: A Fairer Scheme*, above n. 20, p. 57.

69 Accident Compensation Act 2001 sch. 1, cls 66, 70, 76.

70 Ibid, sch. 1, cl. 54. Permanent impairment is defined by cl. 54(1)(c) as a personal injury resulting in 'a degree of whole-person impairment of 10% of more'. Assessment of permanent impairment is based on ACC guidelines and American Medical Association guidelines – see Accident Compensation Corporation, 'Impairment Assessment Lump Sum/Independence Allowance Operational Guidelines' (2014) <https://www.acc.co.nz/assets/contracts/imp-og.pdf>.

71 Todd (ed.), *The Law of Torts in New Zealand*, above n. 2, p. 87. Lump sum payments for loss of faculty were replaced in 1992 with a graduated 'independence allowance'. Lump sum payments for emotional loss and pain and suffering were abolished on the grounds that they were 'very difficult to administer in a fair and consistent manner, reflecting the essential problem of assessing monetary compensation for a non-economic loss' – see Birch, *Accident Compensation: A Fairer Scheme*, above n. 20, p. 52. These kinds of lump sum payments have not been reintroduced.

72 Accident Compensation Act 2001 sch. 1, cl. 56.

73 Ibid, sch. 1, cls 64–65.

74 Ibid, s. 3(c).

this goal,[75] and claimants have a responsibility to co-operate with the rehabilitation plan.[76]

The ACC Scheme disputes resolution process is now quite different from the process under the original 1972 legislation.[77] The 1982 legislation introduced an inquisitorial review process. However, since the 1992 legislation, the dispute resolution process has had a more adversarial approach.[78] Claimants can apply to ACC for a review of its decisions on a claim, delay in processing a claim, or any of its decisions under the Code of ACC Claimants' Rights.[79] Employers can apply for a review of whether a claimant's injury is work-related. Levy payers can apply for a review about any levies paid or deemed payable. Prompt turnaround times are required by the legislation – a decision (with reasons) must be made within 28 days.[80] If ACC does not schedule a review hearing within three months of a review application being lodged then (barring any delays caused by the applicant) the applicant's claim will automatically be successful.[81] Either party can appeal against a review decision to the District Court (though ACC rarely appeals).[82] In practice, if ACC cannot resolve the dispute internally (i.e. without a hearing, and before a review application is filed), then the review application is delegated to one of three alternative dispute resolution providers.[83]

---

75 Ibid, s. 70; Todd (ed.), *The Law of Torts in New Zealand*, above n. 2, p. 79.

76 Accident Compensation Act 2001 s. 72.

77 Todd (ed.), *The Law of Torts in New Zealand*, above n. 2, p. 96.

78 A reason for the change from inquisitorial to adversarial dispute resolution was a philosophical change from a welfare system to an insurance contract under the 1992 legislation – see Todd (ed.), *The Law of Torts in New Zealand*, above n. 2, p. 96.

79 Accident Compensation Act 2001 s. 134.

80 Ibid, s. 144.

81 Ibid, s. 146.

82 Ibid, s. 149; Dean, 'Independent Review of the Acclaim Otago (Inc) July 2015 Report Into Accident Compensation Dispute Resolution Processes', above n. 62.

83 Until recently, FairWay Resolution Limited was the only dispute resolution provider used for reviews (aside from a law firm that handled reviews in one small New Zealand city). FairWay was an independent Crown entity, but became employee-owned in 2017 following Miriam Dean QC's independent review and perceptions that FairWay was insufficiently independent from ACC. In 2019, ACC announced that it would also work with two other dispute resolution service providers – the Independent Complaint and Review Authority Ltd and Talk Meet Resolve. See New Zealand Government, 'FairWay Change Positive for Staff and Customers' (2017) <https://www.beehive.govt.nz/release/fairway-change-positive-staff-and-customers>. ACC, 'We're Changing How We Handle Customer Reviews' (2019) <https://www.acc.co.nz/newsroom/stories/were-changing-how-we-handle-customer-reviews/>.

Appeal to the High Court and Court of Appeal is possible with leave but only on questions of law.[84]

4.2. FUNDING

The ACC Scheme's funding models have changed significantly over its history. Issues of funding have been closely linked over time to public conceptions of the ACC Scheme,[85] and where the scheme fits within the (often jurisdictionally different) definitions of insurance, welfare and social insurance.

The original costing of the ACC Scheme was carefully calculated in the Woodhouse Report on the basis that existing compulsory worker compensation and motor insurance levies should be diverted to fund the new accident compensation scheme.[86] This, in combination with savings made by self-insurers (like the Government), and savings to social security and healthcare budgets, would come close to financing the new scheme. The remaining gap would be closed by contributions from newly covered groups – self-employed and motor vehicle licence-holders. The Woodhouse Report had identified administrative cost concerns with allowing social insurance schemes to be administered by private insurance companies, who retained profits from contributions paid into a scheme.[87]

Funding for the ACC Scheme has always been based on a combination of levies on activities and out of the general taxation pool.[88] The scheme currently operates on a full funding model, with a pay-as-you-go model for pre-2001 non-earner injuries.[89] A pay-as-you-go model for funding

---

84 Accident Compensation Act 2001 ss. 162–163.

85 Richard Gaskins, 'Accounting for Accidents: Social Costs of Personal Injuries' (2010) 41 *Victoria University of Wellington Law Review* 37, 37.

86 Royal Commission to Inquire into and Report upon Workers Compensation, *Compensation for Personal Injury in New Zealand*, above n. 13, p. 171.

87 Ibid, p. 181.

88 Todd (ed.), *The Law of Torts in New Zealand*, above n. 2, pp. 98–99.

89 Accident Compensation Corporation, 'Annual Report 2017', above n. 3. 'Our broad financial sustainability objective is to ensure each levied account is in a fully funded solvency position. Full funding means that, at any point in time, the value of our investment portfolio is enough to pay for the future costs of every claim we have received to date. The exception to this full funding objective is the costs of Government-funded non-earners' injuries incurred prior to 1 July 2001. These are funded on a pay-as-you-go basis.'

the whole ACC Scheme was utilised in the 1980s and 1990s, but this was changed by the 1998 legislation.[90]

ACC manages five different accounts that relate to specific types of injuries: the Work Account (for work-related injuries, including private domestic workers and the self-employed), the Earners' Account (for injuries to earners that are not work-related, motor vehicle injuries or treatment injures), the Motor Vehicle Account (for motor vehicle injuries), the Non-Earner Account and the Treatment Injury Account.[91] The first three Accounts are funded by levies on personal income (earnings), business income, vehicle fuel and vehicle registration.[92] The Non-Earner Account (covering children, social welfare recipients, students and visitors) is funded by the Government out of general taxation.[93] The Treatment Injury Account is funded by both the Earners' and Non-Earners' Account, depending on whether the injured person is employed.[94]

The late Sir Owen Woodhouse in recent years suggested that funding should move back to a pay-as-you-go model, because this would enable the Woodhouse Report's requirement of administrative efficiency to be met.[95] He claimed that the original notion of social insurance had been ignored by those who viewed ACC as analogous to commercial insurance. ACC's current reporting data and statements certainly reflect that the organisation takes a commercial insurance approach to its financial operations and management.[96] Sir Woodhouse said a return

---

90 As noted already, the 1998 legislation introduced a degree of privatisation to the ACC Scheme by allowing private insurers to compete for the provision of work-related injury cover. It was necessary to introduce a full funding requirement to ensure private insurers had 'sufficient assets to meet their contractual obligations.' An Insolvent Insurers Fund was to be established to ensure statutory entitlements continued to be paid if 'an insurer has insufficient assets to meet its obligations under accident insurance contacts.' See Accident Insurance Bill (203-1) 1999 (n. 22) iii.

91 Accident Compensation Corporation, 'What Your Levies Pay for' <https://www.acc.co.nz/about-us/how-levies-work/what-your-levies-pay/>.

92 Accident Compensation Act 2001 ss. 167, 213, 218.

93 Ibid, s. 227(2).

94 Ibid, s. 228; Accident Compensation Corporation, 'What Your Levies Pay for', above n. 91.

95 Owen Woodhouse, 'The ACC Concept' <http://docs.business.auckland.ac.nz/Doc/ACC-Forum-2011-17-Woodhouse-ACC-Concept-Paper-revised.pdf>.

96 Accident Compensation Corporation, 'Annual Report 2017', above n. 3; Accident Compensation Corporation, 'Service Agreement 2017/18' (2017) <https://www.parliament.nz/resource/en-NZ/PAP_75186/92e34677ae6c78c38354d975e2ad5eb774ab2c66>; Accident Compensation Corporation, 'Statement of Intent 2015–2019' (2015) <https://www.acc.co.nz/assets/corporate-documents/ACC6969-Statement-of-intent-2015-2019.pdf>.

to pay-as-you-go funding and amalgamating the funding accounts would make it realistic to consider extending the system to sickness and incapacity, thus fulfilling the original vision of the Royal Commission. This point neatly encapsulates the conflicting views within New Zealand of whether ACC should be thought of as a type of insurance (similar to private insurance, but compulsory and with a single monopoly provider) or as a type of social insurance (like social security systems in many continental European jurisdictions).[97]

The ACC Scheme model of a compulsory levy payment to a state monopoly insurer (that is operated in a similar way to a private insurance company) is similar to the funding model of New Zealand's Earthquake Commission ('EQC'). This illustrates the New Zealand government's preference for a private insurance-style approach to the long-term funding of large risks, with coverage applied by default across most of the population. New Zealand is a country on the 'Pacific Ring of Fire' prone to earthquakes, volcanic eruptions and other natural disasters. The EQC provides cover for insured residential property damaged by earthquakes and other natural disasters.[98] Insured homeowners[99] pay a community-rated EQC premium as part of their private insurance cover – the private insurance companies pass this levy on to the EQC.[100] The EQC finances its risk through a savings vehicle called the Natural Disaster Fund and reinsurance purchases from international financial markets. EQC's liabilities are government-guaranteed, which is where taxpayer support becomes relevant. The costs of claims associated with a series of major earthquakes in recent years have fully exhausted the Natural Disaster Fund, and in the 2018–19 financial year the EQC had to call on the government guarantee for the first time.[101] In order to rebuild the Natural

97 Connell, 'Community Insurance versus Compulsory Insurance: Competing Paradigms of No-Fault Accident Compensation in New Zealand', above n. 57.

98 Earthquake Commission, 'The Natural Disaster Fund' <https://www.eqc.govt.nz/about-eqc/our-role/ndf>.

99 Home insurance is not compulsory in New Zealand, but it is commonly required by mortgage providers. EQC cover is also not compulsory, but is added by default to all home insurance policies.

100 The flat-rate EQC premiums means that there is near-total earthquake/natural disaster cover in New Zealand (around 98%), compared with a vastly lower rate of cover in other seismically active locations like Japan, California and Italy. See Cuong Nguyen and Ilan Noy, 'Insuring Earthquakes: How Would the Californian and Japanese Insurance Programs Have Fared after the 2011 New Zealand Earthquake?' (2019) Disasters.

101 The EQC received NZ$125 million (excluding goods and services tax) in three tranches, in order to be able to continue settling claims. See EQC Earthquake

Disaster Fund, the EQC changed its risk financing strategy in 2017 to a fully-funded model (like the ACC Scheme). This means that premiums charged to customers should match the expected liabilities of the scheme and the cost of administering the scheme. However it is expected that it will take until 2030 to rebuild the Natural Disaster Fund, barring any other major disaster events.[102]

5. THE IMPACT OF ACC ON NEW ZEALAND'S LEGAL SYSTEM

5.1. THE EFFECT OF ACC ON RELATED LEGISLATION

5.1.1. Social Security Legislation

The ACC Scheme, with its social insurance-type model and income-related payments, is quite different to the means-tested basic safety net provided by the wider New Zealand social security system. The Woodhouse Report itself saw merit in the idea of modifying or supplementing New Zealand's social security system with a form of income-related benefits (with a view to merging the ACC Scheme with the social security system) but could not anticipate whether this was likely to happen.[103]

However, there are some links and parallels between the ACC Scheme and the social security system. For example, both the 2001 Act and social security legislation have an abatement regime to encourage benefit/compensation recipients to return to paid work without risking the loss of their statutory payments.[104]

There is also a relationship between the ACC Scheme weekly compensation and New Zealand superannuation (pension) payments – superannuation can affect how long a claimant can receive the ACC Scheme weekly payments, and a claimant may be required to choose between receiving ACC payments and receiving superannuation.[105]

Commission, 'Annual Report 2018–19' (2018) 6 <https://www.eqc.govt.nz/sites/public_files/documents/publications/EQC-Annual Report-2018-19.pdf>.

102 Ibid, 41.

103 Royal Commission to Inquire into and Report upon Workers Compensation, *Compensation for Personal Injury in New Zealand*, above n. 13, p. 106.

104 Todd (ed.), *The Law of Torts in New Zealand*, above n. 2, p. 81; Accident Compensation Act 2001 sch. 1, cl. 51.

105 Accident Compensation Act 2001 sch. 1, cl. 52.

A recent official review of the New Zealand social welfare system has recommended a reassessment of the relationship between the ACC Scheme, social welfare and the health and disability system.[106] The ACC itself is delaying any major overhaul of the relevant legislation until it has received complete advice from these various expert groups.[107]

5.1.2. Health and Safety Legislation

Injury prevention is a key focus of the 2001 Act and ACC's activities. Minimising the incidence and impact of injury on the community is one of the express purposes of the 2001 Act.[108] There has been an increasing focus on safety and injury prevention over the ACC Scheme's legislative history, for both social good reasons and in order to minimise claim costs to ACC. The general unavailability of tort damages and other remedies for personal injury means that there is no common law incentive for a defendant to avoid wrongful conduct. There is correspondingly a complementary relationship between the ACC Scheme and New Zealand health and safety legislation.

A primary function of ACC is to promote injury prevention measures that reduce the incidence and severity of personal injury.[109] However, ACC is not legally responsible for ensuring compliance with health and safety measures. In practical terms this means that ACC's focus is targeted financial investment in injury prevention. This means investment in community programmes that seek to reduce the incidence of every kind of injury, including motorcycle and driver safety education, first aid training, sports injury prevention and programmes that aim to prevent sexual violence. ACC is also considering financial incentives (probably levy reductions) to encourage improved health and safety performance.[110]

The blanket effect of the ACC Scheme has deeply affected the shape of safety and liability legislation in New Zealand. Personal injuries caused

---

106 Welfare Expert Advisory Group, 'Whakamana Tāngata – Restoring Dignity to Social Security in New Zealand' (2019) <www.weag.govt.nz>.

107 Michael Fletcher, 'Towards Wellbeing? Developments in Social Legislation and Policy in New Zealand' (2018) <http://www.mpisoc.mpg.de>. The ongoing Royal Commission of Inquiry into Historical Abuse in State Care and in the Care of Faith-based Institutions may also make recommendations on compensation and redress that intersect with ACC Scheme legislation.

108 Accident Compensation Act 2001 s. 3.

109 Ibid, s. 263.

110 Accident Compensation Corporation, 'Annual Report 2017', above n. 3, p. 21.

by a defective product, for example, are not treated differently to another type of personal injury for the purposes of the victim's compensation. The injured person will likely be eligible for coverage under the ACC Scheme, but due to the statutory bar the injured person will not be able to sue the defective product manufacturer or distributor for compensatory damages in relation to their injury. Product safety is regulated by the Fair Trading Act 1986, and the Consumer Guarantees Act 1993 provides a general consumer rights framework. There are civil and criminal penalties for breaches of the Fair Trading Act,[111] whereas the Consumer Guarantees Act mandates simpler practical remedies for consumers.[112] The Commerce Commission is the relevant regulator for product safety, and sets mandatory safety standards (via the Fair Trading Act) for a very small number of products. The Commerce Commission is the most frequent plaintiff (and prosecutor) in proceedings involving an alleged breach of the Fair Trading Act. Because the issue of compensation for injury is disconnected from liability in New Zealand, consumer protection and product safety legislation is also philosophically disconnected from the ACC Scheme. Tort liability under negligence may also be relevant in this area, remembering of course that the ACC Scheme litigation bar will block any cases involving personal injury.

Detailed workplace health and safety law is enshrined in legislation separate to the ACC Scheme, and its enforcement is the responsibility of a separate agency (that reports to the same government minister responsible for the ACC Scheme). In 2015, Parliament passed the Health and Safety at Work Act ('HSWA'), one of the most significant reforms to workplace health and safety in decades. The incentive for this legislative reform was to improve New Zealand's poor health and safety performance compared to similar jurisdictions (such as the UK and Australia).[113] The HSWA introduced amendments to the Accident Compensation Act 2001 to enable ACC to work collaboratively with WorkSafe, New Zealand's new workplace safety regulatory agency.[114]

---

111 Fair Trading Act 1986 s. 40.

112 Additionally, the Sale of Goods Act 1908 provides various implied warranties and conditions in contracts for the sale of goods. However, the parties can contract out of the statute's provisions either expressly or by their conduct or trade usage.

113 New Zealand Government, 'A Blueprint for Health & Safety at Work' (2013), p. 5 <https://www.mbie.govt.nz/assets/f02d850266/working-safer-blueprint-for-health-and-safety.pdf>. The New Zealand government has set a target of a 25% reduction in workplace injuries and fatalities by 2020.

114 Accident Compensation Act 2001 s. 264A; Health and Safety at Work Act 2015 s. 196.

Earlier health and safety legislation also aimed to complement the ACC Scheme.[115] An example of practical collaborative injury prevention activities by ACC and Worksafe are online toolkits for businesses to manage health and safety risks.[116] WorkSafe is the agency responsible for bringing prosecution proceedings for breaches of the HSWA. WorkSafe is also responsible for administering and enforcing legislation relating to mines rescue, hazardous substances, electricity and gas. ACC's role in health and safety law is therefore one of collaboration and financial investment, rather than enforcement.

New Zealand's comparatively poor workplace health and safety outcomes naturally begs the question of whether the no-fault ACC Scheme results in worse preventative safety outcomes, compared to a liability-based system. A 2008 independent review of the ACC Scheme noted that there is no consistent systematic evidence of a liability-driven deterrence effect on injury.[117] That review noted that ACC had a relatively small role in the area of prevention compared with other accident compensation schemes internationally.[118] The 2015 health and safety legislative reforms and the creation of a new regulatory agency can be seen as fulfilling many of the 2008 ACC Scheme review's recommended structural changes to New Zealand's approach to health and safety. ACC's injury prevention activities should be viewed as (potentially) victim-centred and directly connected to reducing the incidence of claims and thus improving the fund's financial position. Actions to punish or sanction the person or company who caused the injury are outside of ACC's ambit.[119]

---

115 Tennent, *Accident Compensation Law*, above n. 2, p. 348.

116 Worksafe, 'Role and Responsibilities' <https://worksafe.govt.nz/about-us/who-we-are/role-and-responsibilities/>.

117 PricewaterhouseCoopers, 'Accident Compensation Corporation New Zealand Scheme Review', p. vi <https://accfutures.org.nz/uploads/sites/accfutures/files/images/pricewaterhousecoopersaccreport.pdf>. Interestingly, on the issue of system costs, the PwC review noted that evidence indicated 'that access to common law benefits, even where significantly limited in nature, has been one of the primary drivers of cost blow-outs in workers compensation schemes in Australia.' In relation to treatment injury, that review noted that there is evidence that no-fault schemes have a positive patient safety impact in the long run.

118 Ibid, p. vi.

119 A proposal to amend the ACC Scheme statutory bar to allow ACC to bring subrogation actions against manufacturers in cases of product failure is set out in Trish O'Sullivan and Kate Tokeley, 'Consumer Product Failure Causing Personal Injury Under the No-Fault Accident Compensation Scheme in New Zealand-a Let-off for Manufacturers?', *Product Safety, Consumers' Health and Liability Law Conference* (Springer 2017) <https://doi.org/10.1007/s10603-018-9383-2>.

5.1.3. *Criminal Legislation*

Some court decisions related to compensation and other damages for crime victims have had a direct effect on criminal sentencing legislation.[120] Crime victims who suffered an ACC-covered personal injury can avoid the statutory bar and top up the 20% shortfall in their compensation losses by way of a reparation order under criminal sentencing legislation. The 2001 Act also now enshrines the availability of exemplary damages actions for criminal personal injury victims, regardless of the defendant's conviction status. These are examples of anomalies in New Zealand law that mean ACC-covered crime victims will sometimes have different or better remedies available to them than other crime victims.

5.2. THE EFFECT OF ACC ON TORT LAW

The classic view (and explicitly stated in the relevant legislation) is that the ACC scheme is a social contract, which removes the right to sue in cases of personal injury for damages under the common law, in return for comprehensive community cover.[121] The recommendation of the Woodhouse Report was to create a statutory replacement for the 'lottery' of the negligence common law action. The resulting legislative product has fundamentally altered the course of New Zealand tort law by effectively eliminating the most common wrongful act that common law damages are sought for in other jurisdictions.[122] Under New Zealand tort law, there are generally two categories of damages available – general damages and special damages. Special damages can be objectively assessed in monetary terms, whereas general damages seek to compensate a more intangible loss. Exemplary (i.e. punitive) damages are available to punish a defendant that is guilty of outrageous wrongdoing. The New Zealand approach to damages is generally more flexible than the English approach to exemplary damages.[123] Notably, exemplary damages are expressly still available under the 2001 Act for the ACC Scheme cases. Unlike Australia

---

120 See the cases discussed under section 5.2.1 below.

121 Accident Compensation Act 2001 s. 3; Todd (ed.), *The Law of Torts in New Zealand*, above n. 2, p. 22; Tennent, *Accident Compensation Law*, above n. 2, p. 6.

122 Accident Compensation Act 2001 ss. 317 and 318. These are the provisions in the legislation that create the statutory bar against common law proceedings for personal injury.

123 Todd (ed.), *The Law of Torts in New Zealand*, above n. 2, pp. 69, 1340.

and the UK, aggravated damages (awarded to compensate the plaintiff's feelings or dignity, or where the plaintiff's sense of injury is increased by the defendant's later bad conduct) are not available in New Zealand – courts have folded the category under the heading of general damages.

5.2.1. Tort Law Damages Still Available for ACC-Covered Personal Injury

The ACC Scheme provides personal injury victims with a replacement for common law compensatory damages, but the legislation expressly leaves open the possibility of exemplary damages for ACC-covered personal injury,[124] and commentary and case law say that vindicatory damages might also be possible.[125]

The latter type of damages can be swiftly dealt with. Vindicatory damages aim to vindicate a victim's right to inviolability of the person and mark the wrong that has been done. New Zealand case law relevant to this area is limited, and the judiciary has been hesitant to open the door to this category of damages actions. *Re Chase*[126] related to a person who was shot dead by police in the execution of a search warrant. The victim's estate brought a claim for damages, including exemplary and nominal damages. The Court of Appeal rejected the claim for nominal damages on the grounds that such an award could allow for abuse of process by those seeking to circumvent the spirit of the ACC Scheme statutory bar against compensatory damages actions. More recently, the High Court arrived at a similar conclusion in *P v Attorney-General*, while still leaving the door open to the possibility of vindicatory damages in principle.[127]

The continuing availability of exemplary damages for personal injury, despite the statutory bar, was affirmed soon after the ACC Scheme's introduction in *Donselaar v Donselaar.*[128] However this scope was affected by a conjoined set of decisions from the Court of Appeal, which

---

124 Accident Compensation Act 2001 s. 319.

125 Todd (ed.), *The Law of Torts in New Zealand*, above n. 2, pp. 72–73.

126 *Re Chase* [1989] 1 NZLR 325. This case should be compared with the English House of Lords decision *Ashley v Chief Constable of Sussex Police* [2008] UKHL 25, which arrived at the opposite conclusion to *Re Chase.*

127 *P v Attorney-General* (2010) NZHC 959 [59–67]. This case concerned a civil damages claim against the government by a man who alleged he was sexually assaulted by a colleague while they were both working on board a Royal New Zealand Navy ship.

128 *Donselaar v Donselaar* [1982] 1 NZLR 97.

found that a conviction or acquittal in a criminal proceeding prevented (because of the common law principle against double jeopardy) a later civil claim for exemplary damages in relation to that act.[129] The effect of this decision was that victims (whose personal injury was caused by a crime) would no longer be able to bring a claim for exemplary damages (unless the prosecution did not proceed). In response, Parliament introduced what is now s. 319(2) of the 2001 Act. This allows for a claim of exemplary damages where the defendant's behaviour has caused personal injury, regardless of the defendant's conviction status. This creates an anomaly whereby crime victims who have suffered ACC-covered personal injury can sue for exemplary damages, whereas other crime victims who suffered no personal injury (but suffered property loss, for example) are barred from bringing an exemplary damages claim because of the common law principle of double jeopardy.

On a related note, there is also one significant exception to the general bar on compensatory damages claims for personal injury. Parliament has given crime victims the ability to sidestep the statutory bar and top up their ACC compensatory losses by way of a reparation order under criminal sentencing legislation. Section 35(2) of the Sentencing Act 2002 was an explicit intervention by Parliament to amend Supreme Court precedent in *Davies v Police*.[130] In *Davies*, the Supreme Court overturned a sentence of reparation on the appellant that made up the shortfall between the victim's lost earnings and the weekly compensation received under the ACC Scheme. The majority judgment of the Supreme Court noted that if reparation could be ordered under sentencing legislation to make up for perceived inadequacies in the ACC Scheme, then crime victims would stand outside the ACC statutory bar on civilly wronged victims seeking compensation through the courts. The court viewed such a result as incompatible with the social contract created by the ACC Scheme. One academic commentary on *Davies* and the resulting parliamentary intervention has suggested that inconsistent outcomes between victims of injury may be acceptable as long as all receive adequate compensation.[131] However this seems unsatisfactory because Parliament is sanctioning different levels of compensation for different categories of victims – in

129 *Daniels v Thompson* (1998) NZCA 3.

130 *Davies v Police* (2009) NZSC 47; Victims of Crime Reform Bill 2011.

131 Simon Connell, 'Justice for Victims of Injury: The Influence of New Zealand's Accident Compensation Scheme on the Civil and Criminal Law' (2012) 25 *New Zealand Universities Law Review* 181, 320.

effect violating its own principle of fairly compensating different victims of unexpected misfortune.[132]

New Zealand courts have thus attempted to vigorously restrict damages actions that aim to 'top up' compensation already received under the ACC Scheme. The subsequent statutory interventions by Parliament are philosophically troubling. In relation to exemplary damages, Todd argues that if crime victims are treated inadequately by the statutory scheme, then the problem should be resolved by raising the benefits available to crime victims under ACC.[133] The original goal of the Woodhouse Report was a scheme that provided real and adequate compensation, without regard to fault or cause. If a universal no-fault compensation scheme falls short for some classes of victims, then surely the logical conclusion is that the statutory scheme is therefore failing for all classes of victims. Compensation levels and scope should be remedied by the legislature or ACC, rather than re-opening the door to common law remedies.

The presence of s. 319(2) of the Accident Compensation Act and s. 32(5) of the Sentencing Act reveals that there are still tensions among the judiciary, legislature and general public about the concept of 'no fault' and what the ACC social contract means. It is not clear which conceptions of justice are supposed to have priority when considering how the ACC Scheme overlaps with civil and criminal law.[134] This is an area that would benefit from legislative restatement.

5.2.2. *Damages Available for Non-ACC Covered Personal Injury*

If a personal injury is not eligible for cover under the 2001 Act, then the victim may proceed with a common law compensatory damages. The key issue here will be the definition of personal injury. As noted above, there is generally no cover for gradual processes, disease, heart attacks, the ageing process, and many types of mental injury.

One of the most important judgments in relation to non-ACC covered personal injury is the Court of Appeal decision in *Queenstown Lakes District Council v Palmer*.[135] This case makes it clear that the key

---

132 For a similar argument in the context of an earlier critique of the ACC Scheme, see James A. Henderson, 'New Zealand Accident Compensation Reform' (1981) 48 *University of Chicago Law Review* 781, 794.

133 Todd (ed.), *The Law of Torts in New Zealand*, above n. 2, p. 72.

134 See generally Connell, 'Justice for Victims of Injury: The Influence of New Zealand's Accident Compensation Scheme on the Civil and Criminal Law' above n. 131, p. 181.

135 *Queenstown Lakes District Council v Palmer* [1998] NZCA 190.

issue is whether the claim for damages arises directly or indirectly from personal injury, within the statutory definition of personal injury. This case is the precedent that a common law claim will be possible in relation to a non-covered injury.

In that case, an American tourist, Mr Palmer, survived a river-rafting accident in the Queenstown area that tragically killed his wife. He suffered serious mental injuries (post-traumatic stress disorder, depression and an associated speech impediment), but no physical injury, and he brought a common law action for damages in relation to his own mental injuries. The question to be answered was whether Mr Palmer's claim for compensatory damages was prevented by the ACC Scheme statutory bar. Mr Palmer was not seeking damages in relation to his wife's death (which fell within the definition of personal injury) – he was seeking damages in relation to his own mental injuries which he suffered as a result of the alleged breach of duty of care by the defendants (Queenstown Lakes District Council and the rafting operator).

Thomas J found that the statutory bar did not apply to Mr Palmer. His Honour noted that the purpose of the ACC Scheme statutory bar against common law claims was to prevent injury victims being compensated twice over (once under statute, and then via the common law) – its purpose was not to prevent personal victim injuries from receiving any compensation at all. Where there is no cover by the scheme, then the right to sue at common law will be revived.

An effect of the case is that a secondary or non-covered victim might end up recovering far more in compensatory damages than an ACC Scheme-covered victim. Thomas J acknowledged this but noted that such anomalies or injustices 'are inherent in the scheme of the Act under which the quantum of compensation is limited relative to the quantum of common law damages which would have been available but for the Act.' He noted that this type of problem would arise when 'a line is drawn between injuries arising from accidents and other injuries and conditions which are not attributable to accidents.'

5.2.3. *Damages Available for Other Types of Torts and Civil Wrongs*

The effect of the ACC Scheme's statutory bar is that compensatory damages in New Zealand tort law are largely centred on compensation for loss or damage to property, and economic (pecuniary) loss.[136]

136 Todd (ed.), *The Law of Torts in New Zealand*, above n. 2, p. 1314.

The courts have also recognised the novel possibility of public law civil wrong damages for the breach of the New Zealand Bill of Rights Act 1990.[137] In relation to the ACC Scheme, the Code of ACC Claimants' rights does not currently include damages as possible remedy for a breach of the code.[138] There is perhaps scope for a public law damages claim for breach of the Code of ACC Claimants' Rights – Todd has questioned generally whether Bill of Rights damages and associated damages will be extended to other areas.[139]

5.3. THE IMPACT OF ACC ON NEW ZEALAND SOCIETY

It is difficult to accurately assess the impact of the ACC Scheme on New Zealand in contrast to an alternative reality where the previous common law system had been allowed to continue. A government-commissioned 2008 review of ACC by the Australian branch of accounting firm PricewaterhouseCoopers attempted to compare the overall value added by the ACC Scheme compared with fault-based tort liability or mixed no-fault and tort systems found in other comparable jurisdictions (in particular Canada, the US and Australia).

The review concluded that the ACC Scheme overall had a positive economic and social value to New Zealand, for roughly 8% more cost than a 'no-ACC' scenario.[140] These benefits include:[141]

- In terms of economic values: an increased labour pool; potentially higher labour productivity; reduced long-term spending on healthcare

137 See *Simpson v Attorney General* [1994] 3 NZLR 667.

138 Code of ACC Claimants' Rights 2002, above n. 29, Part 4.

139 Todd (ed.), *The Law of Torts in New Zealand*, above n. 2, p. 1336. It should be recognised that some social security law commentary has noted that the rights in the Code appear to derive from the ACC legislative entitlements rather than from human rights – see Māmari Stephens, 'The Right to Social Security' in Margaret Bedggood and Kris Gledhill (eds), *Law into Action Economic, Social and Cultural Rights in Aotearoa New Zealand* (Thomson Reuters 2011), p. 148.

140 PricewaterhouseCoopers, 'Accident Compensation Corporation New Zealand Scheme Review', above n. 117, p. vi. 'Total ACC contributions (excluding pre-1999 residual funding) for 2006/07 were $2,620 million. Over the same period we estimate the cost of the alternative scenario (including premiums workers' compensation premium costs, premiums for motor injury and other fault-based insurances, and additional health expenditure and increased social transfers) to be around $2,430 million. This gives an estimate of net additional ACC costs of $190 million. Importantly, this is less than our estimate of the value added by ACC, even if we consider only those values which are measurable.'

141 Ibid.

and other government services; legal cost savings; increased participation and increased tourism activity.

- In terms of social values: improved equity in distribution of resources; improved social inclusion and cohesion; lower rates of poverty; improved quality of life for injured persons and people associated with them; and increased participation in volunteer activities.

6. CASE STUDIES DEMONSTRATING THE LIMITS AND COMPLEXITIES OF A UNIVERSAL SCHEME

6.1. THE GENERAL TENSION OF COVERAGE AND THE EFFECT OF THE STATUTORY BAR

As noted above, common law damages will still be available where the personal injury is not covered by the ACC Scheme, or alternatively (and more rarely) where non-compensatory damages are sought. A number of cases have tested the margins of coverage for personal injury victims either seeking ACC compensation for their injuries, or conversely, the right to sue for common law damages.

Some examples of where common law claims may be possible in special cases outside the ACC Scheme definition of personal injury include:

- Mental injury for secondary victims[142] and some types of sexual misconduct.[143] Mental injury caused by some types of sexual crimes, specified in the legislation, may be covered.[144]
- Non-accidental injury such as the inhalation of gases;[145] the ingestion of bacteria caused by negligence (unless it is a treatment injury or employment-related disease); or the failure to provide an adequate diet.[146]

---

142 *Queenstown Lakes District Council v Palmer*, above n. 135.

143 *L v Robinson* [2000] NZLR 499 (High Court).

144 The leading Court of Appeal case on this topic, *KSB v Accident Compensation Corporation* [2012] NZCA 82 delved into a tricky quasi-criminal area relating to a complainant's conception of consent and it is not clear how case law will continue to develop in this area. For a more detailed discussion, see Todd (ed.), *The Law of Torts in New Zealand*, above n. 2, pp. 49–51.

145 *Rinnai New Zealand Ltd v Pickard* CA13/06, 10 August 2006.

146 *Williams v Chief Executive, Dept of Corrections* [2013] NZHC 3509.

- Disease that is not work-related, treatment injury or indirectly relates to another personal injury – such as a dependant's claim related to cancer caused by smoking.[147]
- Special treatment injury related cases include the costs of raising an unwanted child and some types of clinical trials. This is considered in more detail at section 6.2 below.

It can be difficult factually for a court to determine which of the victim's injuries are covered and which are not – where it is difficult to divide them up, the statutory bar will generally apply.[148] If the injury is ACC-covered, but there is no compensation under the statute, then the statutory bar still applies and a common law claim will be barred.[149]

There are disparities in compensation between those who are eligible for ACC Scheme cover (because their ailment fits the statutory definition of personal injury) and those who can only rely on New Zealand's wider social security system (because they have no prospect of recovery in tort). The income-linked payments available under the ACC Scheme are more generous than the flat-rate benefits available for sickness or invalidity under the welfare system. The Woodhouse Report noted that drawing a line between accidental injury and sickness or diseases was a mixed question of law and medicine and recommended further study by medical and legal experts.[150] These concerns also fit within a wider argument about whether New Zealand should take a rights-based approach to social policy and the social security framework.[151]

The lack of coverage for mental trauma victims under the ACC Scheme was recently brought into sharp focus by the 2019 Christchurch mosque terrorist attack. After a public and political outcry about the lack of mental trauma cover for some victims of the terrorist attack, the government minister responsible for ACC sought Cabinet approval to extend the fund's coverage to relevant mental trauma victims. A key argument behind this proposal was that ACC had the necessary claims management infrastructure in place to compensate the relevant victims (because it was already handling claims from eligible physical personal injury victims

---

147 *Pou v British American Tobacco (New Zealand) Ltd* [2006] 1 NZLR 661 (Court of Appeal).

148 *P v Attorney-General* (2010) NZHC 959.

149 *van Soest v Residual Health Management Unit & Ramstead* [1999] NZCA 206.

150 Royal Commission to Inquire into and Report upon Workers Compensation, *Compensation for Personal Injury in New Zealand*, above n. 13, pp. 20, 41.

151 See generally Stephens, 'The Right to Social Security', above n. 139.

of the terrorist attack). However, the proposal was not implemented by government, in part it seems because the Treasury identified (accurately) that it would lead to glaringly unequal treatment of different victims. The Treasury noted that it would be better to review the purpose of ACC generally in tandem with other healthcare, disability and social welfare legislative reforms.[152]

The failure of Parliament since to enact the second stage of the Woodhouse Report's recommendations means that New Zealand has – via inaction – chosen to develop two parallel and unequal systems for compensating incapacity. This is illustrated in *Trevethick v Ministry of Health*, a case concerning a woman suffering from multiple sclerosis, who claimed that her inability to claim more generous financial support via the ACC Scheme was a discrimination based on her disability and therefore prohibited by New Zealand's human rights legislation.[153] The Court of Appeal, rejecting her claim, said that this was a permissibly justified discrimination,[154] because there was a clear choice by Parliament that the costs of illness would be covered by the public health system and/or private insurance and not by ACC.

A recent High Court decision has tested the bounds of the ACC Scheme's scope for gradual process diseases by permitting cover where current medical knowledge means that the ailment can fit within the wording of the legislation. *Calver (Estate of Trevarthen) v ACC*[155] concerned a woman who had died of mesothelioma following childhood exposure to asbestos via her father, an electrician. ACC had declined cover on the basis (in its view) that mesothelioma was an ineligible non-workplace gradual process condition.[156] Her Honour Justice Mallon relied on known medical evidence and international mesothelioma-related case law, which showed that mesothelioma could, theoretically, be caused by a single exposure to asbestos. She held that the development of mesothelioma was indeed an accidental personal injury resulting from that exposure (and thus qualified for ACC Scheme cover). Expert medical evidence showed there was no current scientific knowledge about what exact dosage level

152 Ministry of Business Innovation and Employment, 'Extended Mental Health Support for Those Affected by the 15 March 2019 Terrorist Attack'; Cabinet Business Committee, 'Minute of Decision CBC-19-MIN-0014'.

153 *Trevethick v Ministry of Health* (2008) NZCA 397.

154 New Zealand Bill of Rights Act 1990 s. 5.

155 [2019] NZHC 1581. This case is currently under appeal.

156 Accident Compensation Act 2001 s. 26(2). There is no cover under the ACC Scheme for injuries resulting from non-workplace gradual processes or disease.

or accumulation would lead to the development of mesothelioma – one exposure could quite possibly be sufficient to lead to a latent diagnosis of mesothelioma cancer.[157] Standing ACC precedent on the definition of personal injury requires consideration of the claimant's whole condition and says that personal injury will exist so long as there are physical impacts (even progressive ones).[158] The sub-definition of an accident in the legislation (that was applicable in this case) says that an injury meets the 'accident' requirement where there is 'the inhalation of any solid, liquid, gas, or foreign object on a specific occasion'.[159] Justice Mallon took an appropriately generous approach to the plain meaning of this sub-definition,[160] and concluded that 'a specific occasion' could include multiple single exposures to asbestos fibres.[161] Therefore Ms Trevarthen's mesothelioma could be properly considered as qualifying for ACC Scheme cover – it flowed from an accident (asbestos fibre inhalation) that lead to personal injury (her eventual mesothelioma), and was *not* a gradual process. The case shows that judges are willing to take a facts-based approach to scheme coherency, but this will have practical expansion consequences that must be managed.

6.2. TREATMENT INJURY

The area of treatment injury provides many examples of the ACC Scheme's limits and complexities. There has been coverage under the ACC Scheme for injuries resulting from medical treatment since the original 1972 legislation. The scope was originally very wide, then strictly tightened under the 1992 legislation, and then relaxed again slightly in the 2000s. Injury resulting from medical treatment was not specifically defined in the original legislation, but in practice an informal definition emerged that embraced the two concepts of 'medical error' (incorrect treatment/medical negligence) and 'medical mishap' (rare adverse

---

157 *Calver v Accident Compensation Corporation* (2019) NZHC 1581 [98].

158 *Allenby v H* [2012] NZSC 33. In *Allenby v H*, pregnancy was found to be an ACC-covered personal injury for a mentally ill patient who became pregnant after sterilisation. However, there was only cover in relation to the pregnancy itself and its associated physical impacts, not for the costs to the mother of raising the child.

159 Accident Compensation Act 2001 s. 25(1)(b).

160 *Harrild v Director of Proceedings* [2003] 3 NZLR 289 (CA) at [19], [37] and [130] requires judges to look for a generous, unniggardly interpretation of legislation.

161 *Calver v Accident Compensation Corporation*, above n. 157, [106].

treatment outcome).[162] The courts, applying these practical principles, followed a general trend of extending the category of medical error.

The New Zealand government's 1991 policy review of the ACC Scheme took a negative view towards the lack of a statutory definition for medical misadventure, claiming it was 'open to widely varying interpretations'.[163] The 1992 legislation, which introduced specific categories of covered personal injury, included a category called 'medical misadventure'. The court-adopted definitions of 'medical error' and 'medical mishap' were included as part of the new statute, as well as further complex requirements. Upon review a decade later, the medical mishap criteria were found to be confusing and arbitrary; meanwhile the medical error category required considerations of fault (in contrast to the no-fault ethos of the rest of the ACC Scheme) and was found to have resulted in a 'blaming culture'.[164]

Coverage for medical injuries under the ACC Scheme has been relaxed since 2005, into the wider concept of 'treatment injury'.[165] The transformation of 'medical misadventure' into the more relaxed 'treatment injury' also indicated broader changes in the ACC Scheme's general philosophy.[166] However, there is still considerable complexity involved in the determination of whether a personal injury will be a covered 'treatment injury'. The negligence-related concepts of 'mishap' and 'error' will still play a part in determining whether there has been a treatment injury.[167] This problematic inability to 'stamp out' fault has been directly acknowledged in recent District and High Court decisions, particularly in relation to the failure to treat (or to provide treatment in a timely manner), and therefore still requires further legislative or appellate court clarification.[168] The overlap between medical injury and illness

---

162 Ken Oliphant, 'Beyond Misadventure: Compensation for Medical Injuries in New Zealand' (2007) 15 *Medical Law Review* 357, 360.

163 Birch, *Accident Compensation: A Fairer Scheme*, above n. 20, p. 31.

164 Oliphant, 'Beyond Misadventure: Compensation for Medical Injuries in New Zealand', above n. 162, pp. 357, 370.

165 Section 32 of the Accident Compensation Act defines treatment injury as a personal injury suffered by a person who is being treated by a registered heath professional, that is caused by the treatment, and not a necessary part or ordinary consequence of the treatment (taking into account all the circumstances).

166 Oliphant, 'Beyond Misadventure: Compensation for Medical Injuries in New Zealand', above n. 162, pp. 357, 359.

167 Todd (ed.), *The Law of Torts in New Zealand*, above n. 2, pp. 54–55; Joanna M. Manning, 'Plus Ça Change, plus C'est La Même Chose: Negligence and Treatment Injury in New Zealand's Accident Compensation Scheme' (2014) 14 *Medical Law International* 22.

168 *Accident Compensation Corporation v Ng* (2018) NZHC 2848; *Crawford v Accident Compensation Corporation* (2019) NZACC 77.

means this complexity is likely to remain for as long as sickness is not covered under the ACC Scheme.

The current scope of coverage for treatment injury under the 2001 Act is:

- personal injury that is a treatment injury;[169]
- a secondary infection passed on by a treatment injury victim;[170]
- personal injury caused by treatment for another covered injury;[171]
- treatment injury caused by a gradual process, disease or infection,[172] including where that is a consequence of treatment for a covered injury;[173]
- a cardiovascular or cerebrovascular episode that is treatment injury.[174]

Treatment injury will not include personal injury caused by an underlying health condition, solely attributable to a resource allocation decision or results from the personal unreasonably withholding or delaying consent.[175] A treatment injury is not considered an accident for the purposes of the legislation.[176]

6.2.1. DePuy *and the International Reach of the Statutory Bar*

Treatment injuries involving products manufactured by multinational healthcare companies may have an impact on victims in multiple jurisdictions. This leads to interesting results when an international treatment injury issue (and corresponding mass liability tort multi-jurisdiction action) comes into conflict with the no-fault nature of the ACC Scheme. An interesting recent case which highlights this dilemma and shows the absolute nature and wide reach of the statutory bar is *McGougan v DePuy International Limited.*[177]

This case related to hip implants manufactured by DePuy that were later discovered to have safety and operational problems. The plaintiffs in

169 Accident Compensation Act 2001 s. 20(2)(b).
170 Ibid, ss. 20(2)(c), 32(7).
171 Ibid, s. 20(2)(d).
172 Ibid, s. 20(2)(f).
173 Ibid, s. 20(2)(h).
174 Ibid, s. 20(2)(i).
175 Ibid, s. 32(2).
176 Ibid, s. 25(2).
177 *McGougan v DePuy International Limited* (2016) NZHC 2511; *McGougan v DePuy International Limited* (2018) NZCA 91.

this case represented a larger group of 38 New Zealanders who received DePuy hip implants in New Zealand, between 2006 and 2009. DePuy is a company registered in England and does not carry out business in New Zealand. The hip implants in question were designed and manufactured in England and distributed in New Zealand by related companies. The problems suffered by the plaintiffs due to the hip implants were covered by the ACC Scheme as treatment injuries, and the plaintiffs had therefore received various entitlements and benefits from ACC. However the plaintiffs had sought further compensatory damages from DePuy via personal injury proceedings in England.[178] The English judge determined that New Zealand law applied to the claims, and that the ACC Scheme statutory bar prevented the plaintiffs from seeking common law compensatory damages.[179] The question to be decided for the New Zealand High Court was whether a common law claim for compensatory damages could be brought in New Zealand relating to ACC Scheme-covered injuries, where the conduct that resulted in the claims (the manufacturing of faulty hip implants) occurred outside New Zealand (in England).

Both the New Zealand High Court and Court of Appeal agreed with the English court and found that the plaintiffs' claims were barred by the 2001 Act. The court said that the plaintiffs' injuries occurred in New Zealand (an interpretation consistent with private international law principles) and focusing on the place of the defendant's conduct would lead to ambiguity and unacceptable uncertainly. The plaintiffs also argued that the ACC Scheme's 'integrity and economic viability' would be compromised if DePuy could escape liability, because DePuy had contributed nothing to the scheme by way of levies (because they did not carry out business in New Zealand), giving DePuy an 'unexpected windfall'. Collins J disagreed and said linking levies to tortious liability was at odds with the no-fault comprehensive nature of the ACC Scheme. Justice Collins also pointed to the scheme's rehabilitative goals and the scheme's funding model (which is linked to the type of injured victim rather than the type of putative defendant).[180] The 'windfall' argument was

---

178 In jurisdictions such as the US and Ireland, courts have awarded very large amounts of compensatory damages to plaintiffs injured with the faulty DePuy hip implants.

179 *Allen & others v DePuy International Ltd* [2015] EWHC 926 at [87].

180 Collins J in *McGougan v DePuy International Limited* (2016) NZHC 2511 also quoted at [54] a 1974 Torts and General Law Reform Committee report which noted that 'Dangerous and defective products produce a number of injuries, yet once the accident compensation scheme is in force, those enterprises whose products cause injuries will not be directly liable to finance the risk in the same manner as the industry operator is called upon to finance the risk of injuries to earners.'

rejected on the grounds that the ACC Scheme's focus is on the victim's rehabilitation. Justice Asher in the Court of Appeal affirmed this, and pointed out the continued availability of exemplary damages, despite the tort bar.[181]

The High Court and Court of Appeal's conclusions in *DePuy* are a sound statutory interpretation of the current bar against common law action. The New Zealand plaintiffs' position may seem inequitable compared to similar classes of victims internationally (some of whom have received large damages sums from DePuy) but the answer to this is surely that the plaintiffs have benefited from efficient compensation and access to rehabilitation via the ACC Scheme. That answer is less watertight when one considers that Parliament has made allowances under criminal sentencing legislation for crime victims to 'top up' their ACC Scheme compensation by way of reparation order (a type of criminal punishment). One is left wondering: does Parliament think crime victims are more deserving of extra compensation than treatment injury victims?

6.2.2. Pregnancies and Unwanted Births as Treatment Injury

Cases involving unplanned and unwanted pregnancies, births and stillbirths have raised delicate policy questions.

Negligently caused stillbirth will be covered by the ACC Scheme, and the medical or treatment injury will be viewed as being suffered by the mother (meaning a common law claim for compensatory damages will be barred).[182]

In relation to pregnancy generally, recent case law has clarified that an unwanted pregnancy itself may be a kind of covered personal injury, but the ongoing obligations and costs of child-rearing (specifically, childcare costs) will not lead to ACC Scheme cover. Historically, pregnancy was viewed by New Zealand courts as a natural physiological condition until a turnabout by the Supreme Court. In *Allenby v H*,[183] pregnancy was found to be an ACC-covered personal injury for a mentally ill patient who

---

181 *McGougan v DePuy International Limited* (2018), above n. 177, [29].

182 *Harrild v Director of Proceedings* [2003] 3 NZLR 289. A later judgment found that a child born alive who suffered antenatal injuries will be the relevant personal injury victim, instead of the mother – *C v Accident Compensation Corporation* [2011] NZAR 389.

183 *Allenby v H* [2012] NZSC 33.

became pregnant following sterilisation. However, there was only cover in relation to the pregnancy itself. In *J v Accident Compensation Corporation*,[184] a woman who became pregnant following a failed sterilisation sought loss of earnings compensation in relation to childcare. As a single mother with a low-wage job, she could not afford childcare costs that would enable her return to work. She had received ACC Scheme income replacement earnings for 11 weeks post-birth. The social welfare benefits she was subsequently receiving were much less than equivalent ACC Scheme earnings compensation. The majority judgment limited the definition of 'injury' to the pregnancy itself and held that it was not the purpose of the ACC Scheme to compensate for 'all consequences that may follow an accident'.[185] Because the appellant required no further rehabilitation and there was no longer an issue in relation to her own health, she had no entitlement to compensation for her other losses related to the care of her child. This appears to be the correct result on a simple statutory interpretation approach, but it certainly fails to recognise the impact to a woman of ongoing economic losses stemming from motherhood and its physical effects.[186]

6.2.3. *Clinical Trials*

There is a gap in the ACC Scheme in relation to individuals who are injured in clinical trials. There will only be ACC Scheme cover where the claimant did not agree in writing to participate, or where the trial has ethics committee approval (and the trial was not conducted principally for the manufacturer or distributor's benefit).[187] The lack of ACC Scheme cover for injured participants in industry clinical trials has been labelled as a serious policy misstep.[188] ACC Scheme coverage may depend

---

184 *J v Accident Compensation Corporation* (2017) NZCA 441.

185 Ibid, [42].

186 Anthea Williams, 'Wrongful Birth and Lost Wages: J v Accident Compensation Corp' (2018) 2 *New Zealand Women's Law Journal* 295.

187 Accident Compensation Act 2001 s. 32(5) and (6).

188 Joanna M. Manning, 'Does the Law on Compensation for Research-Related Injury in the UK, Australia, and New Zealand Meet Ethical Requirements?' (2017) 25 *Medical Law Review* 397, 427 <https://academic.oup.com/medlaw/article-abstract/25/3/397/3769302>. Manning nevertheless argues that the New Zealand model is best when compared with the UK and Australia, and that a publicly funded no-fault compensation fund is the best way to compensate for research-related injury. One can draw an analogy between the risk assumed by trial participants for the benefit of society, and the Woodhouse Report's notion of socially encouraged risks (mainly in relation to motor vehicles).

on whether a person is allocated to a standard or trial treatment arm in an industry-sponsored trial.[189] A clinical trial participant not covered by ACC may only have recourse to much less generous industry guidelines on compensation for their injury, or the possibility of a common law claim.

7. DISPUTE RESOLUTION ISSUES: RECENT CHANGES TO ENABLE BETTER ACCESS TO JUSTICE

Since the ACC Scheme's implementation, court access for ACC Scheme-covered claimants has been limited. This can be seen as complementary to and fulfilling the statutory bar to replace the common law action 'lottery' to enable swift and real compensation for personal injury victims (as an aid to their rehabilitation). The 2001 Act allows anyone who is declined cover or entitlements to challenge that decision. The dispute resolution process is described above at section 4.1.

In 2015, the New Zealand government commissioned an independent review of accident compensation dispute resolution processes.[190] This was in response to a July 2015 report by Acclaim Otago, an advocacy group representing disabled persons in relation to their ACC claims.[191] The Acclaim Otago report made a comprehensive assessment of ACC dispute resolution processes, and identified problems with access to law, access to medical evidence, the sense of being heard, and access to representation. The resulting 2016 independent review report by Miriam Dean QC made a series of recommendations (that were wholly adopted by the New Zealand government[192]) to improve ACC dispute resolution processes.

The recommendations of the review are summarised below. They reveal the value of transparency, good procedure and a strong sense of

189 Manning, 'Does the Law on Compensation for Research-Related Injury in the UK, Australia, and New Zealand Meet Ethical Requirements?', above n. 188, p. 412.

190 New Zealand Government, 'Government Focused on Access to Justice for ACC Clients' (2015) <https://www.beehive.govt.nz/release/government-focused-access-justice-acc-clients>.

191 Acclaim Otago, 'Understanding the Problem: An Analysis of ACC Appeals Processes to Identify Barriers to Access to Justice for Injured New Zealanders' (2015) <http://www.acclaimotago.org>.

192 New Zealand Government, 'Further Work to Improve ACC Dispute Resolution' (2016) <https://www.beehive.govt.nz/release/further-work-improve-acc-dispute-resolution>.

fairness – in other words, that dispute resolution outside the courts should meet the same high standards as traditional avenues of justice:

- *Data and evidence*[193] – The review was critical of ACC's inability to provide comprehensive and reliable data based on its activities; including cover, entitlements and costs of defending appeals. It noted that lack of quality data makes it difficult to assess whether claimants face a barrier to accessing justice. The review recommended that ACC explore better ways to analyse data about its claims and disputes.
- *Access to law*[194] – Many claimants represent themselves in the ACC appeal process, and Acclaim Otago said they found it difficult to access the necessary legal information. The review recommended funding a third-party voluntary legal information website to provide access to all relevant case law and a practical primer for claimants. The review also recommended that FairWay, ACC, the judiciary and the government use legal communication tools better to educate claimants about the dispute resolution process and understand better how claims and appeals are decided.
- *Access to medical evidence*[195] – The review found that this was a complex area to deal with, involving issues of best practice in both law and medicine. In line with the review's other findings, it recommended establishing better procedures (including dialogue between experts), easier access to costs and making the independence of medical experts known.
- *The sense of being heard*[196] – This was an area that revealed the importance of good procedure and the optics of independence and impartiality. FairWay was at that time the company that provided dispute resolution services to ACC. There were perceptions among claimants that ACC had insufficient independence from FairWay and its reviewers. These perceptions did not reflect an actual bias by FairWay in favour of ACC, but the review recommended changes to resolve this perception. FairWay has since been transferred from Crown ownership to employee ownership,[197] and two other

---

193 Dean, 'Independent Review of the Acclaim Otago (Inc) July 2015 Report Into Accident Compensation Dispute Resolution Processes', above n. 62, pp. 13–14.
194 Ibid, pp. 36–39.
195 Ibid, pp. 42–50.
196 Ibid, pp. 20–33.
197 New Zealand Government, 'FairWay Change Positive for Staff and Customers' (2017) <https://www.beehive.govt.nz/release/fairway-change-positive-staff-and-customers>.

companies provide dispute resolution services for ACC cases.[198] Other recommendations included an improved review process with clear published guidelines, increased review costs for claimants and improvements to ACC's procedural conduct as a defendant. The concerns raised by Acclaim Otago and the review's recommendations show that alternative dispute resolution mechanisms, no matter how flexible or cost-effective, must compare favourably with the independence and quality of the judiciary to enable claimants to feel that they are being treated fairly.

- *Access to representation*[199] – ACC Scheme legislation and case law is complex, but only a small number of New Zealand lawyers have expertise in this area. The best and most experienced lawyers are usually retained by ACC. Conversely, Acclaim Otago estimated that around 60% of claimants represented themselves. The lack of legal expertise in this area is perhaps an unintended consequence of removing the legal profession from the sphere of personal injury law generally. The review recommended more ACC-funded quality independent advocacy services and giving the District Court power to appoint counsel to represent claimants in exceptional cases.

The review agreed with Acclaim Otago that the ACC Scheme appeals system should be considered with a human rights-based approach, but further examination was beyond the scope of the review.[200]

8. THE FUTURE OF THE ACC SCHEME

The ACC Scheme is held up by both proponents and opponents of no-fault compensation funds, and leading international common law commentary considers it to be an open question whether no-fault is desirable in principle.[201] The scheme has had a politically buffeted

198 ACC, above n. 83.

199 Dean, 'Independent Review of the Acclaim Otago (Inc) July 2015 Report Into Accident Compensation Dispute Resolution Processes', above n. 62, pp. 52–58.

200 Ibid, p. 16.

201 Mark Lunney, Donal Nolan and Ken Oliphant, *Tort Law: Text and Materials*, 6th edn (Oxford University Press 2017), p. 1003. The conclusions of this legal commentary should be compared with the favourable view of no fault systems found in the cost-based analysis of the ACC Scheme by PricewaterhouseCoopers, 'Accident Compensation Corporation New Zealand Scheme Review', above n. 117, p. vi.

growth into maturity, but has a strong financial position[202] and enjoys widespread support among all sectors of New Zealand society.

The ACC's immediate goals continue the themes, present since the 1992 legislation, of safety/reduction of injuries, rehabilitation and economic efficiency.[203] The corporation is currently working to improve its processes and make case management more customer-focused.[204] The major financial and operational challenge facing the ACC Scheme in the coming decades is the ageing of the New Zealand population and in particular its workforce.[205] Increasing injury rates in addition to more chronic disease among an ageing population will bring into sharp focus the current exclusion of sickness from the ACC Scheme.

The extension of the ACC Scheme to include other types of physical ailments and incapacity has been a long-simmering undercurrent to various policy and legislative changes. It also has a very practical financial impact on individuals whose circumstances and ailments fall on the edge or outside of the statutory definition of personal injury. This is illustrated by chronic health conditions like diabetes and obesity, an ongoing public health challenge for New Zealand. The contradiction of New Zealand's 'two-tier' incapacity structure has been recognised in recent years by ACC itself,[206] but there is a notable legal and policy void about the appropriate next steps. The efficient, principled and sustainable development of the ACC Scheme justifies consideration and explanation by the legislature (with the input of ACC and other relevant bodies) about whether the scheme can and should be extended to include sickness and other ailments. At the same time, there should be a parallel wholesale consideration of social welfare legislation, with the aim of remedying the lop-sided levels of compensation available to individuals, depending on the cause of their misfortune.

After all, as a half-century has passed, it is useful to consider how New Zealand society, law and political thinking has changed since the

---

202 Accident Compensation Corporation, 'Annual Report 2017', above n. 3, p. 3.

203 Accident Compensation Corporation, 'Statement of Intent 2015–2019', p. 12.

204 Accident Compensation Corporation, 'Briefing to the Incoming Minister', p. 13.

205 PricewaterhouseCoopers, 'Accident Compensation Corporation New Zealand Scheme Review', above n. 117, p. vi. There is some official recognition already by ACC that New Zealand's ageing population is having an impact on claims growth – see Accident Compensation Corporation, 'Annual Report 2017', above n. 3, p. 36.

206 Accident Compensation Corporation, 'Financial Condition Report' (2013), p. 83 <https://www.acc.co.nz/assets/corporate-documents/financial-condition-report-2013.pdf>.

Woodhouse Report. Is there a common consensus for the extension of the scheme to cover other types of ailments, as the Woodhouse Report envisaged? Do the social and legal settlements underpinning the scheme as a compensation fund need to be recast to reflect social insurance best practices found in other jurisdictions? The uniqueness of the New Zealand accident compensation fund model was based on the isolated and prosperous jurisdictional quirks of its founding era. Although the Woodhouse Report itself did consider social security and occupational insurance systems elsewhere, the authors made it clear that the Report's proposals were unique and specifically designed for the New Zealand jurisdiction.[207] Social welfare in New Zealand is still financed from general taxation and since 1968 no separate social welfare tax or contribution has been payable.[208] Aside from the ACC Scheme, New Zealand has resisted further development of its social welfare and security structures toward a social insurance model.[209]

Quality data is an important tool in the development of effective evidence-based policy and law. One can assume that ACC has, over its history, gathered a broad body of information about injuries, compensation, rehabilitation and dispute resolution. This data should more actively inform decision-making by legislators about the ACC Scheme's future development. As noted earlier, an independent review of ACC's dispute resolution practices criticised ACC's inability to provide comprehensive and reliable data based on its activities. Recent academic commentary from the UK has similarly noted that closer attention to ACC data could lead to better safety outcomes and understanding of which incentives

---

207 Royal Commission to Inquire into and Report upon Workers Compensation, *Compensation for Personal Injury in New Zealand*, above n. 13, p. 25.

208 *Laws of New Zealand* Social Welfare (online ed.), para. 7.

209 As of late 2017, there were no proposals by the New Zealand government and relevant social security ministry for a major social welfare policy change towards a social insurance approach. The Social Security Act 2018 featured no significant policy changes to its predecessor. The 2017 election led to a change in government, and the New Zealand Labour Party (a social-democratic political party, and main partner in the new coalition government) have indicated that they plan to amend the principles of the Social Security Act. See 'New Zealand Labour Party Social Development Manifesto 2017' (2017) <https://d3n8a8pro7vhmx.cloudfront.net/nzlabour/pages/8578/attachments/original/1504834539/Social_Development.pdf?1504834539>. New Zealand can be described as a 'reluctant welfare state', like the UK, Ireland, Australia and Canada – see Michael Belgrave, 'Social Policy History: Forty Years On, Forty Years Back', *Affording our Future Conference* (2012) <https://www.victoria.ac.nz/sacl/centres-and-institutes/cpf/publications/pdfs/1.8-Belgrave-paper.pdf>.

affect relevant institutional and individual behaviour.[210] Such evidence would certainly aid the settlement or reframing of well-trodden arguments about which compensation framework has adequate deterrence or effectiveness. Data might also help lawmakers and policymakers to understand the true limits of the ACC Scheme's utility, and where other social security, insurance or tort law structures could play a greater role.

An over-focus on funding costs and matching ACC costs to revenues since the 1980s tends to ignore the ACC Scheme's social benefits and leads to a reversion to the pre-Woodhouse language of common law and workers' compensation.[211] Should economic efficiency, social security or human rights-based principles guide the ACC Scheme, its funding and its future development? New Zealand's currently underdeveloped (compared to continental European jurisdictions)[212] social security system – both structurally and philosophically – makes this a difficult question to answer, and thus plan the future of the ACC Scheme. Certainly, the reforms to ACC through the 1980s and 1990s can be explained with reference to a wider enthusiasm by New Zealand legislators for the theory of free market efficiency. Under the privatisation prism, the beneficial reduction in social costs by ACC tend to be ignored in favour of minimising the programme costs of ACC levies.[213] A thorough assessment by Government, with contributions from wider society, of the purpose of both ACC – as a compensation fund, social insurer and/or monopolistic private insurer – and the social welfare system, is required.[214]

---

210 Sonia Macleod and Christopher Hodges, *Redress Schemes for Personal Injuries* (Hart Publishing 2017), p. 47.

211 Richard Gaskins, 'Accounting for Accidents: Social Costs of Personal Injuries' (2010) 41 *Victoria University of Wellington Law Review* 37, 43. Gaskins at para. 44 claims that a common-law way of thinking has re-emerged in the New Zealand legislature, that seeks to relieve a levy payer because he or she did not cause the injury. It is certainly hard to disentangle privatisation 'creep' here from quite worthy goals of incentivising good health and safety practices.

212 The co-ordination between ACC and social security is not as good as what is found in European systems, but generally better than what is found in the US and Australia. See PricewaterhouseCoopers, 'Accident Compensation Corporation New Zealand Scheme Review', above n. 117, p. xvii.

213 Gaskins, 'Accounting for Accidents: Social Costs of Personal Injuries', above n. 211, pp. 37, 49.

214 The New Zealand Law Foundation has recently funded research on the possibility of extending the ACC Scheme to include coverage for sickness and incapacity. See New Zealand Law Foundation, '2017 Winners of the Foundation's Annual Awards Announced' (2017) <http://www.lawfoundation.org.nz/?p=8474>.

A review of the ACC Scheme should also consider whether it was appropriate for the legislature to enshrine in statute better remedy possibilities for crime personal injury victims (i.e. compensation top-ups via reparation orders and the possibility of exemplary damages regardless of a defendant's conviction status). In a universal system, even small changes to entitlements and remedies will translate into real financial differences for different categories victims. Such changes, without wider consideration of their effects, introduce contradiction and uncertainty to the heart of the legislative regime.

Geoffrey Palmer, a former New Zealand Prime Minister who has been intimately involved with the ACC Scheme and its changes over the decades, has noted that 'now is the time for an enduring and sustainable policy on accident compensation that is based on a broad community consensus.'[215] Issues such as the elimination of fault-based concepts from treatment injury, justice between categories of victims and access to justice concerns cannot be resolved by piecemeal reform – a twenty-first-century consensus on the future of New Zealand's no-fault universal accident compensation fund is required. Input about the future of the scheme should surely also be informed by population health best practice and legal-medical research and data. New Zealand's social security goals for the twenty-first century and how ACC fits within or complements those goals also need to be considered and clearly addressed. These various issues reveal the present impasse for the future development and expansion of the ACC Scheme – that will not be solved by piecemeal legislative adjustments or policy silence.

[215] Geoffrey Palmer, *Reform: A Memoir* (Victoria University Press 2013), p. 216. See also Geoffrey Palmer, 'A Retrospective on the Woodhouse Report: The Vision, the Performance and the Future' (2019) 50 *Victoria University of Wellington Law Review* <https://ssrn.com/abstract=3472722>.

REMEDIES UNDER SPANISH TORT LAW AND THE ROLE OF COMPENSATION FUNDS

Rosa M. GARCIA-TERUEL*

* I wish to thank the editors for allowing me to publish this chapter, Ms Larissa Vanhooff for all the recommendations and I also give thanks to Professor Dr Sergio Nasarre for his guidance. Of course, the responsibility for any errors in the resulting work remains my own.

1. GENERAL OVERVIEW OF COMPENSATORY MECHANISMS IN SPAIN

The person who damages another must be liable according to the legal framework of the Spanish Civil Code (SCC). The SCC foresees a fault-based liability system in its art. 1902 of the SCC – thus requiring the fault or negligence of the tortfeasor[1] –, although other specific legal provisions regulate strict liability for certain cases (e.g. the liability of the possessor of an animal under art. 1905 of the SCC or the strict liability for car accidents in the event of personal injuries under art. 1.1 of RDL 8/2004[2]). In these cases, the victim is not required to prove the negligence of the tortfeasor, which may help her to claim for compensation (*pro damnato* principle).

Article 1902 of the SCC establishes that it is the person who causes damages to another that is the one liable. Thus, the victim may directly claim compensation against the tortfeasor. However, this compensation may be granted through different means that aim to compensate or to palliate the victim, normally in cases of unidentified or insolvent tortfeasors. For example, through social security benefits (mainly regulated in RDL 8/2015[3]), insurances (some of them compulsory for the tortfeasor, such

---

1 Although fault is generally required to make someone liable for damages, this requirement declines in cases of strict liability (car accidents, hunting). In addition, Spanish case law considers that there must exist a reversal of the burden of proof in risky activities (*teoría del riesgo*), so it is the tortfeasor who has to prove his or her diligence (such as in theme parks with attractions or in the case of fireworks). See, regarding this case law, the judgment of the Supreme Court (hereafter, STS) of 25.3.2010 (RJ 2010, 4347) and STS 16.12.2009 (RJ 2009, 529).

2 RDL 8/2004, 29 October, on the civil liability and insurance of motor vehicles. Spanish Official Gazette (hereafter BOE) No. 167, 5.11.2004.

3 RDL 8/2015, 30 October, on the Consolidated Social Security Act. BOE No. 261, 31.10.2015. Some of the social security benefits that can be admitted are widows' or orphans' pensions and temporary or permanent disability pensions, regardless of whether or not this incapacity was caused by a work-related accident. For a more in-depth analysis of social security benefits and its relationship with Spanish tort law, see S. Nasarre Aznar, 'Law of Torts – Spain' in F. Hendrickx (ed.), *International Encyclopaedia of Law* (Kluwer Law International 2016), pp. 262 and ff.

as the one for car accidents[4]) and through different types of funds, which is the object of this chapter. Consequently, compensatory mechanisms can be divided in Spain as following:

1. Traditional compensation through a direct claim against the tortfeasor, which is based on art. 1902 of the SCC or on special regulations relating to civil liability.[5] In this section, one can include either liability requiring fault (*negligencia*) or strict liability systems (*responsabilidad objetiva*).
2. Public aids. Although they are not strictly considered a compensation for damages, they can alleviate the victim.[6] Apart from the general social security benefits (for example, temporary and permanent disability under RDL 8/2015), the government may create *ad hoc* aids for certain cases, such as the ones for women that are victims of domestic violence (art. 27 of the Organic Act 1/2004[7]). In some cases, these aids may oblige the victim to waive his/her right to claim compensation against the tortfeasor, since the Public Administration can, after paying the victim, subrogate to her position. This is the case of the benefits paid to victims of terrorism or for those paid to patients infected with AIDS at a public hospital[8] (see below).
3. Compulsory and optional insurances. Some sectors may potentially cause damages, so the law compels them to arrange an insurance policy to cover possible damages to third parties. The victim may, in case of an accident, claim compensation directly from the insurer

---

4 Established in art. 1 of RD 1507/2008.

5 Article 1902 of the SCC is considered the basis of tort liability in Spain. However, specific legislations are regulated both in the SCC and in specialised rules. For example, art. 1905 of the SCC regulates liability for damages caused by animals (strict liability, thus without requiring fault), art. 1910 of the SCC (strict liability for objects that fall from a house), art. 17 of the Act on Building Regulations (*Ley de la Ordenación de la Edificación*, regarding damages to buildings due to the construction process), or arts 32 and ff. of Act 40/2015, on the Public Sector (*Ley del Régimen Jurídico del Sector Público*, regarding the liability of public administration).

6 In this sense, Díez-Picazo considered that social security benefits were not strictly a part of tort law, but a mechanism to alleviate victims. L. Díez-Picazo, *Derecho de daños* (Civitas 1999), pp. 62–63.

7 Organic Act of 28 December 2004, on Measures for protection against gender violence. BOE No. 313, 29.12.2004.

8 Note that the Public Administration could be liable due to the presence of infected blood in public hospitals (arts 32 and ff. of Act 40/2015; see STS 25.4.2007, RJ 2007, 3532), but these benefits worked as a covert transaction. A. Azagra Malo, *Daños del amianto: litigación, aseguramiento de riesgos y fondos de compensación* (Instituto de Ciencias del Seguro, Fundación Mapfre 2011).

(art. 76 of Act 50/1980, on the Insurance Policy[9]). This is the case of motor vehicles, aircrafts, nuclear energy, hunting, ships, the promoter of timeshare dwellings, construction sector, health services, etc.

4. Compensation funds (*fondos de compensación*). A compensation fund is an entity that manages public or private funds to cover a certain group of damages without taking into account the fault of the tortfeasor.[10] In this situation, and to ensure that the victim is fully compensated, legislation can regulate compensation funds to cover a certain amount of damages, while reducing judicial costs.[11] These funds are usually created to provide compensation in cases of mass torts[12] (large class action lawsuits), i.e. a product which causes widespread damages, since the funds of the tortfeasor may be insufficient to cover all the damages.[13] They can also be created to cover damages that, due to their nature, the government considers deserves special protection, such as in cases of terrorist attacks,[14] or in cases where the tortfeasor is not identified, such as in some car accidents.[15] This is a way for society to share the burden of these damages, leaving aside an in-depth analysis of the fault committed by the tortfeasor, and thus their creation depends on a legislative policy matter.[16] Note that, although they may be useful for compensating victims, both funds and compulsory insurances have also been criticised for causing more public spending and a possible moral

---

[9] BOE No. 250, 17.10.1980.

[10] A. Ruda González, *El daño ecológico puro. La responsabilidad civil por el deterioro del medio ambiente, con especial atención a la Ley 26/2007, de Responsabilidad Medioambiental* (Thomson Reuters Aranzadi 2008).

[11] K. Fiore, 'No-Fault Compensation Systems' in M. Faure (ed.), *Encyclopedia of Law and Economics* (Edward Elgar 2009), Vol.1.

[12] M. Farris, 'Compensating Climate Change Victims: The Climate Compensation Funds as an Alternative to Tort Litigation' (2010) 2(2) *Sea Grant Law and Policy Journal* No. 49–62.

[13] Note that the tortfeasor would be liable with all her current and future assets (art. 1911 of the SCC), but even they may be insufficient to cover mass torts.

[14] As happened with the World Trade Center Victims' Compensation Fund of 2001. As will be seen below, Spain has not opted for the creation of a compensation fund in case of terrorist attacks. See L.S. Mullenix, 'Designing compensatory funds: in search of first principles' (2015) 3(1) *Standford Journal of Complex Litigation*.

[15] See, regarding these aids and funds in Spain: V. Múrtula Lafuente, 'Causalidad alternativa e indeterminación del causante del daño en la responsabilidad civil' (2006) 351 *Indret*.

[16] R. De Ángel Yagüez, *Tratado de responsabilidad civil* (Civitas 1993), p. 63.

hazard: that is to say, the phenomenon whereby being insured alters the tortfeasors' incentives to take due care.[17]

Indeed, these alternative mechanisms to compensate victims have gained importance in recent years and become an essential part of tort law, in particular, in those higher-risk sectors that may potentially cause damages. An example of this importance is the recommendations to the Commission on Civil Law Rules on Robotics,[18] which establishes that, in the case of robots' liability, 'an insurance system could be supplemented by a fund in order to ensure that reparation can be made for damage in cases where no insurance cover exists'. This type of fund, according to the recommendations, could be a general one or an individual one depending on the type of robot (autonomous vehicles, care robots, medical robots, etc.).

Therefore, the aim of this chapter is to analyse the availability of these compensation funds in Spain and their role in today's tort law, while examining the importance of other mechanisms to compensate victims of key mass accidents in this country.

2. COMPENSATION FUNDS, A SOLUTION WHICH IS NOT REPRESENTATIVE OF THE OPTIONS USED TO COMPENSATE VICTIMS

As in other legal systems,[19] a general regulation for compensation funds does not exist in Spain, meaning that they are created by special rules and on a case-by-case basis and with different requirements and characteristics. However, in any case, compensation funds are not a representative mechanism for the compensation of victims in the case of mass damages in Spain, which are more often met through compulsory insurances or even public aids financed by the national budget. That is why, as well as analysing some of the compensation funds that operate in Spain, the most representative public aids for mass accidents are also covered in this chapter.

---

17 C. Parsons, 'Moral Hazard in Liability Insurance' (2003) 28(3) *The Geneva Papers on Risk and Insurance* No. 448–471 and, regarding Spanish Law, Díez-Picazo, *Derecho de daños*, above n. 6, p. 188.

18 Report with recommendations to the Commission on Civil Law Rules on Robotics (2015/2103(INL)).

19 See the other chapters of this book regarding other EU countries.

2.1. THE MAIN PLAYER IN COMPENSATION FUNDS IN SPAIN: THE INSURANCE COMPENSATION CONSORTIUM

Initially created to cover riot risks during the Spanish Civil War (1936–1939), the Insurance Compensation Consortium (in Spanish, *Consorcio de compensación de seguros*, hereafter CCS) was set up permanently in 1954.[20] CCS coverage has been widened over time: from natural risks (e.g. floods, earthquakes) to terrorist damages, car accidents, hunting torts, etc.

The CCS is nowadays a public business institution, with its own legal entity, attached to the Ministry of Economy and Competitiveness, under the Directorate-General for Insurance and Pension Funds. RDL 7/2004[21] regulates the CCS bylaws and establishes that it works under the principle of compensation (art. 3).

The CCS has a double nature in tort law:[22]

- It works as a guarantee fund, that is to say, the CCS may compensate the victim when she or he cannot be compensated through a direct claim to the tortfeasor or through an insurance policy. This is the case with car accidents (see below). In this occasion, moral hazard cannot be considered a drawback of this fund,[23] since the tortfeasor is the one who has to compensate the victim and the CCS only does so in certain cases when the former cannot pay. In this vein, Ruda[24] highlights the role of the CCS and establishes that 'the Spanish state is clearly an insurer of last resort'. The CCS covers the following damages as a guarantee fund:
  - Extraordinary risks: natural accidents, terrorism, rebellion, damages by the police or the military in periods of peace, etc.[25]

---

20 Consorcio de Compensación de Seguros, *The Spanish Extraordinary Risk Coverage System* (Report 2016), p. 3.

21 RDL 7/2004, of 29 October, on the Statues of the Insurance Compensation Consortium. BOE No. 267, 5.11.2004.

22 This legal nature is confirmed by art. 18 of RDL 7/2004, when it says that the function of the CCS is to work as a guarantee fund. In addition, art. 20 of RDL 7/2004 establishes that it can also work as an insurer or reinsurer.

23 Azagra Malo, *Daños del amianto: litigación, aseguramiento de riesgos y fondos de compensación*, above n. 8, pp. 216–217.

24 A. Ruda, 'Regulating risk through private law: the Spanish approach' in M. Dyson, (ed.), *Regulating Risk through Private Law* (Intersentia 2018), p. 161.

25 Article 1 of RD 300/2004, of 20 February, on the Regulation of extraordinary risks insurance. BOE No. 47, 24.2.2004. These damages can be also compensated through the European Union Solidarity Fund.

- Car accidents, provided that the vehicle is unidentified, uninsured, or the car was stolen.[26]
- Damages to volunteer firefighters.[27]

- But, at the same time, it also works as a direct insurer or reinsurer regarding nuclear and agricultural damages. It is thus governed, as are regular insurers, by the Private Insurance Supervisory Act.[28]

2.2. EXTRAORDINARY RISKS

Extraordinary risks, such as natural disasters, cannot be compensated through traditional mechanisms of tort law since no liable tortfeasor exists. That is the reason why one of the functions of the CCS is to compensate these damages. According to art. 6 of RDL 7/2004, the CCS covers personal and property damages caused by extraordinary risks provided that the victim has a property, life or accident insurance and that said policy does not cover them. Thus, it is necessary to have an insurance policy to be compensated for natural disasters and, when this policy does not cover these risks (which is standard practice, because it is difficult to calculate the probability that these events will occur[29]), or the insurer is in bankruptcy (art. 8.1 of RDL 7/2004), the CCS will step in to cover these damages. Note that it is funded by supplementary premiums in insurance policies (art. 7 of RDL 7/2004).

The damages caused by the following extraordinary risks can thus be recovered from the CCS (art. 6.1):

- Earthquakes, seaquakes, floods, volcanic eruption, atypical cyclonic storms and the fall of astral bodies and meteorites. For example, the CCS compensated victims of the 2011 Lorca earthquake with a total

26 Second Council Directive 84/5/EEC obliged Member States to regulate an institution with the aim of covering damages in cases of car accidents (such as one caused by an unidentified vehicle). Thus, art. 1.4 of this Directive establishes that 'Each Member State shall set up or authorise a body with the task of providing compensation, at least up to the limits of the insurance obligation for damage to property or personal injuries caused by an unidentified vehicle or a vehicle for which the insurance obligation provided for in paragraph 1 has not been satisfied'. As a consequence, the CCS was adapted to comply with these functions, and it has been regulated according to the requirements established by successive Directives on car accidents.

27 Regulated in art. 46 of Act 43/2003, *Ley de Montes*. BOE No. 280, 22.11.2003.

28 Act 20/2015, of 14 July, on the Private insurance and reinsurance Supervisory Act. BOE No. 168, 15.7.2015.

29 See E. Barrero, *El Consorcio de Compensación de Seguros* (Tirant lo Blanch 2000), pp. 175 and ff.

amount of more than €412 million.[30] CCS also expects to compensate victims of floods in Murcia during the autumn rainfalls of 2019.[31]
- Damages due to terrorism, rebellion, sedition and riots.
- Damages caused by the army or the police in times of peace.

However, compensation is excluded in some cases, such as when the damaged thing had a pre-existing defect, or in cases of armed conflicts, during a state of national emergency, for damages due to nuclear energy,[32] damages due to demonstrations, or damages due to the mere course of time (art. 6.3 of RDL 7/2004). That is why legal disputes often arise regarding the obligation of the CCS to compensate victims. For example, in the judgment of the Court of Appeal (hereafter SAP) in Granada on 15.11.2013,[33] a dwelling was demolished by the rain and wind, but, at the same time, it was in a bad state of repair. As a consequence, the court decided that the CCS did not have to pay compensation, because this damage could be excluded according to art. 6.3 of RDL 7/2004. However, in other cases the court compelled the CCS to grant compensation to the victim: in SAP Barcelona 14.11.2001,[34] there was a bank robbery by the terrorist group GRAPO. Taking into account that this organisation had been recognised as a terrorist group, the court understood that the damages had to be compensated by the CCS. Also, STS 22.11.2000[35] granted compensation to a businessman whose dwelling was set on fire by a group of people, as this act was considered to be a riot.

2.3. ROAD ACCIDENTS

The most important function of the CCS is the role it plays in compensating road-accident victims and, apart from the general rules of RDL 7/2004

---

30 Nevertheless, some problems arose regarding the amount of compensation and the information to victims. See Murcia.com. *IU denuncia que el Consorcio de Compensación de Seguros se niega a facilitar información a los afectados por los terremotos de 2011 en Lorca*, 10.11.2017. Available at: <https://www.murcia.com/lorca/noticias/2017/11/10-iu-denuncia-que-el-consorcio-de-compensacion-de-seguros-se-niega-a-facilitar-informacion-a-los-afectados-por-los-terre.asp>.

31 See Murcia.com. *Lluvias y fuertes vientos en la Región de Murcia: cuándo reclamar por los daños de esta nueva DANA*, 03.12.2019. Available at: https://www.murcia.com/region/noticias/2019/12/03-lluvias-y-fuertes-vientos-en-la-region-de-murcia.asp.

32 However, the CCS covers the compensation that cannot be covered by the insurance of nuclear damages, being a reinsurer of this type of damage (art. 9 of RDL 7/2004).

33 AC 2013, 2286.

34 AC 2002, 977.

35 RJ 2000, 9298.

(essentially in art. 11), RDL 8/2004,[36] on civil liability and the insurance of motor vehicles, is also applicable in these cases. This Act not only foresees the role of the CCS in car accidents, but also the road-accidents liability regime[37] and the tables for the assessment of personal injuries (tariffication scheme), which were recently amended through Act 15/2015.[38] Again, the CCS may compensate victims of road accidents when the tortfeasor is unidentified or the insurance is unable to make the required payment. This fund is financed by receiving 50% of funds raised through traffic fines (art. 3.4 of RDL 8/2004). Thus, the CCS covers road-accident damages that occur in Spain in the following cases:

- In cases of an unidentified tortfeasor, the CCS covers personal injuries. When personal injuries are significant (death or incapacity – spending at least seven days at the hospital), it is possible to recover damages to property too.[39] If not, victims cannot be compensated for these property damages. The CCS is not only required to pay compensation when an unidentified vehicle directly runs over a person or a car. By way of example, the Supreme Court also compelled the CCS to pay for damages caused by an oil stain left on the road by an unidentified car (STS 22.10.2009[40]).
- In cases of uninsured vehicles, provided that the tortfeasor's car is registered in Spain. However, the CCS does not cover damages to the drivers and other users of the tortfeasor's vehicle, since they ought to have known that the car did not have an insurance policy (art. 11.1.g of RDL 8/2004). In this sense, see STS 28.11.2013,[41] which granted

36 BOE No. 267, 5.11.2004.

37 For personal injuries, the tortfeasor is subject to strict liability. Regarding damages to property, a fault-based system is established. However, when the accident causes damages to property and it does not involve a collision between two vehicles, there is a reversal of the burden of proof of negligence (art. 1 of RDL 8/2004).

38 BOE No. 228, 23.9.2015. Note that this tariffication scheme is compulsory in the field of road accidents, but courts usually use these figures as an orientation to assess personal injuries arising from other accidents. See M. Martín-Casals, 'An Outline of the Spanish Legal Tariffication Scheme for Personal Injury from Traffic Accidents' in H. Koziol and S. Jaap, *Liber Amicorum Pierre Widmer* (Springer 2003), pp. 235 and ff.

39 The former art. 10 of the Fifth Motor Directive (Directive 2009/103/EC) introduced this requirement, and so RDL 8/2004 regulates the compensation of damages to property when significant personal injuries have been caused. Every legislation defines what 'significant injuries' means. Member States can also regulate a deduction of €500, which has to be paid by the victim.

40 RJ 2009, 5705.

41 RJ 2013, 7876.

damages to the two-year-old son of a woman killed while travelling in a car without insurance. Note that if the uninsured vehicle causes damages, both the driver and the owner of the car can be personally liable for them (art. 1.3 of RDL 8/2004).

- In cases where the tortfeasor is driving a stolen vehicle that has insurance. The CCS does not cover damages to the drivers and other users, since, of course, they should have known that the car was stolen (art. 11.1.g of RDL 8/2004).
- In cases where the insurer is in bankruptcy. However, the CCS only covers damages that should be covered by a compulsory insurance, but not the additional coverages offered by an optional premium policy (STS 19.2.1996[42]).

The victim does not need to prove that the tortfeasor does not want to or cannot pay the damages to claim compensation against the CCS (art. 11.5 of RDL 8/2004). However, the CCS does not have to compensate the victim when the accident is excluded from the field of application of RDL 8/2004. In particular, RDL 8/2004 is only applicable in accidents caused by a traffic event (*hecho de la circulación*) involving motor vehicles. The definition of a 'traffic event' and a 'motor vehicle' can be found in RD 1507/2008,[43] which establishes that:

- Motor vehicles are those that can move on the surface of the earth and that are powered by a motor, including mopeds, special vehicles, trailers and semi-trailers, and those that require an administrative authorisation to travel on public roads. Trains, trams, toys and wheelchairs are excluded (art. 1 of RD 1507/2008).
- A traffic event is one caused by the risk created by driving motor vehicles. This is applicable when these events happen in garages and parking lots, public or private roads or land suitable for urban or interurban traffic circulation, as well as roads that, without having the characteristics necessary for traffic circulation, are of common use. Sports events (car racing in racing tracks), traffic events due to industrial or agricultural work and car accidents in ports and airports are not considered a 'traffic event' and are thus excluded from this system of liability. In addition, the use of a motor vehicle as an instrument to commit a crime is not considered a traffic event either (art. 2 of RD 1507/2008).

---

42 RJ 1996, 1259.

43 BOE No. 222, 13.9.2008.

That is the reason why courts decide not to grant compensation to the victim when the accident is excluded from RDL 8/2004. For example, STS 9.3.2012[44] ruled on an accident in which an unidentified vehicle ran over the victim. It appeared that this accident was a crime, as ten minutes before the accident the victim had argued with a group of people in a bar. So, the tortfeasor therefore did not want to use the car as a means of transport, but as an instrument to commit a crime. In the same vein, SAP Cádiz 3.11.2009[45] ruled that burning an abandoned car that caused damages was not considered a traffic event (*hecho de la circulación*), and so the CCS did not have to pay compensation. On the other hand, STS 21.3.2007[46] decided to grant compensation to the victim because, although the car was used to run over a person, it was being used as a mode of transport and, in this case, the CCS had to pay compensation to the victim's relatives.

2.4. DAMAGES TO VOLUNTEER FIREFIGHTERS

In case of fire, apart from professional firefighters, volunteer firefighters can also help to extinguish a fire.[47] According to art. 49 of the *Ley de Montes*, the Central Government, through the CCS, has to grant coverage for damages suffered by volunteer firefighters, regardless of their professional status.

The Order issued on 3 August 2001[48] regulates this compensation and establishes in art. 1 that the CCS will cover personal injuries suffered by people who help with the task of extinguishing fires. These damages are funded through supplementary premiums charged by the General

44 RJ 2012, 5441.

45 JUR 2010, 45419.

46 RJ 2007, 2125.

47 Some of these may not have any training, but they are also covered by this fund. However, there may be other volunteer firefighters that have to pass a competitive entrance examination in order to be appointed, but they are considered neither civil servants nor employees. According to Catalan Decree art. 2.1 of No. 8/2015 (DOGC No. 6800 of 30.1.2015), volunteer firefighters are those that, due to their social charity, provide altruistic functions of fire prevention, extinction and salvation, within the corresponding unit of the competent department, and they have the right to be insured for accidents during their work. As a consequence, those that overcome the entrance exam will be both insured and compensated by the CCS, if applicable.

48 BOE No. 221, 14.9.2001.

Directorate of Nature Conservation of the Spanish Ministry of the Environment. The assessment of the personal injuries is also established in this Order: in the event of death, the CCS compensates the victim's relatives with €31,553. A large amount is established for permanent disability (depending on the severity, up to €47,329).

2.5. COMPENSATION FUND FOR ENVIRONMENTAL DAMAGES

In 2007, Act 26/2007[49] was passed, entering into Spanish Law Directive 2004/35/CE and thereby establishing the polluter-pays principle. Act 26/2007 included a system of strict liability for purely environmental damages,[50] that is to say, it only covers damages to the environment, being not applicable in the event personal injury or any type of property damage (art. 5.1).[51] In addition, apart from regulating this liability, arts 33 and 34 created two funds: the Compensation Fund for Environmental Damages (*fondo de compensación de daños medioambientales*, art. 33) and the National Fund for Repairing Environmental Damages (*fondo estatal de reparación de daños ambientales*, art. 34).

The CCS manages the Compensation Fund for Environmental Damages. Article 33 of Act 26/2007 establishes that it has the nature of a compensation fund (*fondo de compensación*), which is created with the supplementary premiums applied to environmental damages insurances. This fund aims to cover those damages that, having occurred during the period that the insurance was valid, their effects appear once the insurance policy has lapsed. As a consequence, this fund refers to latent damages that the insurance cannot cover (due to a claim-made clause, art. 73 II of Act 50/1980), opting for this mechanism that may

49 Act 26/2007, on environmental liability. BOE No. 255, 24.10.2007.

50 However, this strict liability regime is only applicable to damages caused by companies involved in certain high-risk activities (waste management, transportation of dangerous goods). Regarding other types of business activity, due diligence has to be proven by the company, but negligence is still required (art. 3).

51 Environmental damages suffered by individuals in these cases may be recovered under art. 1902 of the SCC, art. 1908 of the SCC, or injunctions such as the '*acció negatòria*' of the Catalan Civil Code (arts 544-4 to 544-7 Book V of the Catalan Civil Code, Act 5/2006). See Nasarre Aznar, 'Law of Torts – Spain', above n. 3, pp. 197 and ff.

ensure compensation even when the tortfeasor does not have funds.[52] However, art. 44 of RD 2090/2008,[53] on the Regulation of Environmental Liability, establishes some exceptions. For example, this fund does not cover those damages that the former insurance policy did not cover; nor those caused by abandoned polluting premises. A time limitation term of 30 years is also included, in such a way that if the damage does not appear within 30 years of the date of expiration of the insurance, it cannot be recovered through this fund. The Compensation Fund for Environmental Damages also covers the damages when the insurer is in a bankruptcy proceeding.

On the other hand, the National Fund for Repairing Environmental Damages is financed through the Spanish General Budget and is under the management and supervision of the Ministry of the Environment. In this case, it aims to cover the costs of implementing measures for the prevention and compensation of damages to national natural resources, such as rivers and the sea, when the tortfeasor cannot be liable under Act 26/2007, that is to say, when no one is at fault (in the cases when the law requires negligence to establish liability) and the former had authorisation to use certain materials that were not considered pollutants. Damages to public goods whose titleholder is one of the Spanish autonomous regions, may also be covered if the region in question participates in the financing of the compensation fund (art. 34.2 of Act 26/2007).

2.6. FORMER COVERAGES

Until 2009, the CCS also covered damages that cannot be recovered through the compulsory travel insurance (e.g. damages caused to a person who is travelling on public transport) or the compulsory hunting insurance (e.g. damages caused by a hunter). However, art. 1 of Act 6/2009[54] abrogated this CCS function and nowadays the damages that cannot be covered either through a direct claim against the tortfeasor, or against the insurer, cannot be recovered.

---

52 N. Alvarez Lata, 'Responsabilidad civil por daños al medio ambiente' in F. Reglero Campos and J.M. Busto Lago (eds), *Tratado de responsabilidad civil* (Thomson Reuters Aranzadi 2014).

53 BOE No. 308, 23.12.2008.

54 BOE No. 161, 4.7.2009.

3. OTHER FUNDS THAT ARE NOT MANAGED BY THE *CONSORCIO DE COMPENSACIÓN DE SEGUROS*

3.1. FUNDS OF A DIFFERENT NATURE

Under Spanish law, there are other types of funds that are not managed by the CCS, although not all of them have a tort-law nature. The only one related to torts is the Fund for Defective Products (see below). Some other funds with a different nature are the following:

- The Salary Guarantee Fund (*Fondo garantía salarial*, FOGASA): this fund ensures workers receive their wages and their redundancy payments when the employer is declared insolvent. FOGASA compensates each worker with up to €8,383 for wages, and €25,498 for redundancy payments (2019). FOGASA is mainly funded with social security contributions from public and private companies that employ workers (art. 33 of RDL 2/2015[55]).
- The Deposit Guarantee Fund (*Fondo de garantía de depósitos*): it protects deposits made by investors and banking service users (savings accounts, current accounts, fixed-term deposits and securities deposits) covering up to €100,000 of losses due to the insolvency of a bank (RDL 16/2011[56]). It is mainly financed through contributions from associated institutions (e.g. all the credit entities in Spain must be associated, art. 5.1 of RDL 16/2011).
- The Investments Guarantee Fund (*Fondo de garantía de inversiones*): it protects investments other than bank deposits when the relevant firm becomes insolvent and thus the investor cannot recover its investments (art. 198 of RDL 4/2015, on the Securities Market).[57]
- The Alimony Guarantee Fund (*Fondo de garantía de alimentos*). This fund guarantees children receive unpaid alimony,[58] provided that this alimony payment is recognised by a Spanish court after a separation,

---

55 RDL 2/2015, of 23 October, on the Statute of Workers. BOE No. 255, 24 October 2015. FOGASA regulation follows Directive 2008/94/EC.

56 BOE No. 249, 15.10.2011.

57 BOE No. 255, 24.10.2015. This fund was created following the requirements of Directive 1997/9/EC.

58 According to art. 142 of the SCC, alimony are foods, accommodation, clothing, medical assistance and education.

divorce or marriage annulment, or by a legally approved agreement (art. 2.2 of RD 1618/2007[59]). That is to say, when one of the parents of a child under 18 has the obligation to pay alimony and he or she does not do so, the children may ask the Alimony Guarantee Fund for a compensation. However, the family unit of the minor cannot exceed a certain annual income and the amount granted as a compensation is €100 a month for up to 18 months.[60]

- Compensation fund for relegation in a football league (RDL 5/2015[61]): in order to improve the promotion and operation of the competition and contribute to the promotion of sport in general, each club participating in LaLiga (the Spanish football league), in any of its categories, shall contribute annually in proportion to the income obtained by the joint commercialisation of broadcasting rights. Thus, 3.5% of these broadcasting rights will be used to finance a Compensation Fund that can benefit football teams that are relegated from their category. 90% of this amount is assigned to teams that are relegated from the first division, and the remaining 10% to those relegated from the second division (art. 6).

3.2. COMPENSATION FUND FOR DEFECTIVE PRODUCTS OR SERVICES

Liability for defective products is regulated in arts 135 and ff. of Spanish RDL 1/2007,[62] which establishes a strict liability regime[63] for damages caused by a defective product. The tortfeasor's liability for damages

59 RD 1618/2007, of 7 December, on the organisation and functioning of the Alimony Guarantee Fund. BOE No. 199, 14.12.2007.

60 Note that this amount only represents half of the alimony due, when both parents earn €1,000. See an alimony calculator for courts at: <http://www.poderjudicial.es/cgpj/es/Servicios/Utilidades/Calculo-de-pensiones-alimenticias/Tablas-orientadoras-para-determinar-las-pensiones-alimenticias-de-los-hijos-en-los-procesos-de-familia-elaboradas-por-el-CGPJ>.

61 BOE No. 104, 1.5.2015.

62 RDL 1/2007, of 16 November, of the General Law for the Defence of Consumers and Users and other complementary laws. BOE No. 287, 30.11.2007. This is a consolidated act that gathers all the former legislation on consumers that was transposed into Directive 85/374/ECC, on product liability.

63 RDL 1/2007 does not expressly establish the strict liability regime. However, following art. 4 of Directive 85/374/ECC, the victim only needs to prove the damage, the defect and the causal relationship between them. In addition, the explanatory statement of the Directive confirms that the liability for defective products is a non-fault one.

resulting in a death or personal injury and caused by identical items with the same defect is limited to an amount of €63,106,270 (art. 141.2 of RDL 1/2007).

In addition, RDL 1/2007 also regulates the liability for defective services (arts 147–149) in such a way that whoever provides a service to a consumer shall be liable unless he/she can prove due diligence (reversal of the burden of proof of the fault). Moreover, when the service is associated with a 'dangerous' activity, a strict-liability regime is applicable. The services subjected to this strict-liability regime are, in any case, sanitary services, the repair and maintenance of household appliances, the repair of elevators and motor vehicles, repairs in dwellings, the installation and maintenance of gas and electricity and those services related to a means of transport.

According to art. 131 of RDL 1/2007,

> The Government, after a hearing involving the interested parties and the consumers and users' associations, may establish a system requiring compulsory insurance to cover civil liability derived from the damages caused by defective products or services and the foundation of a guarantee fund that totally or partially covers damages consisting of death, intoxication and personal injury.

That is to say, this article allows the government to not only oblige companies to have a compulsory insurance, but also gives it the possibility of requiring the creation of a compensation fund (a guarantee one) that covers only the following damages: death, intoxication, and personal injuries. Note that this possibility is not included in Directive 85/374/ECC, but the government has not yet created it. That is to say, nowadays it is neither compulsory to have an insurance policy for damages caused by defective products or services,[64] nor has the government created a compensation fund to cover them.

3.3. BILL TO CREATE A COMPENSATION FUND FOR THE VICTIMS OF ASBESTOS

Many productive sectors, such as the construction industry, have been using asbestos, a cheap mineral appreciated for its properties. However,

---

64 Although, some sectors that may potentially cause damages for defective products or services have their own compulsory insurance. For example, the compulsory travel insurance (art. 10 of RD 1575/1989), or the one for elevators (art. 10 of RD 1314/1997).

it was not until the twentieth century that the associated health hazards were discovered: when inhaling it, it may cause lung cancer among other diseases. According to the WHO,[65] asbestos causes more than 107,000 deaths every year.

Spain prohibited this material through an Order dated 7.12.2001,[66] but by that moment many workers had already inhaled it, suffering adverse effects, and many constructions still contain this material.[67] Damages caused by asbestos led to mass tort claims (class action suits) in several countries, and so some of them created compensation funds to cover these damages.[68] In Spain, the number of judgments regarding asbestos damages was also considerable (according to Azagra, approximately 190 judgments between 1996–2010[69]) but this disaster was faced through general social security benefits and direct claims against the companies where victims used to work with this material.[70]

Several sectors, represented by academia,[71] victims associations[72] and even by regional governments[73] asked for the regulation of a compensation fund to cover these damages. It was not until 2017 that the government decide to pass Bill No. 125/000005[74] to regulate this fund, which was debated in Parliament but, due to the end of the legislative period, this Bill expired. Stakeholders are now waiting for a new legislature to recover the Bill.

---

65 World Health Organization, *Asbesto crisotilo* (2015). Available at: <http://apps.who.int/iris/bitstream/handle/10665/178803/9789243564814_spa.pdf;jsessionid=EB598D81DE694BC94617E60438078D0F?sequence=1>.

66 BOE No. 299, 14.12.2001.

67 For example, undergrounds in Madrid were constructed with asbestos, and are still working: <http://www.lavanguardia.com/local/madrid/20180307/441329165618/trenes-amianto-madrid-asciende-90.html>.

68 In France, the *fons d'indemnisation des victimes de l'amiante* (2001), in Belgium, the *Asbestfonds* or *fons d'amiante* (2006), in the UK (Workers Compensation Act 1979), etc. See the other chapters of this book regarding other EU countries.

69 Azagra Malo, *Daños del amianto: litigación, aseguramiento de riesgos y fondos de compensación*, above n. 8, p. 31.

70 A. Azagra Malo and M. Gili Saldaña, 'Guia InDret de jurisprudencia sobre responsabilidad civil por daños del amianto' (2005) 2 *Indret* 18.

71 Azagra Malo, *Daños del amianto: litigación, aseguramiento de riesgos y fondos de compensación*, above n. 8, p. 266.

72 See ASFAMI –Association of victims of asbestos. 'Creación de un fondo de compensación para las víctimas del amianto' (2018). Available at: <http://afectadosamianto.com/2017/10/31/creacion-del-fondo-de-compensacion-para-las-victimas-del-amianto/>.

73 Such as the Basque Parliament. <https://www.noticiasdegipuzkoa.eus/2019/05/03/economia/euskadi-vuelve-a-exigir-a-espana-un-fondo-de-compensacion-por-amianto#Loleido>.

74 Available at: <http://www.congreso.es/public_oficiales/L12/CONG/BOCG/B/BOCG-12-B-8-1.PDF>.

According to the Bill, the Fund for the Compensation of Victims of Asbestos had legal personality and capacity, being under the control of the Ministry of Social Security (art. 1.2). Its aim was the full compensation of damages, provided that the Social Security department has recognised that the claimant is suffering from an occupational disease, or that she has been damaged by asbestos in Spain.

Article 3 established that the fund had the following resources:

- The contributions from public or private employers that employ workers (they would have been obliged to contribute according to art. 11.a).
- Contributions from mutual insurances for workplace accidents and occupational diseases (they would have been obliged to contribute according to art. 11.b).
- The amounts obtained by the fund thanks to its subrogation to liability claims.
- Transfers fixed in the Spanish General Budget.
- Any others created by the law.

The victim had to start an administrative procedure to ask for compensation. Once granted the compensation, the Fund for the Compensation of Victims of Asbestos would have been subrogated to all the rights that the victim had to take legal action against the entities that should fully or partially compensate the damage (art. 18).

4. THE LACK OF COMPENSATION FUNDS FOR MASS ACCIDENTS IN SPAIN AND THE ROLE OF PUBLIC AIDS

4.1. OVERVIEW

As has been seen in this chapter, the role of compensation funds is limited in Spanish law. There have been mass accidents, which do have a fund in other countries (e.g. the one for asbestos sufferers in Belgium) but not in this legal system. In addition, the ones that are regulated have a restrictive nature, so they cover damages only in particular circumstances: for example, the CCS only compensates victims when the insurance cannot do so. Whilst the fund for defective products or services is still not working more than ten years after it received legal recognition.

However, this lack of funds does not imply that victims do not have options for seeking compensation when the tortfeasor or the insurer do not comply. The Spanish legal system usually prefers to provide public aids to the victim, meaning that less compensation funds are regulated than in other countries where the role of insurances is more important.[75]

4.2. VICTIMS OF VIOLENT OR INTENTIONAL CRIMES

Act 35/1995[76] regulates the payment of compensation through public aids to the Spanish or EU citizens that are victims of violent or intentional crimes in Spain.[77] Although in 1995 this country had not ratified the European Convention on the Compensation of Victims of Violent Crimes (1983), the explanatory statement of Act 35/1995 referred to this convention in the following way:

> Convention No. 116, of the Council of Europe, of 24.11.1983, on compensation of victims of violent crimes should be highlighted. Its entry into force occurred in 1988 and although not yet signed by Spain, it constitutes a legal reference of the first order in the treatment of this matter.

It was six years later that Spain decided to ratify the European Convention.[78]

Act 35/1995 covers both direct (death, personal injuries and mental or physical damages) and indirect damages (e.g. the ones suffered by the victims' relatives). Physical and moral damages caused by crimes against sexual freedom can also be covered through this aid, even when no violence was used to commit them (art. 1.2 of Act 35/1995).

---

75 For example, while in the US victims of the 11 September terrorist attack were compensated through a compensation fund (World Trade Center Victim's Compensation Fund), Spain prefers to provide social security benefits to these victims (see below). In this sense, Moréteau explains that 'the American social welfare system is underdeveloped by comparison to similarly developed countries, victims being often left with no resources and having therefore a strong incentive to sue any available tortfeasor'. O. Moréteau, 'Catastrophic Harm in United States Law: Liability and Insurance' (2010) 58 *American Journal of Comparative Law*, No. 13. See also Mullenix, 'Designing compensatory funds: in search of first principles', above n. 13.

76 BOE No. 296, 12.12.1995.

77 Note that Act 4/2015, on victims of a crime, also regulates some rights for any kind of victim, such as the right to be informed about their rights and any possible aids they can apply for (art. 5.1).

78 Through the Instrument of Ratification of the European Convention on Compensation to the Victims of Violent Crimes. BOE No. 312, 29.12.2001.

The way to compensate victims under this regime is the following:

- The compensation is to be paid by the Spanish Ministry of Economy (art. 8.1). The Ministry can also provide the aid to the victim before the judges decide who the tortfeasor is and which compensation should be granted to the victim, working as an advanced payment (art. 10).
- In case of death, the victims' relatives can receive this aid. However, they share the compensation: the spouse receives half of the amount and children the other half. If the victim did not have a spouse or children, her parents will receive it. The compensation has a fixed value of 25 Spanish minimum wages. For example, if the victim dies in 2019, relatives will receive a maximum of €315,000 (€12.600 x 25). In any case, the amount received by the victim cannot be higher than the compensation established by the court.
- In case of personal injuries, they may be constitutive of the permanent or temporary disability of the victim. In case of temporary disability, she will receive double the daily minimum wage. In case of permanent disability, the amount will depend on its severity (between 40 and 135 monthly minimum wages).
- In any case, the victim has only one year from when the crime was committed to ask for this aid. This term works as a statutory limitation period, so it can be interrupted during the criminal procedure (art. 7.1).
- The government subrogates the victim regarding the action for damages against the tortfeasor (art. 13).

4.3. VICTIMS OF TERRORIST ATTACKS

Act 29/2011, on the recognition and protection of victims of terrorist attacks,[79] introduces public aids that can be granted to people who suffer damages due to terrorist attacks. As in victims of violent crimes, the victims of a terrorist attack are both the direct victim as well as the victim's relatives in case of the death of the former (arts 4.1 and 4.2). In addition, victims of damages to property and the ones threatened by a terrorist can also be granted compensation through these aids (arts 4.3 and 5).

[79] BOE No. 229, of 23.9.2011. Before the legislation of 2011, there existed Act 32/1999, on victims of terrorist attacks (BOE No. 242, 9.10.1999), which also provided aids for this type of victim.

Apart from the general right of information (art. 8), urgent medical care (art. 9), physiological assistance (art. 8), the right to be informed about public aids and compensation (art. 11), compensation for funeral expenses (art. 12) and consular assistance (art. 13), victims may also claim compensation directly from the Ministry of the Interior.

The compensation in this case works as following:

- In case of death, the victims' spouse and children can receive this aid (half for the spouse, half for children). Unlike victims of violent crimes (see above), in cases where the victim does not have a spouse or children, not only can the parents receive compensation, but also grandchildren, siblings and grandparents, in this order (art. 17).
- This compensation is paid in the form of public aid. However, when the amount of this allowance is below the compensation granted by the court, the government may satisfy the difference payable to the victim (art. 20). In this case, the government subrogates the victim and thus can claim the reimbursement of these expenses from the tortfeasor (the terrorist). It is compulsory for the victims to assign the civil claims to the government in order to receive the compensation (art. 21.2).
- Material damages to dwellings, commercial or industrial premises, vehicles and to trade unions and political parties' headquarters can also be compensated (art. 23). In this case, the compensation is to be paid by the General State Administration, unless other administrations or insurer cover these damages (subsidiary liability).
- The amount of the compensation is established in annex I. For example, in the event of death, the family has a right to a payment of €250,000.

4.4. VICTIMS OF THE PRESTIGE (OIL SPILL DISASTER)

In November 2002, the oil tanker Prestige sunk in front of the Galician coast. The collapse of the ship caused an oil spill, and was one of the most important environmental disasters that has occurred in Spain, affecting the Spanish, Portuguese and French coasts. The proceedings held to decide the criminal and civil liability of this case took ten years, and almost 2,000 victims asked for compensation,[80] most of them fishermen.

---

80 El País. *El desastre del prestige en 10 cifras.* <https://politica.elpais.com/politica/2017/11/16/actualidad/1510845980_483459.html>.

Four people were found liable: the ship's captain (both criminal and civil) according to art. 3 of the International Convention on Civil Liability for Oil Pollution Damage (hereafter CLC[81]). The insurer (The London Steamship Owners Mutual Insurance Association), but with the limit established in the insurance policy; Mare Shipping Inc (ship's owner) and also the International Oil Pollution Compensation Funds (STS of 14 January 2015[82]), a fund that operates when damages are higher than the amount that the tortfeasor can or has to compensate.[83]

However, the Spanish government reacted before the court's decision took place and passed RDL 4/2003,[84] creating social benefits that function as an advanced payment.[85] But this RDL has been considered to be a mechanism to protect the government against civil liability claims:[86] victims had to accept the assessment of the damages made by the government; the victim had to sign a waiver of his/her right to claim liability (art. 5.1); the government was thus entitled to claim compensation against the tortfeasor (the ship's captain and the owner of the Prestige), the insurer, or even against the International Oil Pollution Compensation Funds. Thus, this international fund did not pay the victims directly, but rather the Spanish government. Note that the compensation has not yet been paid (2019[87]).

4.5. VICTIMS OF BLOOD CONTAMINATED WITH HEPATITIS C AND HIV

Between 1980–1995, more than 1,800 Spaniards were infected with HIV or Hepatitis C due to contaminated blood. Most of these infections were

---

81 Adoption: 29 November 1969; Entry into force: 19 June 1975; Being replaced by the 1992 Protocol: Adoption: 27 November 1992; Entry into force: 30 May 1996.

82 RJ 2016, 4120.

83 Article 4 of the International Convention on the Establishment of an International Fund for Compensation for Oil Pollution Damage, 1992. Spain ratified this convention.

84 BOE No. 148, 21.6.2003. This piece of legislation was complemented one year later with RDL 4/2004. These aids were partially financed by the International Oil Pollution Compensation Fund.

85 In any case, these compensations were satisfied through soft loans to the victims, with the government being entitled to receive due compensation after the judgment. See also J.L. Pulido, 'Compensation by the Coastal State -The Prestige Disaster' in J. Basedow and U. Magnus (eds), *Pollution of the Sea. Prevention and Compensation* (Springer 2007).

86 A. Rubí and J. Piñeiro, 'El blindaje del Gobierno en la crisis del Prestige' (2003) 169 *Indret.*

87 It was not until December 2019 that the compensation in charge of the insurer began to be distributed. ABC. *España da por perdidos 1.500 millones de las indemnizaciones*

contracted in public hospitals, so the liability of laboratories, public administration and private medical centres was put into question.

The government passed several acts to provide social benefits to the victims that were infected in public hospitals:

- Act 14/2002[88] for victims of Hepatitis C: this Act provides social aids for the victim or their relatives in case of death (children, spouse or parents). However, the amount of compensation is limited to €18,030 (art. 2) and, to access these aids, the victim has to waive the right to exercise any type of claim against the Public Administration or its respective staff (i.e. doctors, nurses), for medical negligence or other forms of liability, related to the fact that the victim was infected with Hepatitis C while under public care.
- RDL 9/1993:[89] it provides special aids for victims damaged by blood contaminated with HIV prior to the establishment of compulsory HIV testing. The amount of compensation was assessed in art. 2 of RDL 9/1993 and, in order to receive it, the victim had to waive his/her right to make a claim against the Public Administration or its personnel. In fact, those victims that had obtained a judgment determining the liability of the Public Administration could not apply for these aids (arts 3.2 and 3.3).
- In the Autonomous Region of Catalonia, Final Disposition 37th of Act 3/2000[90] regulated some social benefits for victims of contaminated blood infected in Catalan public hospitals. In this case, the victim also has to waive the exercise of all types of claims against the Public Administration, authorities and workers.[91]

4.6. VICTIMS OF THALIDOMIDE

During the 1950s and 1960s, many children were born with malformations due to the side effects of some medications containing thalidomide.

del Prestige. 02.12.2019. Available at: <https://www.abc.es/espana/galicia/abci-espana-perdidos-1500-millones-indemnizaciones-prestige-201912020134_noticia.html>.

88 BOE No. 135, 6.6.2002.

89 BOE No. 130, 1.6.1993.

90 Official Gazette of Catalonia (DOGC) No. 3144, 22.5.2000.

91 See the problems of these aids at J.C. Seuba Torreblanca, 'Ayudas a los contagiados por el VHC en el sistema sanitario público' (2003) 3, *Indret*.

After some years of litigation, RD 1006/2010[92] introduced a number of social aids for victims of thalidomide.

However, its scope of application is quite narrow: it only provides social aids to victims who were born between 1960–1966, provided that thalidomide was or could be what caused the malformations. In addition, the amount of compensation depends on the degree of disability: between €30,000 and €100,000, and the victims only had months to claim these aids (until September 2010). Parliament has also been debating the possibility of increasing these aids, not only in relation to their amount but also with regard to the number of victims entitled to ask for them.[93]

5. CONCLUDING REMARKS

Compensation funds are not representative of the mechanisms used for compensating victims in Spain, a country which prefers other remedies in cases of massive damages. While other countries decided to create a fund to cover certain damages (e.g. terrorist attacks, asbestos damages), Spain opted for providing victims with social security benefits, requiring compulsory insurances or other types of social aids. Thus, compensation funds are certainly a new phenomenon in Spanish tort law, although the CCS has been working in key sectors (natural disasters and road accidents) since the last century, when directives on road accidents required it to compensate these uncovered damages.

The compensation funds that are regulated in this country are conceived as a guarantee fund: the fund may compensate the victim when she or he cannot be compensated through a direct claim to the tortfeasor or through an insurance policy, as happens with road accidents or with the Compensation Fund for Environmental Damages. With respect to the fund for natural disasters (extraordinary risks), the victim may only ask for a compensation when she or he has arranged an insurance policy that does not cover these risks. In short, these regulated funds usually work when the victim has no option to receive compensation from other sources. Moreover, case law shows that these regulated funds even imply a certain

92 BOE No. 190, 6.8.2010.

93 La Vanguardia, 'El PP incluye ayudas millonarias en los Presupuestos a afectados por la talidomida' 11 June 2018. Available at: <http://www.lavanguardia.com/vida/20180611/4525969783/pp-incluye-ayudas-millonarias-en-los-presupuestos-a-afectados-por-talidomida.html>.

tendency to settle liability disputes in court (which is in fact precisely what compensation funds want to avoid), since conflicts arise when determining whether the CCS has to compensate the victim or not.

Due to some of the shortcomings of the social security benefits regulated for certain damages, more and more sectors, represented both by academia and by stakeholder associations, recommend the regulation of compensation funds, such as the victims of asbestos (there was a draft bill to create a fund for them). Indeed, social security benefits usually establish a certain amount (usually low) to alleviate victims; to access these aids, the victim has to waive her right to claim against the tortfeasor; and normally they cover only personal injuries (except, for example, victims of terrorist attacks).

The law maker has also taken into account these shortcomings and in the last years has regulated some compensation funds, such as the one for environmental damages (2007) or the one for defective products or services, which still has to be implemented. Nevertheless, this legislative response to key mass accidents or damages is slow when compared to other legal systems that regulated some compensation funds years ago. Further developments on this topic will show whether some of the bills to create compensation funds are finally implemented, and whether this country, taking into account the stakeholders' recommendations, will continue opting for social security benefits ahead of these funds.

COMPENSATION FUNDS IN THE UNITED KINGDOM

Ken OLIPHANT*

* This chapter was initially written in 2016 and updated selectively for the present publication.

1. INTRODUCTION

In the UK, as in perhaps all mature legal systems, compensation for victims of misfortune comes from a number of different sources. The following may be regarded as the most important:

- Social security
- Private insurance
- Tort law
- A surprisingly wide variety of other compensation funds and schemes

The last-mentioned – the focus of this chapter – are created because of perceived gaps of cover in, or shortfalls in the compensation offered by, the other three sources.[1] Each of the three suffers from its own specific limitations – affecting either the scope of cover provided or the amount of compensation paid.

Social security provides only a minimum level of support and compensation payments are targeted on needs, rather than losses. In general, only pecuniary rather than non-pecuniary needs are addressed. The benefits provided may be means tested.

---

1 In English, one tends to refer to a 'compensation scheme' rather than a 'compensation fund'. Compensation schemes need not make use of a specific fund or have distinct management of its own assets: cf. workmen's compensation (1897–1948), based on private insurance; in other contexts, contributions to the compensation fund may be paid out of the general operating budget of a government department.

The major limitation of private insurance, by contrast, is that it is voluntary, so the coverage it provides is incomplete. (In some contexts – for example, in respect of motor vehicles – third-party liability insurance is compulsory, but this is to ensure the effectiveness of the remedies granted by tort law, so the insurance here is not an *independent* source of compensation.) In practice, there are limits on what first-party (or loss) insurance will cover, especially because of the moral hazard problems that arise if insurance benefits are too attractive. For example, the benefits payable under income protection insurance in the event of unfitness to work will not replace the insured's full lost income for the remaining part of his or her working life but will likely be limited to a specified percentage of pre-disability earnings.

In considering the scope of the compensation provided in the UK by the law of tort, it should be noted in the first place that the system is predominantly fault-based. In comparison with other European countries, there is very little strict liability. Fault-based liability applies even in respect of road traffic accidents. In respect of work-related injuries and illnesses, there is no workers' compensation. The erstwhile system was abolished in 1948 on the theory that occupational injuries and illnesses should not be distinguished categorically from those arising in other contexts; instead, all should be brought within a universal social security system. This increased the importance of the remedy provided by tort law, and that importance increased as the real value of social security benefits diminished over time.[2] From the final years of the nineteenth century until very recently, the courts interpreted statutory health and safety requirements as laying down strict duties whose contravention was actionable in damages without the need to prove fault.[3] But in 2013 this strict liability was abolished by statute and the injured worker must now prove fault in order to succeed in an employers' liability claim.[4]

It is worth adding that the scope of tortious State and public authority liability is also very limited in the UK.[5] In general, there is no liability in

---

2 See generally Richard Lewis, 'Employers' Liability and Workers' Compensation: England and Wales' in Ken Oliphant and Gerhard Wagner (eds), *Employers' Liability and Workers' Compensation* (de Gruyter 2012).

3 Lewis, 'Employers' Liability and Workers' Compensation: England and Wales', above n. 2, paras 109 and ff.

4 Enterprise and Regulatory Reform Act 2013 s. 69.

5 See generally Ken Oliphant (ed.), *Public Authority Liability in Comparative Perspective* (Intersentia 2016).

damages for supervisory or investigative failures as the courts have ruled consistently that the responsible authority owes no *duty of care* even to foreseeable victims – as highlighted in recent cases about negligent police investigations and delayed responses to 999 emergency calls.[6] Further, English law recognises no principle of equality in the distribution of public burdens (*égalité devant les charges publiques*) whereby the State may be required to pay compensation to those injured by its lawful activities.[7]

2. COMPENSATION SCHEMES: A CHRONOLOGY

To give a flavour of the range of special compensation schemes recognised now or in the past in English law, it may be useful to provide a chronological survey. In fact, such schemes have a long – perhaps, surprisingly long – history, dating back at least as far as the Riot Act of 1714.[8] This statute, a response to the public disorder caused by the accession of George I, Elector of Hannover, to the British throne on the death of Queen Ann, put an obligation on the local community – the 'hundred' – to compensate for damage caused to buildings in the course of a riot. Though this compensation provision gathered little attention from modern writers, it was again put in the spotlight in the aftermath of riots in London and Birmingham in 2011, following which the scope of the entitlements under the Act, and the burden of the liability, were litigated to the Supreme Court.[9] Even before judgment, Parliament passed the Riot Compensation Act 2016 to clarify the law.[10]

---

6 See especially *Michael v Chief Constable of South Wales Police* [2015] UKSC 2, [2015] AC 1732. In such cases, there may be a claim for damages by way of just satisfaction under the Human Rights Act 1998.

7 See Ken Oliphant, 'The Liability of Public Authorities in England and Wales', no. 47 and ff, in Oliphant (ed.), *The Liability of Public Authorities in Comparative Perspective*, above n. 5.

8 The Act is the source of the familiar phrase, 'to read the Riot Act': an official would read aloud a text prescribed in the statute, requiring the dispersal of any group of 12 or more persons who were 'unlawfully, riotously, and tumultuously assembled together'. The text read: 'Our sovereign lord the King chargeth and commandeth all persons, being assembled, immediately to disperse themselves, and peaceably to depart to their habitations, or to their lawful business, upon the pains contained in the act made in the first year of King George, for preventing tumults and riotous assemblies. God save the King.'

9 *Mitsui Sumitomo Insurance Co (Europe) Ltd v Mayor's Office for Policing and Crime* [2016] UKSC 18, [2016] AC 1488 (applying s. 2 of the Riot (Damages) Act 1886).

10 Implementing the recommendations of Neil Kinghan, 'Independent Review of the Riot (Damages) Act 1886: Report of the Review' (2013).

Other significant landmarks in the development of compensation rights in the UK include the following:

- The Workmen's Compensation Act 1897, establishing the system of workers' compensation that survived until 1948.
- The introduction of compulsory motor liability insurance in the Road Traffic Act 1930, ensuring the effectiveness of tort remedies against negligent motorists.
- The creation of the Motor Insurers' Bureau in 1946, providing compensation for victims of uninsured drivers, and later for hit-and-run victims.
- The creation of the welfare state in 1948, absorbing workmen's compensation – and at the same time expanding the previously limited scope for employers' liability claims in tort.[11]
- The creation of the Criminal Injuries Compensation Scheme (CICS) in 1964.
- The Vaccine Damage Act 1979; and in the same year the first of the various schemes offering compensation to the victims of asbestos (the Pneumoconiosis etc. (Workers' Compensation) Act 1979).
- In 1988, the establishment of the first of the various schemes offering compensation to the victims of contaminated blood (this dealing with HIV; later schemes deal with Hepatitis C).

Further analysis of these schemes is provided below to the extent necessary to elucidate their main characteristics and the differences between them.

3. CHARACTERISTICS OF COMPENSATION SCHEMES

Perhaps the most distinctive characteristic of compensation schemes is that they are context specific. They are restricted in scope by reference to the cause of the injury or damage, the type of injury or damage suffered, and/or by the occasion of its occurrence.

- *By cause of injury*: criminal injuries, vaccine injuries, blood transfusions, oil pollution, banking/insurance/pensions fund failure, etc.

[11] Especially through the abolition of the defence of common employment: Law Reform (Personal Injuries) Act 1948 s. 1.

Sometimes the scheme can be narrowly limited to a specific agent, as in the case of asbestos, thalidomide, and foot and mouth disease (FMD).

- *By type of injury*, for example Hepatitis C or HIV infection (from blood transfusion, etc.), pneumoconiosis (etc.) or mesothelioma (from workplace exposure), or the slaughter of livestock (because of FMD).
- *By occasion of occurrence*, as in the case of work accidents and occupational diseases.

It may be noted that these different factors may be applied in combination (e.g. *type of injury plus cause* or *type of injury plus occasion*).

Other typical (though perhaps not universal) characteristics include:

- Entitlement to compensation is on a no-fault basis, though (as with criminal injuries and compensation for accidents caused by uninsured or untraced motorists) compensation may be for injury caused by *someone's* fault, while it may be the case that the recognition of the right to compensation was motivated, at least in part, by a desire to head off civil claims for damages based on fault on the part of the State (as has been suggested in respect of criminal injuries compensation).
- Streamlined procedures (quick, cheap, making use of administrative tribunals rather than courts).
- Compensation is paid out of a distinct compensation *fund*, not from general taxation revenues.

4. POINTS OF DISTINCTION BETWEEN COMPENSATION SCHEMES

A number of points of distinction may be observed as between different compensation schemes. Regarding the compensation to be paid, is it to cover the victim's losses in full or only partially? If the latter, is the compensation a fixed amount or subject to a cap? Another set of differences relates to the effect of the scheme on entitlements in tort law or under social security. Does the scheme exclude those alternative claims or can they be combined? If the latter, are the recoveries from different sources set off or accumulated, and/or is the scheme subrogated to the victim's rights against the 'responsible' party? Lastly, regarding funding, is the financing for the scheme to come from those whose activities cause or create the risk of the injuries covered by the scheme, or their insurers, is it to come from potential victims, or is the taxpayer to foot the bill? Almost all permutations of these variables are to be found amongst the special compensation schemes to be found in the UK today, as the more detailed analysis below will show, though it is hard to discern any particular pattern in or logic behind them.

5. THE MAIN COMPENSATION SCHEMES IN THE UNITED KINGDOM BY THEMATIC CLUSTER

5.1. ASBESTOS-RELATED DISEASE

Compensation for asbestos-related disease comes from a variety of different sources, including social security (industrial injuries disablement benefit) and tort law (employers' liability/EL claims). There are also three separate compensation funds for the benefit of asbestos victims, while the Financial Services Compensation Scheme (FSCS) offers relief for employers and insurers who face an undue payment burden.[12]

Additionally, there are dedicated trust funds for asbestos victims – notably, that set up for those who brought claims against the former asbestos producer, Turner and Newall, and related companies (now part of Federal-Mogul).[13] As schemes of a private character, they will not be considered further in the present chapter.

5.1.1. Dust-Related Diseases

The Pneumoconiosis etc. (Workers' Compensation) Act 1979 established a compensation scheme providing lump sum payments to sufferers of certain dust-related industrial diseases, subject to various conditions. The awards are for victims of occupational exposure to asbestos who cannot or have not taken civil action because their former employer has stopped trading.

---

12 See further Ken Oliphant, 'The Changing Landscape of Work Injury Claims: Challenges for Employers' Liability and Workers' Compensation', paras 56 and 63 and ff. in Oliphant and Wagner (eds), *Employers' Liability and Workers' Compensation*, above n. 2; Alan Mckenna, 'An overview of the legal landscape of negligently inflicted asbestos related conditions' [2011] *Journal of Personal Injury Law* 205.

13 The T&N UK Asbestos Trust and The EL Trust: see <https://tandnasbestos.org.uk>.

The asbestos-related[14] diseases included under the Act are:

- Pneumoconiosis (including asbestosis), referring to a variety of diseases of the respiratory tract owing to the inhalation and retention of dust particles;
- Diffuse mesothelioma: a cancer of the lining of the lungs or abdomen associated almost exclusively with asbestos;
- Bilateral diffuse pleural thickening (benign thickening of the lining of the lungs) (not to be confused with (less serious) pleural plaques); and
- Lung cancer (primary carcinoma of the lung) if accompanied by asbestosis or bilateral diffuse pleural thickening.

Awards vary according to age and degree of disablement (as assessed by a medical advisor on a percentage scale) and at time of writing ranged from £3,051 for 10% disablement in a sufferer aged 77 or more to £86,607 for 100% disablement in a sufferer aged 37 or less.[15] The total compensation payable by this scheme in 2010, the last year for which it was possible to find a figure, was £37,611,000.[16]

Only people who receive Industrial Injuries Disablement Benefit (IIDB) are eligible to receive a payment under the 1979 Act. IIDB is a non-contributory social security benefit paid to employees who become disabled through an accident at work or as a result of one of some 70 specified occupational diseases. The general minimum degree of disablement required is 14% (payable as 20%). For diffuse mesothelioma and asbestos-related lung cancer, disablement is stipulated to be 100%. There is a maximum payment of (at time of writing) £168 per week, equating to an annual total of £8,736. IIDB may be combined with other social security benefits, such as Constant Attendance Allowance (maximum £134.40 per week), Exceptionally Severe Disablement Allowance (£67.20 per week) and either an Unemployability Supplement (£103.85 per week) or a Reduced Earnings Allowance (maximum £67.20 per week).[17] So the total annual amount paid could be up to £24,619.40 (£473.45 per week).

---

14 The Act also covers other types of pneumoconiosis such as silicosis and kaolinosis, as well as byssinosis, a reactive airways disease of cotton, flax and hemp workers.

15 Pneumoconiosis etc. (Workers' Compensation) (Payment of Claims) Regulations 1988, SI 1988/668, Schedule, as substituted by Pneumoconiosis etc. (Workers' Compensation) (Payment of Claims) (Amendment) Regulations 2015, SI 2015/503, reg.2(5).

16 Department of Work and Pensions, 'Pneumoconiosis etc. (Workers' Compensation) Act 1979 and 2008 Mesothelioma Scheme', April 2011, p. 4.

17 See <http://www.gov.uk/industrial-injuries-disablement-benefit>.

5.1.2. *2008 Mesothelioma Scheme*

A separate scheme applies to those who suffer mesothelioma from non-occupational exposure to asbestos.[18] It provides lump sums for:

- those exposed to asbestos from a relative (e.g. from their overalls);
- environmentally (e.g. living near a factory using asbestos);
- the self-employed; and
- those who cannot trace specific exposure to asbestos, but there is nothing to suggest that they were not exposed to asbestos in the UK.

The aim was to ensure faster compensation payments, including up-front financial support within six weeks.[19] The cost of the compensation is met through compensation recovery whereby payments (under this scheme and under the 1979 scheme) are recovered by the State if a civil claim for compensation is subsequently successful.[20] Payments under the 2008 scheme are intended to correspond to what can be afforded out of the projected compensation recovery amounts, and are supposed to increase as those funds allow.[21]

At time of writing, rates of compensation varied from £13,295 (for those aged 77 or over at the date of diagnosis) to £85,580 (for those aged 37 or under).[22] The total amount of compensation paid under the scheme in 2010 was £8,006,000.[23]

5.1.3. *Diffuse Mesothelioma Payment Scheme*[24]

This further scheme was introduced by the Mesothelioma Act 2014 and established by the Diffuse Mesothelioma Payment Scheme Regulations 2014, SI 2014/916, following a Department of Work and Pensions

---

18 Part 4 [ss. 46 and ff] of the Child Maintenance and Other Payments Act 2008. The provisions followed a public consultation in 2006.

19 Child Maintenance and Other Payments Act 2008: Explanatory Notes, para. 10 (referring to the Secretary of State's announcement of proposals in March 2007).

20 Social Security (Recovery of Benefits) Act 1997.

21 Child Maintenance and Other Payments Act 2008: Explanatory Notes, paras 11 and 392 and ff.

22 <https://www.gov.uk/diffuse-mesothelioma-payment/what-youll-get>.

23 Department of Work and Pensions, 'Pneumoconiosis etc. (Workers' Compensation) Act 1979 and 2008 Mesothelioma, Scheme' April 2011, p. 4.

24 See <http://mesoscheme.org.uk/>.

consultation of 2010.[25] (As regards the Department's rejection of a wider employer's liability fund, see below.)

The scheme is intended to deal with the problem that employees negligently exposed by their employer to asbestos, who contract diffuse mesothelioma decades after the exposure, are often in practice unable to recover compensation: by virtue of the passage of time no solvent employer remains to be sued, and the employee is often unable to trace any insurer who was providing EL insurance to their employer at the material time.[26]

The scheme makes payments to eligible people with diffuse mesothelioma and eligible dependants of people who have died from diffuse mesothelioma before making an application to the scheme. People will be eligible for a scheme payment if they were first diagnosed with diffuse mesothelioma on or after 25 July 2012 (which was the date when the government responded to the consultation and made its intentions clear) as a result of negligent exposure to asbestos at work in the UK. The scheme is only open to people who have not brought an action against a relevant employer or employer's EL insurer because they are unable to do so. In addition, in order to be eligible to claim from the scheme, applicants must not have received damages or a specified payment in respect of diffuse mesothelioma and must not be eligible to receive a specified payment from another source.[27]

The scheme is funded by a levy on insurance companies that are currently active in the EL insurance market. The amount of the levy to be paid by each insurer is determined by reference to each insurer's market share in a recent 12-month period.[28]

The scheme provided for by the Act does not allow for payments to be made to persons with long-tail industrial diseases other than diffuse mesothelioma. The government stated that it considers this condition to be unique, in particular because of its near universal fatality, the speed of death following diagnosis and its causation arising exclusively from exposure to asbestos.[29]

Payments under the scheme are in the form of a single, once and for all, lump sum.[30] The amount of the lump sum was initially intended to

---

25 Department of Work and Pensions, 'Accessing compensation: Supporting people who need to trace Employers' Liability Insurance – public consultation' (2010).
26 Mesothelioma Bill [HL] Explanatory Notes.
27 Ibid, para. 13.
28 Ibid, para. 15.
29 Ibid, para. 17.
30 Regulation 19(2).

be 80% of an average civil claim for mesothelioma, but the amount was increased to 100% of average civil claims for new diagnoses on or after 10 February 2015 under new compensation rules brought in on that date. This resulted in an increase of up to £54,000 a person.[31] Payments now range from £87,061 (for those aged 90 and over at the time of diagnosis) to £271,120 (for those aged 40 and under).[32]

5.1.4. Contribution for Mesothelioma Claims

Additional compensation in respect of mesothelioma may be paid by the Financial Services Compensation Scheme (FSCS), but this is distinctive in that it makes payments to *employers* and *their insurers* rather than to the victims of the disease. It does so in cases where the employer (or insurer) cannot enforce its contribution (i.e. recourse) rights against other responsible persons on being found liable to pay damages in a tort mesothelioma claim.[33] The same problem arises as for victims: the long latency period may mean that other responsible persons have ceased to trade or cannot be identified. This was the case, for example, in *Barker v Corus (UK) plc*,[34] where insolvent employers were responsible for 83% of total asbestos exposure. The House of Lords in that case ruled that each employer's liability should be proportionate to their contribution to the overall exposure, meaning that the defendant employer paid only 17% of full damages.[35] This left the victim undercompensated, and Parliament legislated almost immediately to ensure that liability in mesothelioma cases would be 'joint and several' (i.e. solidary or *in solidum*).[36] This relieves the victim of the risk of the insolvency (etc.) of a former employer or the latter's insurer. So, in *Sienkiewicz v Greif (UK) Ltd*,[37] where the defendant was responsible for only 15% of the exposure to asbestos, and 85% was environmental exposure, the claimant nevertheless recovered 100% damages.

---

31 DWP Press Release, 'Mesothelioma sufferers' compensation boosted by extra £54,000' (10 February 2015).

32 https://www.mesoscheme.org.uk/payment-tarrif-2015-onwards/.

33 See further Oliphant, 'Changing Landscape of Work Injury Claims: Challenges for Employers' Liability and Workers' Compensation', above n. 12, paras 63 and ff.

34 *Barker v Corus (UK) plc* [2006] UKHL 20, [2006] 2 AC 572.

35 The liability is for material contribution to risk: *McGhee v National Coal Board* [1973] 1 WLR 1; *Fairchild v Glenhaven Funeral Services* [2002] UKHL 22, [2003] 1 AC 32.

36 Compensation Act 2006 s. 3.

37 [2011] UKSC 10, [2011] 2 AC 229.

As a quid pro quo, where an employer is unable to recover contribution or indemnity from other responsible parties, the shortfall on recovery is to be made good out of the financial services compensation fund which (inter alia) guarantees payments in the event of an insurer's insolvency.[38]

5.2. HEALTHCARE PROVISION (VACCINES AND BLOOD)

English law places significantly less reliance on compensation funds in the area of healthcare provision than French law.[39] The two particular categories in which specific compensation rights are granted are vaccine damage and infection from contaminated blood.

5.2.1. *Vaccine Damage*

A separate compensation scheme for vaccine damage was introduced by statute in 1979.[40] The rationale was that vaccine injury is the very occasional price that society pays for the benefit of defeating disease through national vaccination programmes. The compensation entitlement maintains public trust in the system and encourages participation in it. (Vaccination is not compulsory.)

The scheme pays a fixed sum of £120,000, but the compensation entitlement is limited to cases of severe (i.e. 60% or greater) disablement resulting from vaccination against specified diseases. Despite criticism of the scheme in Parliament, there are no current plans to reform it.[41]

5.2.2. *Infection with Hepatitis C or HIV by NHS Blood*

During the late 1970s and early 1980s more than 1,200 people with haemophilia were infected with HIV through their clotting factor treatment and around 100 people with other conditions were infected with HIV through treatment with NHS-supplied blood products or

---

38 Compensation Act 2006 s. 3(7) and Compensation Act 2006 (Contribution for Mesothelioma Claims) Regulations 2006, SI 2006/3259.

39 Simon Taylor, *Medical Accident Liability and Redress in English and French Law* (Cambridge University Press 2015), p. 64.

40 Vaccine Damage Payments Act 1979, analysed by G. Dworkin, 'Compensation and Payments for Vaccine Damage' [1979] *J Social Welfare Law* 330.

41 See HC Deb 24 March 2015 vol. 594 col. 441WH.

blood transfusions. A large proportion of the victims were also infected with Hepatitis C. This continued until heat treatment of blood products was introduced in 1985 and a screening test for blood donations was developed and introduced in 1991.

This healthcare disaster led in 1988 to the government's establishment of the first of a number of charitable trusts and not-for-profit companies which now provide compensation to victims out of funds provided on an *ex gratia* basis by the government. Up to early 2016, over £390 million had been paid (since 1988); the projected expenditure over the lifetime of the scheme was a further £570 million, with an extra £125 million earmarked for the introduction of reforms announced in 2016.[42]

For HIV, two charitable trust funds were established and funded by the government:

- Macfarlane Trust,[43] established in 1987 (for haemophiliacs infected with HIV as a result of contaminated NHS blood products) (its work was subsequently complemented by that of a not-for-profit company, MFET Ltd, established in 2010,); and
- Eileen Trust, established in 1993 (for non-haemophiliacs infected with HIV through blood transfusion or tissue transfer).

These charities initially paid beneficiaries lump sums of £20,000, to which a further £60,500 was later added by way of out-of-court settlement of claims brought by haemophiliac HIV victims; this further payment was subsequently extended to others infected with HIV through NHS-supplied infected blood.[44] In 2009, an annual payment (rising to £15,500) was introduced. There were also discretionary bereavement payments for dependants on low incomes.

For Hepatitis C victims, compensation came a little later and was initially unfavourable in comparison with that to victims of HIV. The main initial source was the Skipton Fund,[45] a company established in 2004. This compensated for infection with Hepatitis C through treatment

42 See generally Department of Health, 'Infected blood: reform of financial and other support' (2016), available at <https://www.gov.uk/government/uploads/system/uploads/attachment_data/file/494004/Infected_blood_cons_doc.pdf>, para. 0.5.

43 <http://www.macfarlane.org.uk/>.

44 Department of Health, 'Infected blood: reform of financial and other support', above n. 42, ch. 1.

45 <http://www.skiptonfund.org>.

with NHS blood or blood products prior to September 1991, paying lump sums of £20,000 plus (in severe cases) £25,000, but until 2011 it did not make annual payments and provided no support to dependants. A government review in 2010[46] highlighted discrepancies in the treatment of HIV and Hepatitis C and led to reforms, including the provision of further, targeted support for Skipton Fund beneficiaries *and* their dependants via a new fund managed by the Caxton Foundation,[47] established in 2011. Annual payments were also introduced for Hepatitis C victims and the amounts paid were equalised.

The Department of Health initiated a further review of the schemes in early 2016.[48] It criticised the outdated and confusing funding structure, based on five separate entities and requiring some victims to deal with more than one fund. It also criticised differences in payments and policies, as well as the lack of individualised assessment of beneficiaries. Its proposal was for a unified scheme run by a single body under which the existing flat-rate annual payments would be replaced by differential payment levels assigned following individualised assessment. The maximum annual payment would be fixed perpetually at £15,000 and not increased in line with inflation. The proposal was opposed by victims' groups, who feared that most victims would be left worse off financially and in a position of uncertainty because of the unpredictability of individualised assessment.[49] The legitimacy of these concerns was

46 Department of Health, 'Review of the support available to individuals infected with Hepatitis C and/or HIV by NHS supplied blood transfusions or blood products and their dependants' (2010). The review followed the rejection of Lord Archer of Sandwell's call to pay Irish levels of compensation: see Written Ministerial Statement, Department of Health, Anne Milton, 'Support for those affected by contaminated blood' (14 October 2010). See also Department of Health, 'Government response to Lord Archer's Independent report on NHS supplied contaminated blood and blood products' (20 May 2009).

47 Department of Health, 'Infected blood: reform of financial and other support', above n. 42, paras 1.3 and 2.2.

48 Department of Health, 'Infected blood: reform of financial and other support', above n. 42. This followed a report by the All-Party Parliamentary Group (APPG) on Haemophilia and Contaminated Blood (Inquiry into the current support for those affected by the contaminated blood scandal in the UK (2015), available at <http://haemophilia.org.uk/wp-content/uploads/2017/02/appg_hcb_fr.pdf.pdf>) and, in Scotland, the report of the Penrose Inquiry (Penrose Inquiry – Final Report (2015), available at <http://www.penroseinquiry.org.uk/finalreport/pdf/penrose_inquiry_final_report.pdf>).

49 See <https://haemophilia.org.uk>.

recognised by the government, which implemented reforms in 2017. These included increases in the annual payments and the retention of discretionary support, alongside the touted appointment of a single body (the NHS Business Services Authority) to run the now unified scheme. New maxima were established for both Hepatitis C and HIV (£15,655, rising to £18,500 from 2018/19 and then rising in line with inflation) with higher amounts in respect of co-infection (£30,805, rising to £36,500 from 2018/19 and then also rising in line with inflation).[50]

6. MOTOR VEHICLE ACCIDENTS (UNINSURED AND UNTRACED DRIVERS)

The Motor Insurers' Bureau was established by the insurance industry in 1946 in response to Ministry of Transport pressure. (Cynics suggest it was designed to forestall legislative intervention.) The agreement reached with the Ministry requires insurers to contribute, *pro rata* to the amount of their motor business, to a fund from which compensation is paid to victims of uninsured drivers. Compensation was extended to victims of untraced ('hit and run') drivers in 1968.

In 2014, the MIB settled 44,276 claims and paid compensation totalling £280.6 million.[51] The cost of the scheme has reduced significantly in recent years: in 2015 the levy on members was £244 million against a collection high of £417 million in 2008.[52]

The MIB actively pursues recovery of indemnity from the uninsured driver.[53]

---

50 Department of Health, 'Government Response to Consultation on Special Category Mechanism and other support in England' (2017), available at <https://assets.publishing.service.gov.uk/government/uploads/system/uploads/attachment_data/file/666622/Infected_Blood_Consultation_Response.pdf>. In the light of continuing questions about the government's responsibility for the use of infected blood, the UK Prime Minister announced in the same year the establishment of an independent public inquiry into the tragedy: <https://www.gov.uk/government/news/pm-statement-on-contaminated-blood-inquiry-11-july-2017>. See further <https://www.infectedbloodinquiry.org.uk/>.

51 Motor Insurers' Bureau, *Annual Report & Accounts 2014* (2015), pp. 11 and 32.

52 Ibid, pp. 4 and 6.

53 See further Robert Merkin and Jenny Steele, 'Policing Tort and Crime with the MIB: Remedies, Penalties and the Duty to Insure' in Matthew Dyson (ed.), *Unravelling Tort and Crime* (Cambridge University Press 2014).

7. CRIMINAL INJURIES COMPENSATION[54]

The Criminal Injuries Compensation Scheme (CICS) provides compensation in respect of personal injury which is directly attributable to being a direct victim of a crime of violence.[55] The scheme was established in 1964, initially on a non-statutory basis; payments were *ex gratia*. The Scheme was given statutory foundations in 1988. It meets the obligation imposed by Directive 2004/80/EC relating to compensation to crime victims.

The rationale for the scheme is sympathy for the innocent victim of crime. The government has consistently rejected the view that the compensation discharges a *liability* of the State. The Pearson Commission (in its report on *Civil Liability and Compensation for Personal Injury*) concluded that 'compensation for criminal injury is morally justified as in some measure salving the nation's conscience at its inability to preserve law and order'.[56]

The fund is financed from general taxation. Its finances are allocated by the Ministry of Justice.

Compensation was initially awarded at the full level of damages in tort, but a statutory tariff was introduced in 1996. Thereafter, the compensation recovered under the CICS has been calculated differently from that available by way of damages in tort law, and the tariff award no longer based on the personalised assessment undertaken in tort cases. The maximum tariff award is £250,000. This can be supplemented by a contribution towards loss of earnings after the first 28 weeks of loss and other special expenses. The overall maximum is £500,000.[57]

---

54 See generally David Miers, 'Compensating deserving victims of violent crime: the Criminal Injuries Compensation Scheme 2012' (2014) 34 *Legal Studies* 242.

55 The current Scheme was established under the Criminal Injuries Compensation Act 1995. See further Ministry of Justice, 'The Criminal Injuries Compensation Scheme 2012' (2012), available online at <https://assets.publishing.service.gov.uk/government/uploads/system/uploads/attachment_data/file/808343/criminal-injuries-compensation-scheme-2012.pdf>. From a historical perspective, see Ken Oliphant, 'Landmarks of No-Fault in the Common Law' in Willem H. van Boom and Michael Faure (eds), *Shifts in Compensation between Public and Private Systems* (Springer 2007), nos 36–46. The CIC Authority became an executive agency in 2014: Ministry of Justice and Criminal Injuries Compensation Authority, Criminal Injuries Compensation Authority Agency Framework Document, April 2014.

56 Royal Commission on Civil Liability and Compensation for Personal Injury (Chairman: Lord Pearson), *Report*, Cmnd 7054 (1978), para. 1588.

57 Criminal Injuries Compensation Scheme 2012, para. 31.

Calls for more extensive compensation entitlements for victims of terrorism after the 7/7 bombings in London in 2005 were rejected by the government, which reiterated that the CICS is akin to charity rather than the discharge of a liability.[58] However, in 2012, entitlement under the scheme was extended to British citizens and EU (etc.) nationals resident in the UK who are victims of specific acts of terrorism abroad. These include the Brussels airport attack of April 2016 and the Paris attacks of November 2015. The same payment entitlements are recognised as under the regular scheme and they are subject to the same maximum of £500,000.[59]

The Scheme received 32,595 new applications in 2014–2015. It made compensation awards totalling £176.6 million.[60]

8. FINANCIAL SERVICES

8.1. FINANCIAL SERVICES COMPENSATION SCHEME (FSCS)

The FSCS was set up under the Financial Services and Markets Act 2000, becoming operational on 1 December 2001.[61] It is the UK's compensation scheme of last resort for customers of financial services firms authorised by the Financial Conduct Authority (FCA) or the Prudential Regulation Authority (PRA). The FSCS may pay compensation to customers of authorised financial services firms that fail. This will

[58] See further David Miers, 'Rebuilding Lives: Operational and Policy Issues in the Compensation of Victims of Violent and Terrorist Crimes' [2006] *Criminal Law Review* 69.

[59] Ministry of Justice, 'The Victims of Overseas Terrorism Compensation Scheme 2012' (2012). The Scheme was laid before Parliament under s. 54(1) of the Crime and Security Act 2010.

[60] Criminal Injuries Compensation Authority, 'Annual Report and Accounts 2014–15' (2015). [NB. This does not reveal how many claims were accepted/disallowed in the year. 7,584 claims were disallowed because the injury was not serious enough; 2,246 because the injury did not result from a crime of violence. These categories, and other categories of disallowed claims, overlap, preventing calculation of the total number of claims rejected.]

[61] For early evaluations, see Financial Services Authority, 'Financial Services Compensation Scheme reform: Fast payout for depositors and raising consumer awareness', CP09/03, January 2009; FSA, 'Banking and compensation reform, Including feedback on CP08/23, CP09/3, CP09/11 and CP09/16, Policy Statement 09/11', July 2009; Harry McVea, 'The Financial Services Compensation scheme and deposit insurance reform' [2008] *Lloyd's Maritime and Commercial Law Quarterly* 389.

generally be because they have stopped trading and are unable to pay protected claims against them or likely to be 'in default'.[62] The aim is to preserve consumer confidence in the banking system and financial services sector generally. A sceptical opposing view is that the existence of a compensation scheme might mean that alternative options that might be more advantageous to investors, such as a rescue of the collapsed firm, are not explored.[63]

The FSCS has claimed to have protected more than 4.5 million consumers since 2001 and paid out more than £26 billion in compensation. In 2015/16, it paid out £272 million in compensation to consumers as a result of 32,000 claims.[64] The scheme is funded by levies on firms subject to regulation in the financial services sector.

The scheme has three different components:

- Bank deposits are guaranteed up to £85,000 (or £1 million in the case of temporary large deposits, e.g. the proceeds of sale of one's home or a compensation lump sum);[65]
- Protection against insurance company failures, with 100% protection for entitlements under compulsory motor or employers' liability insurance, or under professional indemnity insurance; otherwise 90%; and
- Protection in respect of other financial services, e.g. £85,000 for investments or for home financing (mortgages).

8.2. PENSION PROTECTION FUND (PPF)[66]

The PPF provides financial protection for those whose pension funds fail or who are the victims of fraud. The main fund provides compensation

62 Financial Services Compensation Scheme, 'In Brief: Parliamentary Briefing' (May 2016), p. 2.

63 See A.C. Page and R.B. Ferguson, *Investor Protection* (Weidenfeld and Nicolson 1992), p. 74, cited by Eilis Ferran, 'Dispute resolution mechanisms in the U.K. financial sector' (2002) 21 *Civil Justice Quarterly* 135, 149.

64 Financial Services Compensation Scheme, above n. 62, p. 2.

65 Providing the protection required by EU law: Directive 94/19/EC of the European Parliament and of the Council of 30 May 1994 on deposit-guarantee schemes OJ L135, 31.05.1994; Directive 2009/14/EC of the European Parliament and of the Council of 11 March 2009 amending Directive 94/19/EC on deposit-guarantee schemes as regards the coverage level and the payout delay [2009] OJ L68/3; Directive 2014/49/EU of the European Parliament and of the Council of 16 April 2014 on deposit guarantee schemes (recast) [2014] OJ L173/149.

66 <http://www.pensionprotectionfund.org.uk/>.

to members of eligible defined benefit pension schemes, where the employer became insolvent on or after 6 April 2005, and there were insufficient assets in the pension scheme to cover the PPF level of compensation. It is supplemented by the Financial Assistance Scheme, offering relief to pension scheme members where their scheme started to wind-up between 1 January 1997 and 5 April 2005, and the Fraud Compensation Fund[67] which pays compensation – paid for through a separate levy on all pension schemes – to members of work-based pension schemes of all types whose employers become insolvent and their schemes have lost out financially because of dishonesty. Between 1 April 2015 and 31 March 2016, the fund paid £616 million to pension scheme members.[68]

9. AGRICULTURE

The Animal Health Act 1981 states that the Secretary of State for Agriculture may cause to be slaughtered any animal affected with foot and mouth disease or another specified disease or suspected of being affected, and any other animal that appears to have been exposed to the infection. The Act requires farmers of slaughtered animals to be paid compensation in the value of the animal prior to infection or slaughter (or, in the case of diseases other than foot and mouth, in an amount specified by order of the Secretary of State). Compensation is also to be paid in respect of infected material such as straw destroyed during a cull.[69] The aim is to encourage farmers' participation in slaughter programmes so as to protect agricultural business in general, while relieving those who bear the cost for the general benefit.

Following a major outbreak of foot and mouth disease in 2001, £1,158 million was paid in compensation in respect of the slaughter of

67 Established as the Fraud Compensation Board by the Pensions Act 1995 ss. 78 to 86, repealed with effect from 1 September 2005 but substantially re-enacted in ss. 182 to 189 of the Pensions Act 2004, with further regulation by Occupational Pension Schemes (Fraud Compensation Payments and Miscellaneous Amendments) Regulations 2005, SI 2005/2151 and Occupational Pension Schemes (Fraud Compensation Payments and Miscellaneous Amendments) Regulations 2010, SI 2010/483.

68 Pension Protection Fund, 'Pension Protection Fund Annual Report & Accounts 2015/16', HC461 (July 2016), p. 13.

69 See Animal Health Act 1981 ss.16A, 32A and 36.

over 4.2 million animals; the average payment to the farmers affected was around £125,000; the highest payment was over £4 million.[70]

In the same outbreak, a separate, voluntary Livestock Welfare (Disposal) Scheme was introduced for animals who were not directly affected by foot and mouth disease but could not be moved to alternative accommodation or pasture nor sent to market because of movement restrictions and could therefore have been at risk of suffering because of overcrowding. The scheme made payments to farmers of £205 million for the slaughter of two million animals.[71]

10. REJECTED COMPENSATION SCHEME PROPOSALS

Notwithstanding the introduction of the various compensation schemes described above, the UK has proved reluctant to follow the example of other countries in introducing no-fault compensation schemes of wider scope.

10.1. A NEW ZEALAND-STYLE ACCIDENT COMPENSATION SCHEME

Though the well-known Accident Compensation Scheme introduced in New Zealand in 1974[72] itself drew inspiration from the work of British academic Terence Ison, specifically his 1967 book *The Forensic Lottery*, and had only recently been established at the time of the British Royal Commission into Compensation for Personal Injury chaired in the 1970s by Lord Pearson, Pearson narrowly interpreted its terms of reference so as to preclude it from making a recommendation for or against the adoption of a New Zealand-style scheme in the UK, and the matter has never been close to the legislative agenda again. It may

70 National Audit Office, 'The 2001 Outbreak of Foot and Mouth Disease', HC 939, Session 2001–2002 (2002), para. 4.5. As to difficulties with the administration of compensation payments in paras 4.5 and ff.

71 Ibid, paras 4.22 and ff. See further <http://footandmouth.fera.defra.gov.uk/secure/fmdscience/lwds.cfm>.

72 For a useful overview, see Stephen Todd, 'Forty Years of Accident Compensation in New Zealand' (2011) 28 *Thomas M Cooley Law Review* 189.

in any case be that Pearson's own sympathies were with the existing UK approach based on a mix of tort law and social security, and that he was personally dubious about the abolition of tort effected in New Zealand.

10.2. MOTOR NO-FAULT

A State-administered no-fault compensation scheme for road accidents was first given notable advocacy by two scholars, Elliott and Street, in 1968.[73] In 1978, the Pearson Commission repeated their call[74] and was echoed in its turn by the Civil Justice Review in 1988,[75] but no reform materialised. In 1991, there was a further proposal from the Lord Chancellor's Department (LCD), limited to small claims of £2,500 or less.[76] The LCD believed that the range of road accident victims eligible for compensation would be wider than under the tort system, and that disputes over liability for minor injuries would be greatly reduced. The scheme was to be funded and operated by the insurance industry. Again, the proposal was never adopted.

10.3. NO-FAULT COMPENSATION FOR MEDICAL INJURIES

A report of a public inquiry into a healthcare scandal in Bristol recommended in 2001 the abolition of the law of clinical negligence and its replacement with no-fault compensation.[77] A particular advantage of such a scheme, said the report, was to encourage the open reporting of adverse events and near misses.

---

73 Derek W. Elliott and Harry Street, *Road Accidents* (Penguin 1968). See also Justice, *No Fault on the Roads* (Stevens & Sons 1974); Francis Trindade, 'A No-Fault Scheme for Road Accident Victims in the United Kingdom' (1980) 96 *Law Quarterly Review* 581; Richard Lewis, 'No-Fault Compensation for Victims of Road Accidents: Can it be Justified?' (1981) 10 *Journal of Social Policy* 161; Peter Bartrip, 'No-Fault Compensation on the Roads in Twentieth Century Britain' [2010] *Cambridge Law Journal* 263.

74 Royal Commission on Civil Liability and Compensation for Personal Injury (Chairman: Lord Pearson), *Report*, Cmnd 7054 (1978).

75 Review Body on Civil Justice, *Report*, Cm 354 (1988).

76 Lord Chancellor's Department, 'Compensation for Road Accidents: A Consultation Paper' (1991).

77 Bristol Royal Infirmary Inquiry, 'Learning from Bristol: Report of the Public Inquiry into children's heart surgery at the Bristol Royal Infirmary 1984–1995', Cm 5207(I) (July 2001), ch. 26 para. 35.

However, the Chief Medical Officer, in a follow-up report of 2003,[78] stated that a general no-fault scheme for medical injuries would be too expensive and recommended instead a (much) narrower scheme for birth injuries resulting in severe neurological impairment. Even this more limited suggestion was not taken up by the government, which instead enacted a 'NHS Redress' scheme of dubious utility, which is more a semi-formalised mechanism for settling low-to-medium value tort claims than a distinct compensation scheme. Though enacted,[79] the scheme has not yet been implemented in England (though it was introduced in Wales).[80]

10.4. AN EMPLOYERS' LIABILITY INSURANCE BUREAU (ELIB)

It has been suggested from time to time that there should be an equivalent to the Motor Insurers' Bureau (MIB) in the context of compulsory employers' liability insurance.[81] The creation of an ELIB has been strongly urged by unions and other groups, but consistently rejected by the government. In 2012, the government reiterated that it considered that the running costs would be disproportionate to benefits. It recognised, however, that mesothelioma was a 'unique case', which led to the creation of the Diffuse Mesothelioma Payment Scheme 2014 (above).[82]

10.5. INJURIES ASSOCIATED WITH PRODUCT-RELATED DEVELOPMENT RISKS

In response to a European Commission's Green Paper on Liability for Defective Products, the UK government announced in January 2014

---

78 Chief Medical Officer, 'Making Amends: a consultation paper setting out proposals for reforming the approach to clinical negligence in the NHS' (2003).

79 NHS Redress Act 2006.

80 National Health Service (Concerns, Complaints and Redress Arrangements) (Wales) Regulations 2011, SI 2011/704.

81 See e.g. R.C. Simpson, 'The Employers' Liability (Compulsory Insurance) Act 969' (1972) 35 *Modern Law Review* 63.

82 Department for Work and Pensions, 'Accessing compensation – Supporting people who need to trace Employers' Liability Insurance: Government response to consultation' (July 2012), no. 4.2; This constituted a retreat from the provisional opinion expressed in Department for Work and Pensions, 'Accessing compensation: Supporting people who need to trace Employers' Liability Insurance – public consultation' (2010), paras 58 and ff.

that it has no plans to introduce a special compensation scheme for the victims of defective products in cases where the development risks defence applies. It noted that it would be difficult to assess the likely demand on such a fund.[83]

11. POSSIBILITIES FOR THE FUTURE?

Notwithstanding the failed initiatives just mentioned, it would be too soon to write off the scope for further innovation in the UK in the creation of new compensation schemes. A number of possibilities may be considered.

11.1. A COMPENSATION FUND FOR UNINSURABLE NATURAL DISASTERS

A Belgian Law of 12 July 1976 addresses the issue of compensation of damage caused to private property by natural disasters.[84] According to art. 1 of the Law, specified heads of direct material damage to private personal property or land is to be compensated under specified legal conditions. The damage must occur on Belgian land and be caused by specified natural phenomena. Entitlement extends only to damage that was not and could not be insured against. The fund thus operates as a primary fund and embodies the idea of national solidarity towards the victims of natural disasters.

The UK is exposed to broadly the same risk of natural disaster as its continental neighbours, and its insurance market also experiences difficulty with the provision of cover in particular contexts (e.g. homes built on flood plains). But it prefers to address these issues through *ad hoc* solutions. For example, following flooding in 2013–14, the government announced a package of different forms of support for those affected, including grants to homeowners and businesses to fund flood resilience or resistance measures in respect of flooded property; relief against business rates (taxes) for flooded properties; council tax discounts for flooded homes; and a business support scheme for businesses losing trade

---

[83] UK response to the Commission's Green Paper on Liability for Defective Products, 15 January 2014, Ares(2014)74687, p. 7, available at <http://ec.europa.eu/DocsRoom/documents/1496/attachments/1/translations/en/renditions/pdf>.

[84] See Larissa Vanhoof, 'Compensation Funds in Belgium', section 3.6, in this volume.

as a result of the flooding. The measures were designed to complement existing insurance cover (e.g. by covering the amount of any excess in the insurance policy) and their benefit can be denied to those who failed to insure themselves.[85]

The problem of obtaining insurance cover in flood-affected areas has been addressed by cooperative action between the government and insurers, initially under a Statement of Principles dating from 2000.[86] Under the Principles, insurers had a commitment to continue the cover of their existing customers, but this was intended only as a temporary measure as new insurers could decide to whom they offered flood insurance. Consequently, under a new initiative taken with the government's blessing, insurers established a new joint reinsurance fund, Flood Re, in respect of flood damage claims.[87] Flood Re became operational on 1 April 2016 and it is estimated that it will assist 350,000 households in the UK at risk of flooding.

According to the website:

> Flood Re takes the flood risk element of home insurance from an insurer in return for a premium based on the property's council tax band. In addition, we would charge the insurer an excess on the flood part of the policy of £250. Because Flood Re's activities are subsidised by a levy on insurers of £180m, the premium we charge insurers is below the rates insurers would normally charge on properties at the highest risk of flooding.

11.2. A COMPENSATION FUND FOR TECHNOLOGICAL DISASTERS

A Belgian Law of 13 November 2011 provides a model for the creation of a compensation scheme for bodily injury and pain and suffering resulting from a technological accident.[88] Where the accident has a tortious cause, the scheme is subsidiary in character and seeks reimbursement from the tortfeasor for sums paid out by way of compensation to the victims. Where no such recourse is possible, the fund becomes a primary fund and offers the victims compensation as a matter of social solidarity.

---

85 Department for Communities and Local Government, 'Flood Support Schemes: Guidance Note' (updated December 2014).

86 'Flood Insurance Statement of Principles' (2000).

87 <http://www.floodre.co.uk/>.

88 See Larissa Vanhoof, 'Compensation Funds in Belgium', section 3.7, this volume, and Isabelle Durant, 'Belgium' in Ken Oliphant and Barbara C Steininger (eds), *European Tort Law 2012* (deGruyter 2013), p. 57 no. 1 and ff.

Again, in the UK there is likely to be a preference for *ad hoc* responses to particular incidents in which the tort remedy proves inadequate, rather than the enactment of a general statutory framework.

11.3. INSURANCE FOR THE VICISSITUDES OF LIFE

The possible model here is the form of personal accident insurance known as the *garantie contre les accidents de la vie* offered in French markets since 2000.[89] In the UK, Patrick Atiyah has even gone so far as to argue that '[t]he action for damages for personal injuries should simply be abolished, and first-party insurance should be left to the free market.'[90] One doubts that many would share his enthusiasm for the *abolition* of the tort remedy, but the present author thinks that it would be desirable to encourage the growth of vicissitudes of life insurance as a *complement* to other sources of support. However, one should not be blind to its limitations. In particular, moral hazard problems prevent insurers offering full compensation for all the losses for which one would be entitled to damages in tort – notably, damages for loss of future earnings. In serious injury cases, the victim may lose decades of remunerative employment, but no first-party insurance known of will compensate for all that lost income. In fact, the French policies consulted by the author seem to limit compensation to a maximum of €1 million – not a negligible sum, but well below the future economic loss component of the largest personal injury damages awards.

11.4. TARGETED INTERVENTION BY STATUTE OR *EX GRATIA* COMPENSATION TO ENSURE EQUALITY IN DISTRIBUTION OF PUBLIC BURDENS

Perhaps the most realistic hope for the UK is for a more coherent approach to the creation of compensation schemes, whether on a statutory or

89 See Jean Péchinot, 'La garantie des accidents de la vie', RCA, mai 2000, n°5, Chron. 10.

90 Patrick S. Atiyah, *The Damages Lottery* (Hart Publishing 1997), p. 189. See also John Smillie, 'The Future of Negligence' (2007) 15 *Torts Law Journal* 300. For criticism of Atiyah's approach, see Arthur Ripstein, 'Some Recent Obituaries of Tort Law' (1998) 48 *University of Toronto Law Journal* 561; Joanne Conaghan and Wade Mansell, 'From the Permissive to the Dismissive Society: Patrick Atiyah's Accidents, Compensation and the Market' (1998) 25 *Journal of Law and Society* 284.

ex gratia basis. One guiding principle that no doubt underpins many interventions to date, but has been insufficiently enunciated, is the need to ensure equality in distribution of public burdens: *égalité devant les charges publiques*. It is striking that the official Treasury guidance for creating an *ex gratia* compensation scheme makes no (even implicit) reference to such principle. Under the rules of public finance, establishing an *ex gratia* public compensation scheme requires advance Treasury approval.[91] But the only guidance provided on the establishment of compensation schemes seems to envisage them as a response to maladministration or service failure,[92] and does not address compensation to ensure the fair distribution of public burdens. The present author would therefore propose that the public finance rules be amended so as to allow for the creation of compensation schemes where a benefit to society at large has a cost to particular persons, and compensation to such persons is justified by the need to ensure public participation in a general programme of risk reduction or simply by the desire to express solidarity to victims of disaster.

12. CONCLUSION

As the above discussion shows, the UK's approach to compensation schemes is *ad hoc* and unprincipled. The basis for singling out specific groups for special compensation is rarely enunciated and simply may not exist. The provisions of different schemes, including the benefits they offer, differ considerably – again, without any obvious justification.

Numerous anomalies exist. For example, funds guaranteeing tort compensation rights are accepted in some areas but not others. The Motor Insurance Bureau guarantees tort compensation rights for those injured by the negligence of uninsured and untraced drivers, and the 2014 Diffuse Mesothelioma Payment Scheme guarantees the rights of those exposed to asbestos during the course of employment who are unable to recover compensation for their erstwhile employers because the latter is insolvent and uninsured or cannot be traced. But, at the same time as accepting the desirability of guaranteeing tort compensation to the victims of mesothelioma, the government has rejected the idea of an

---

91 HM Treasury, 'Managing Public Money' (2013, revised 2015), para. 2.3.4.

92 Ibid, ch. 14.

Employers' Liability Insurance Bureau for the protection of all employees suffering the financial consequences of occupational injury or disease because their employer failed to comply with the obligation to insure.

Where compensation schemes are created, there is a suspicion in many cases that the main motivation was to forestall liability claims against the State for its supervisory failures, as with criminal injuries compensation (bearing in mind the courts' denial of any police duty of care in investigating or preventing crime). The special compensation arrangements for vaccination damage and for infection with Hepatitis C or HIV from blood or blood products are perhaps other examples.

The government also seems to be more ready to embrace funds to protect general business interests, such as through financial services compensation and pensions protection, or the provision of compensation for the slaughter of diseased animals, than to compensate for personal injury. Social solidarity seems not, or only rarely, to be a reason for the creation of such schemes.

It seems therefore that there is an urgent need to re-assess the basis on which compensation schemes are created outside the tort and social security systems. As stated above, a key guiding principle could be the need to ensure the fair and equal distribution of public burdens, which should be accepted into English law so as to provide a more principled basis for the creation of new compensation schemes, whether statutory or *ex gratia*, in the future.

COMPARATIVE ANALYSIS OF COMPENSATION FUNDS

Differences, Common Characteristics and Suggestions for the Future

Thierry Vansweevelt, Britt Weyts,
Larissa Vanhooff and Kim Watts

1. INTRODUCTION

The chapters contributed to this volume reveal that although compensation funds are used for many different purposes, they face many of the same legal, procedural and equality challenges.

2. OPERATIONAL FIELD OF COMPENSATION FUNDS

Compensation funds crop up in response to a wide variety of misfortune. Throughout the different contributing countries, some remarkable similarities in the domains that compensation funds cover can be seen.

Examples can be found in most countries of compensation funds in the domain of *traffic accidents*. This is not surprising, however, since the second European Council Directive on motor vehicle insurance requires EU Member States to create a mechanism for compensating personal injury or damage to property caused by a vehicle that is unidentified or not insured.[1] Therefore, these compensation funds share similar traits, especially in relation to the factual circumstances in which they will intervene.

Deposit guarantee funds have also emerged in the analysed jurisdictions, thanks to Directive 94/19/EC of the European Parliament and of the European Council of 30 May 1994 on deposit guarantee schemes.

Notwithstanding EU influence, traffic accident compensation funds and deposit guarantee funds in Member States in fact often pre-dated the relevant EU Directives.

A similar development exists for the compensation of *crime victims*. According to the Council of Europe's European Convention on the Compensation of Victims of Violent Crimes, victims of serious bodily injury or impairment of health directly attributable to an intentional crime of violence and the dependants of persons who have died as a result of such crime should be able to receive compensation.[2] Not all Treaty Members have implemented this Convention in the same manner.

---

1 Second Council Directive 84/5/EEC of 30 December 1983 on the approximation of the laws of the Member States relating to insurance against civil liability in respect of the use of motor vehicles, OJ L008, 11.01.1984, pp. 17–20.

2 Article 2 of the European Convention on the Compensation of Victims of Violent Crimes.

In Belgium, France, the Netherlands and the UK, the compensation mechanism has taken the shape of a compensation fund.[3] Spain on the other hand opted for public aid instead of a fund for the compensation of general crime damage. Terrorist damage on the other hand is regulated by a separate compensation fund in Spain.[4]

Asbestos-related damage, which can be qualified both as occupational damage and *industrial* or environmental damage, has affected multiple European jurisdictions. Several countries have decided that compensation funds are best placed to cope with time bar issues, difficulties in proof of damage and other challenges in asbestos-related damage claims. This includes Belgium, France, the Netherlands and the UK.[5] In Spain, a future compensation fund still lingers in its embryonic stage.[6] A typical characteristic of asbestos compensation funds is that they are conceived as temporary problem fixers, *ad hoc* solutions rather than structural bodies. Germany covers mining damage,[7] another type of industrial damage, with a compensation fund, whereas Belgium introduced a fund-based compensation system for technological accidents.[8]

Several compensation funds have been created to deal with *natural disasters*, however, they are all of a very divergent nature. Belgium shares its rather unique position with Spain in having a fund that intervenes for various natural hazards in a structural way by setting out criteria that apply for disasters to come.[9] Very different is the Dutch approach. There, the compensation system relies on *ad hoc* compensation funds that are created in the wake of a specific disaster, often when State responsibility is assumed. With the WTS a structural solution is offered, however only in cases of natural disasters. On a related note, several countries use compensation funds for damage by wildlife and protected species. This occurs in France, Belgium and Germany.[10]

Finally, there is a diverse picture in the field of *healthcare*-related damage, yet there are some common features. In France, Germany, the UK and Spain there are similar remedies for contaminated blood

3 Vanhooff, pp. 12–13; Knetsch, p. 48; Faure, Hartlief and van Maanen, pp. 73–74 and Oliphant, pp. 176–177.
4 Garcia-Teruel, pp. 154–155.
5 Vanhooff, pp. 13–14; Knetsch, p. 50; Faure, Hartlief and van Maanen, pp. 75–76 and Oliphant, pp. 170–171.
6 Garcia-Teruel, pp. 150–152.
7 Knetsch, p. 50.
8 Vanhooff, pp. 18–19.
9 Vanhooff, pp. 17–18 and Garcia-Teruel, p. 141.
10 Knetsch, p. 50 and Vanhooff, pp. 19–20.

damage and/or specific drugs and vaccinations (e.g. thalidomide).[11] In Spain, again, there is no compensation fund structure used – rather, the public aid approach is preferred.[12] France, followed by Belgium, has broadened the scope of their healthcare compensation fund and both countries now have a structural compensation fund for medical damage.[13]

An important point to note is that there appears to be two different forms of compensation fund structure in the jurisdictions analysed – structural funds established by way of legislation, and *ad hoc* compensation funds. The term *ad hoc* can have several interpretations. From the examples illustrated in this book an *ad hoc* compensation fund can be identified as a compensation fund that was created in an immediate response to a damaging event (often leading to mass damage) and that has been installed by the executive branch of government without undergoing thorough scrutiny by a parliament.

3. PURPOSE AND MOTIVATION FOR COMPENSATION FUNDS

As noted above, compensation funds in the selected jurisdictions provide compensation to individuals for losses in a variety of circumstances. But why was it necessary to create these compensation funds in the first place? Why were the existing tort, contractual, private insurance, social insurance and/or social security frameworks perceived as insufficient to adequately manage the relevant losses? In other words, what can we discern as the *purpose and motivation* behind the analysed compensation funds as alternative loss allocation and redress systems?

One can conclude from the contributions to this volume that compensation funds are created for two key purposes, one *reactive* and one *proactive*. Firstly, there is a *reactive motivation* of avoiding the determination or apportionment of liability using existing civil procedure mechanisms or insurance (because it is either impossible or undesirable for various reasons). Secondly, there can be a *proactive motivation* to create a framework that provides compensation that combines quasi-social security compensation elements via a procedure

11 Knetsch, p. 48 and Oliphant, p. 172.

12 Garcia-Teruel, pp. 156–157.

13 Knetsch, p. 49 and Vanhooff, pp. 15–16.

that is ideally comparable to an efficient private insurance claim. In the second purpose, compensation funds are being used as a mixed-doctrine solution to complex problems.

3.1. REACTIVE PURPOSE: IT IS IMPOSSIBLE TO USE NORMAL COMPENSATION MECHANISMS

This motivation for the creation of a compensation fund stems from situations where it is impossible to use the existing tort system or private insurance system to allocate the losses suffered by the victim. There may be no tortfeasor available or traceable, or the loss was uninsurable. Closely related, but slightly different, is the motivation of a legislature which decides that although there *could* be a compensation solution via existing compensation frameworks, it would be undesirable to force victims to use that route. That slightly different motivation is dealt with in the next subsection.

'Impossibility' is the simplest and most obvious motivation for a compensation fund, and it manifests itself most clearly in the form of a guarantee fund. Examples of compensation funds with this kind of motivation can be found in most of the jurisdictions analysed in this volume:

1. Belgium's Common Guarantee Fund, Disaster Fund, and 'Fund' for Technological Accidents provide compensation for impossible-to-insure-or-sue cases like hit-and-run motor vehicle accidents, uninsurable natural disaster loss, lightning strikes or a bankrupt insurer.[14] The last-resort nature of Belgian's Victim Compensation Fund means compensation will only be available to victims who have no other possible route of compensation.[15] The mandate given to the Fund for Medical Accidents to compensate in cases of uninsured or under-insured medical practitioners reveals that 'impossibility' motivation.[16] Similarly, one aspect of *Fedris*' responsibility is to pay compensation to injured workers in the case of uninsured or inadequately insured employers.

14 Vanhooff, pp. 11–12, 17–19.
15 Ibid, pp. 12–13.
16 Ibid, pp. 15–16.

2. In France and Germany, compensation funds for uninsurable and un-litigatible motor vehicle accidents were established in the mid-twentieth century. In France, this fund (*Fonds de garantie des assurances obligatoires de dommages*) has been extended to include hunting accidents and accidents involving animals. There is also a combined crime and terrorism victims' compensation fund in France which has grown in strength and application over time.
3. The Netherlands' WTS scheme, which provides compensation in cases of designated catastrophes or large accidents which are uninsurable or not covered by another source of compensation.[17] That 'uninsurable' and 'un-sue-able' motivation can also be identified in the Netherlands' compensation funds for violent crime victims (*Schadefonds Gweldsmisdrijven*),[18] air pollution damage,[19] traffic victims (*Waarborgfonds Motorverkeer*),[20] asbestos victims who have no other possible claim route,[21] and other *ad hoc* compensation funds for unexpected natural and man-made disasters.[22] The authors of the Netherlands contribution noted, however, that an increase in insurance possibilities for different kinds of loss would reduce the need for compensation funds with this 'impossibility' motivation.
4. In Spain, a jurisdiction which appears otherwise reluctant to widely embrace compensation funds, the Insurance Compensation Consortium, will compensate victims who have no other possible route of compensation. This includes victims of 'extraordinary' risks like natural accidents, terrorism, *force majeure*-type losses involving the police or armed forces; victims of uninsured and unidentifiable motorists; and also includes volunteer firefighters who suffer loss. Similarly, the impossibility of recovering losses from insolvent employers, financial service providers and former spouses is the motivation for the creation of other niche Spanish compensation funds.
5. The UK's three asbestos-related disease compensation funds are accessible to victims when the former employer in question is no longer trading and thus cannot be sued, or where a victim had non-occupational exposure and thus has nobody to sue. The 'impossibility'

17 Faure, Hartlief and van Maanen, pp. 70–71.
18 Ibid, pp. 73–74.
19 Ibid, p. 74.
20 Ibid.
21 Ibid, pp. 75–76.
22 Ibid, p. 75.

motivation can also be found in the UK's motor vehicle compensation scheme for victims of untraceable or uninsured drivers,[23] and its Criminal Injuries Compensation scheme.[24] Impossibility to fulfil contractual obligations because of insolvency is the motivation for the British compensation funds that apply to regulated financial services.[25]

The compensation fund mechanism can be seen here as being used because the conclusion arrived at by tort law, private insurance or social insurance – that no route to compensation is available due to the circumstances – is perceived as being an undesirable outcome. A compensation fund in this category has a limited purpose, by compensating a narrow group of individuals who suffered loss due to a specific type of tortfeasor or causation event. This purpose does not have wider implications for other individuals who have suffered similar loss because of a different kind of tortfeasor or cause.

This more limited coverage of compensation funds is the simplest to define and does not conflict too much with the surrounding tort and insurance landscape. The purpose of these compensation funds is precisely defined, and the absence or irrelevance of the tortfeasor means that it is less necessary to weigh up concerns of moral hazard or whether successful claimants are being treated more advantageously than other claimants who have suffered similar losses in different circumstances. The factual circumstances applying to these kinds of compensation funds – including natural disaster, terrorism and hit-and-run victims – are likely to garner a sympathetic response from the public, relevant public authorities, politicians and legislators. Thus, this motivation can also be seen as including a social solidarity element.

3.2. REACTIVE PURPOSE: IT IS UNDESIRABLE TO USE EXISTING COMPENSATION MECHANISMS

Some compensation funds reviewed in this volume were created with the purpose of compensating for loss because the ordinary compensation mechanisms are perceived as an inappropriate solution

23 Oliphant, p. 175.
24 Ibid, pp. 176–177.
25 Ibid, pp. 177–179.

to the problem of allocating loss and compensation. Unlike the 'impossibility' motivation, there is not an absence of a possible insurance, tort or other civil claim option. Rather, there was a choice made to use a compensation fund as an alternative mechanism because the potential results of ordinary compensation mechanisms were deemed undesirable by the legislature and society – for example, the unpredictability of whether a tort claim will be successful,[26] a desire to avoid claims against the State and public authorities in relation to public services,[27] or to protect an important industry vulnerable to collapse because of an unexpected crisis.[28]

Examples of this kind of motivation in the compensation funds reviewed in this book include:

1. The Belgian Fund for Medical Accidents' damage fund responsibilities which pays compensation in situations of sheer medical misfortune – but only in cases of severe injury.[29]
2. France's medical compensation fund (*Office national d'indemnisation des accidents médicaux*, or *ONIAM*) pre-dates the Belgian system and also compensates severely injured victims of medical misfortune. Blood infections, drug injury victims and other victims of medical disasters have also been specifically included in the ONIAM system, diverting away potential civil damages claims in these categories of loss.
3. Germany's public health disaster compensation funds (such as those for thalidomide victims and the victims of State-sponsored East German athletic doping) diverted questions of loss and liability away from the courts, because a legislative response was perceived to be a more desirable outcome in those situations.[30]
4. New Zealand's comprehensive personal injury compensation fund, the ACC Scheme, was established because existing compensation options were perceived to be fragmented and leading to injustice and practical anomalies.[31] There was not a specific event or circumstance that motivated the New Zealand fund's creation.

---

26 Watts, p. 98.
27 In relation to the UK see Oliphant, p. 178; in relation to France see Knetsch, p. 52, in relation to the Netherlands see Faure, Hartlief and van Maanen, pp. 80–81; in relation to Belgium see Vanhooff, pp. 23–24.
28 Such as the UK financial services sector see Oliphant, p. 178.
29 Vanhooff, p. 16.
30 Knetsch, pp. 48–49.
31 Watts, p. 98.

5. The UK's compensation scheme for infected slaughtered farm animals is motivated by a desire to ensure farmers voluntarily comply with (and presumably do not launch legal challenges against) agriculture disease control legislation.[32] Similarly, that jurisdiction's unified scheme for vaccine damage and blood infection provides a compensation route for victims that diverts away from potential civil damages claims against the public health service.[33]

3.3. PROACTIVE PURPOSE: EFFICIENT COMPENSATION VIA SIMPLIFIED PROCEDURE

This purpose illustrates a choice by the legislature to create a compensation fund that is a structural approach to the payment of compensation to victims who meet specific criteria. The purpose of the compensation fund is the timely compensation of future, yet-to-be identified victims of certain types of loss. The fund is thus established not only with reference to a group of existing victims, but with future victims in mind. The compensation fund may feature elements of social security, private insurance as well as civil damages claims – meriting the description of a mixed doctrine solution.

- France has favoured such proactive purpose for compensation funds, with both the ONIAM and the *Fonds de garantie des victimes d'actes de terrorisme et d'autres infractions* having a broad scope to process many different types of claims using a model similar to compulsory insurance, in a way that supplements social security.[34]
- The Netherlands' structural approach in designing the WTS, with its specific principles of compensation, illustrates a noble proactive compensation purpose that could have covered many types of catastrophic loss.[35] However it has failed to be of practical use or have wider application to non-natural disasters.[36]

---

32 Oliphant, pp. 179–180.
33 Ibid, pp. 172–175.
34 Knetsch, pp. 55–56.
35 Faure, Hartlief and van Maanen, pp. 69–71.
36 Ibid, pp. 71–72.

- The New Zealand ACC Scheme is the most comprehensive example in this volume of a compensation fund with this proactive purpose.[37] The purpose is illustrated in the fund's streamlined claims procedure, a private insurance-style organisational and funding structure and the fund's income-linked periodic compensation payments to claimants.

The jurisdictions which have used compensation funds with this proactive purpose can be contrasted with the likes of the Netherlands, Spain and Germany. In those jurisdictions, there is evidence instead of legislators adjusting existing insurance, social security and tort structures to better address compensation problems, instead of using the compensation fund option.

It is also notable that the different chapters reveal a stark division between the common law and civil law approaches to loss allocation. Both the UK[38] and New Zealand legislators have chosen not to make a distinction between different types of injuries or apply strict liability, thus elevating the importance of tort law as a means of allocating loss. In the New Zealand case, there was a corresponding choice to create a wide-ranging compensation fund to supplant tort law. In the UK, there was a choice to rely on tort law and fault-based remedies. Therefore, the purpose of supplanting tort law remedies is of greater importance in the New Zealand and UK than it is in the civil law jurisdictions reviewed in this volume.

4. FUNDING OF COMPENSATION FUNDS

This book has shown that compensation funds have different sources of income, with both differences between compensation funds in the same country, as well as differences between countries.

The vast majority of compensation funds are funded by public means in the broad sense of the word. In this large category a distinction can be made between compensation funds that are funded via the general budget, including social security without further specification of the relevant branch and those whose funding is made available via special allocated budget, or collected via taxation or fines.

---

[37] Watts, pp. 98–99.
[38] Oliphant, p. 163.

Funds that are funded by the *general public budget* include the British and Dutch compensation funds for crime victims, the Dutch funds for air pollution and some *ad hoc* disaster funds.[39] The Spanish national fund for repairing environmental damage also receives money from the general budget.[40] In Belgium most compensation funds also receive a share from the national budget or from social security.[41]

In other cases, a *special tax* is raised for the purpose of feeding the fund. Money collected in this way does not come from the general budget, but from a special 'nest egg' reserved for the fund. This system offers the opportunity of carefully selecting the exact source of income and determining the ultimate cost bearers. In other words, lawmakers can make a deliberate policy choice for a certain risk allocation model. For example, in the UK, the Diffuse Mesothelioma Scheme of 2014 places a levy on insurance companies currently active in the employers' liability insurance market.[42] Similarly, the British financial services compensation funds levies firms subject to regulation in the financial services sector.[43]

A few compensation funds receive a percentage of *fines* imposed on criminal offenders where there is a certain connection with the working field of the compensation fund. For example, the Spanish compensation fund for traffic accidents receives a percentage of traffic fines.[44] The Belgian fund for crime victims is funded via fines for larger criminal offences, and the Nature and Environment Fund receives a share of the fines for violation of environmental laws.[45] Here a purposed risk allocation model targeting those who create and sustain risks (but not necessarily harm or create damage) is also seen.

Rarely, and in fact only for traffic accidents, the source of income is purely *private*, regulated directly by the private (insurance) sector. This is the case for the French, Belgian and British compensation funds for traffic accidents: insurance companies active in the motor insurance sector are legally bound to be part of the fund, which is a mutual insurance association, and pay their contribution directly to the fund.[46]

---

39 Ibid, pp. 176–177 and Faure, Hartlief and van Maanen, pp. 73–75.
40 Garcia-Teruel, p. 147.
41 Vanhooff, p. 40.
42 Oliphant, p. 170.
43 Ibid, p. 178.
44 Garcia-Teruel, p. 143.
45 Vanhooff, pp. 33–34.
46 Knetsch, p. 47, Vanhooff, pp. 33–34 and Oliphant, p. 175.

Compensation funds can also receive funding from both private and public sectors. For example, the Dutch compensation fund for traffic accidents is fed by insurance companies and the public budget.[47] The New Zealand ACC's funding is also based on both the general taxation pool and special direct levies on activities.[48]

5. LEVEL OF COMPENSATION

Compensation funds display a wide variety when it comes to the quantum of compensation they offer and to the calculation of damages.

The general idea that compensation funds necessarily equal limited damages, compared to what tort victims usually receive via court action or via insurance, is not necessarily true. For example, in Belgium the fund for medical accidents can offer *full compensation* that is measured according to the standards of court damages.[49] The compensation funds for traffic victims of the EU Member States generally give compensation similar to what a victim would have received from the tortfeasor's insurance, albeit with limitations in specific cases (e.g. limited to personal damage in case of an unidentified driver).[50]

Of course, for reasons of budget, compensation funds are mostly seen as a remedy of last resort and therefore their available budget is correspondingly restricted, resulting in limited damages.

Limited compensation is a multi-headed hydra and can take various shapes, often combining the following features: limited to certain heads of damage, caps and limitations, percentages and fixed amount.

- In most cases compensation is limited to either material or physical damage and often to more *specific heads of damage*, e.g. loss of earning capacity, loss of school year. The French ONIAM, the Dutch WTS, the Belgian and the British Victim Compensation Funds are clear examples of this approach.[51] There may also be an adjustment to how damages for the specific heads of damage are calculated. This can be according to the rule of full compensation (integrity of the damage for that head is awarded) or further restricted in one of the means mentioned below.

---

47 Faure, Hartlief and van Maanen, p. 74.

48 Watts, p. 106.

49 Vanhooff, p. 29.

50 Ibid and Garcia-Teruel, pp. 143–144.

51 Knetsch, p. 61; Faure, Hartlief and van Maanen, p. 70; Vanhooff, p. 29 and Oliphant, p. 172.

- Sometimes the compensation is expressed as a *fixed* and invariable amount of money. The Belgian and Dutch asbestos compensation funds, the Dutch *ad hoc* Bijlmer-fund, the Spanish volunteer firefighter fund (in case of death of the victim) and the British unified vaccine damage, HIV and Hepatitis C compensation scheme all offer fixed damages.[52] It appears that compensation funds created in the wake of a specific harmful event (such as vaccination, contaminated blood transfusion, air plane crash) also tend to award lump sum fixed damages.
- Another frequently used technique consists of applying *franchises and caps* to the damages, in an attempt to minimise the burden to the public budget. The Flemish natural disaster fund and the Belgian victim compensation fund, the French fund for general crime victims, the Spanish financial services fund, the New Zealand system, the British criminal injuries fund and the Dutch fund for traffic victims are a few of the numerous examples of this capping and limiting of compensation.[53] In short, this is a technique with which many countries' compensation funds are familiar.
- A further system of limiting compensation that are found among the contributing countries is limiting the awardable damages to a *percentage of the total damage*. It is applied in the Flemish Disaster Fund, the Spanish Volunteer Firefighter Fund (for permanent disability) and in the New Zealand ACC Scheme (percentage of disability), to name a few.[54]

Finally, some compensation funds award damages on the basis of *equity*. This is so for the Belgian and the Dutch Victim compensation fund.[55]

6. EFFECT OF COMPENSATION FUNDS ON OTHER LOSS ALLOCATION MECHANISMS

Compensation funds do not exist in a vacuum. They are just one element of compensation that could be available when an individual suffers a loss.

---

52 Vanhooff, p. 28; Faure, Hartlief and van Maanen, pp. 74–75; Garcia-Teruel, p. 146 and Oliphant, p. 172.

53 Vanhooff, p. 26; Knetsch, pp. 59–60; Watts, pp. 103–104; Oliphant, p. 176 and Faure, Hartlief and van Maanen, p. 74.

54 Vanhooff, p. 26; Garcia-Teruel, pp. 145–146 and Watts, p. 104.

55 Vanhooff, p. 29 and Faure, Hartlief and van Maanen, p. 73.

As noted in the previous section, compensation funds often do not give an individual full compensation for their complete pecuniary and non-pecuniary losses.[56] Even the broadest types of funds analysed in this volume do not provide compensation for all possible dimensions of an individual's loss. Therefore, an individual who has suffered loss will probably have to consider more than one avenue of compensation. In addition to a payment from a compensation fund, an individual's loss might also be compensated by private insurance, social security or social insurance, tort damages, or contractual and other damages. Depending on the individual and his circumstances, charitable compensation from third parties might also be available. And of course, an individual may choose (possibly through inaction) or be forced to bear the partial or full brunt of his losses himself.

The compensation funds analysed in this volume have different effects on the ability to allocate losses that are not covered by a compensation fund award. However, it can be broadly concluded that there are two categories of relationship between compensation funds and other loss allocation mechanisms. The first is where the compensation fund has a *dominant or active* effect on other compensation options – the compensation fund will be a primary compensation option, and the fact of a compensation fund payment being made will actively affect whether a different source of compensation is also available. In this dominant role, there is a presumption that the compensation fund payment will be appropriate and adequate compensation in most cases for most claimants. In the second type of relationship, the compensation fund takes *a submissive role* – the availability of a compensation fund payment will only be considered after all other compensation options have been exhausted. In this category, the fact of a compensation fund payment being made is thus dependent on the exclusion of other compensation possibilities, rather than affecting the availability of those possibilities. In this secondary mode, there is a presumption that the other or usual compensation structures will be appropriate and adequate in most cases for most claimants, and that a victim receiving compensation fund payment will tend to be an exceptional case.

These dominant and submissive dimensions will be analysed below in relation to four broad categories of non-compensation fund loss

---

56 Pecuniary losses are the clearly quantifiable economic losses suffered by an individual. Non-pecuniary losses can be more difficult to define – they can include pain and suffering, and potential losses of opportunity.

allocation mechanisms: (1) tort and other court-derived compensatory damages; (2) private insurance; (3) social insurance and social welfare; and (4) charitable and humanitarian financial assistance.

6.1. TORT AND OTHER COURT-DERIVED COMPENSATORY DAMAGES

A general prohibition against double recovery can be found in the liability laws and jurisprudence of both civil and common law systems. This means that in many cases a claimant must make a choice between seeking a payment from a compensation fund and making a court claim for compensation in tort or under another head of damages. Some of the compensation funds analysed in this volume, such as New Zealand's ACC Scheme, completely bar a claim in court for compensatory damages for legal policy reasons.[57]

The simplest results emerge when the compensation fund takes a submissive role in relation to tort and other court-based damages. Thus, the guarantee funds analysed in this volume, which all have a subsidiary character and are only available because of the impossibility of any other compensation source, have virtually no effect on other loss allocation mechanisms. Nevertheless, rules requiring claimants to notify the compensation fund of any ongoing court procedure are a useful guard against any unintended instances of double accumulation, even in the context of a guarantee fund.[58]

Where the compensation fund takes a dominant position in relation to tort and other court-based damages, there will need to be a specific and justified choice made about whether it is acceptable to allow double recovery (i.e. a payment from a compensation fund as well as the possibility of a claim for tort or other damages via the courts). Otherwise, unjustified unfairness and discrimination between different categories of victims will result, undermining the doctrinal validity of the compensation fund. Instances from the selected jurisdictions where double recovery has been allowed (either expressly or by omission of a prohibition) all feature inadequate justification. For example, there is no express policy explanation why, under Belgium's Asbestos Compensation Fund, certain categories of asbestos exposure victims can receive both a

57 Watts, p. 111.

58 Vanhooff, pp. 27–28.

compensation payment and make a claim under liability law.[59] In New Zealand, the legislature has expressly – but with no acknowledgment of doctrinal inconsistency – allowed crime victims to 'top up' their ACC scheme compensation payments with a reparation order payment under criminal law.[60] The special treatment afforded to French blood contamination victims, who were allowed to claim compensation from multiple sources, led to inconsistency and uncertainty that was only resolved by a blanket prohibition on double recovery in every instance of French compensation fund legislation.[61]

It can therefore be concluded that the simplest way to manage the interaction between compensation funds and other court-based damages is to give the compensation fund a submissive, subsidiary character. Where this is not possible, because of the purpose and factual scope of the compensation fund, the possibility of double accumulation should be expressly prohibited by the legislative instruments establishing the compensation fund. If such a prohibition does not occur, it automatically undermines the value of the compensation fund payment as full or at least 'real' compensation for the loss. If the legislature considers it justifiable to allow some types of victims to accumulate compensation from multiple sources, this should spark a query of whether the compensation provided via the fund is in fact adequate.

6.2. PRIVATE AND MANDATORY INSURANCE

As with tort and other court-derived damages, where the compensation fund has a submissive role then there will be limited interaction or effect on the compensation available via private and mandatory insurance. The amount of compensation paid via insurance may impact the value of the compensation fund payment, as is the case with Belgium's Fund for Medical Accidents and Common Guarantee Fund. Uninsurable risks, such as natural disaster damage in the Netherlands and Spain, leave a space for a compensation fund to act in parallel with private insurance in limited cases.

A question that remains unanswered is whether compensation funds that have a dominant role remove the necessity of private insurance

59 Ibid, p. 27.
60 Watts, p. 113.
61 Knetsch, p. 62.

in the relevant area of loss, by effectively operating as a monopolistic public insurance for that kind of loss. The issue of moral hazard comes into play here – if a dominant role compensation fund provides too generous a compensation without the payment of any premium, will individuals fail to take out adequate private insurance to cover their losses? Does the reliance, as seen in the jurisdictions reviewed in this volume, on compensation funds to compensate for unusual or extraordinary risks in fact remove any incentive to shape private insurance to better cover these risks? This is a question that must be further analysed from an insurance law perspective. However, the Netherlands chapter authors' critique, which suggests making risks more insurable rather than relying on compensation funds as a solution, touches on these concerns. Other compensation scholars have argued, however, that a reliance upon private insurance as a primary compensation mechanism (with no compensation fund backup) disproportionately affects the poor and vulnerable – because the freedom to be inadequately insured is actually no freedom at all.[62]

6.3. SOCIAL INSURANCE AND SOCIAL WELFARE

There appears to be a relatively interactive relationship between compensation funds and social insurance and social welfare in all the analysed jurisdictions. In France and Germany, we have seen that compensation funds act as a supplement (but not a replacement) to the social security system.[63] Belgium's *Fedris* agency for occupational risks can generally be seen as a part of the social security system, with some compensation fund elements that stand apart from social insurance.[64]

Dominant compensation funds will generally have a direct effect on the availability of other social welfare payments, such as under New Zealand's ACC Scheme.[65] Subsidiary compensation funds, such as the Netherlands' WTS, will only be available when all other compensation sources, including social security, have been exhausted.[66]

62 Peter Cane and James Goudkamp, *Atiyah's Accidents, Compensation and the Law*, 9th edn (Cambridge University Press 2018), p. 466.
63 Knetsch, p. 55.
64 Vanhooff, pp. 16–17.
65 Watts, pp. 109–110.
66 Faure, Hartlief and van Maanen, p. 82.

Because social security compensation is generally paid on the basis of need, and compensation funds make payments on the basis of specified causal elements, this means that it is easy for compensation funds to operate as a supplement to social security without too much doctrinal inconsistency. In Spain one sees that many academics and stakeholders want compensation funds to be used to make up for the shortfall in social security benefits, which would be another example of a complementary role for compensation funds.[67] Compensation funds can also use eligibility for social security as criteria for compensation fund payment eligibility – as seen in the interactivity between the UK's 1979 dust disease compensation fund and disability benefit eligibility.[68]

It can therefore be concluded that there is a somewhat symbiotic relationship between social security/social insurance systems and compensation funds. Other authors in this field have concluded that compensation fund structures are representative of a trend of providing compensation on a wider social basis[69] – an argument leading to the conclusion that compensation funds are in fact a type of social security structure. Yet as the chapters in this volume have shown, there are intrinsic structural differences between compensation funds and social security, such as whether the trigger for eligibility is causal or need-based. The most significant interactions between social security and compensation funds will be in the cases of dominant compensation funds like the New Zealand ACC Scheme, which provide much more generous compensation than the social security.

6.4. CHARITABLE AND HUMANITARIAN FINANCIAL ASSISTANCE

Generally speaking, there is no evidence from the jurisdictions analysed in this volume that a compensation fund will impact on an individual's ability to receive non-public charitable or humanitarian assistance for their loss. The existence of a compensation fund would hopefully minimise the need of a victim to rely upon the charity of their community, in any event.

---

67 Garcia-Teruel, p. 159.

68 Oliphant, p. 168.

69 Sonia Macleod and Christopher Hodges, *Redress Schemes for Personal Injuries* (Hart Publishing 2017), p. 620.

In some cases, the compensation fund itself can be regarded as a kind of charity. Compensation funds established by legislators that are classified as *ex gratia* – i.e. they make payments without any finding of legal obligations – are often viewed by the public authorities administrating them as charitable in nature. The UK's Criminal Injuries Compensation Scheme is an example of such a fund. The expression of social solidarity from the community to victims can be classified as a type of humanitarian assistance, particularly in the cases of Dutch *ad hoc* funds, the enhanced compensation available for terrorism victims under French Guarantee Fund for Victims of Terrorism and Other Offences.

It can therefore be concluded that compensation funds are unlikely to impact on the availability of charitable and humanitarian assistance. In fact, the compensation fund structure itself can be seen as an expression of the State's charity towards victims who have suffered loss in a heinous or morally repugnant way.

7. CONCLUSIONS AND THE POTENTIAL FOR REFORM

7.1. GENERAL CONCLUSIONS

Compensation funds operate where the traditional compensation sources have reached their limit. For example, tort law can only offer redress after proof of fault or negligence, causation and damage. When either of these elements is absent or cannot be proven sufficiently, it follows logically that no compensation can be awarded. In theory this is a logical consequence of tort principles and should not question the functioning of tort as it is exactly the result of a proper functioning of it. However, the sheer existence of compensation funds, as a means of 'closing the compensation gaps', next to other no-fault schemes, is proof of (growing) dissatisfaction with these inherent limits of tort, insurance and social security. Does this conclusion require a call for general compensation law reform? In New Zealand this conclusion did indeed form part of the case for widespread reform and lead to the creation of a super fund.[70] In other countries however, the prospect of general reform of compensation law appears to be a more challenging issue.

70 Watts, p. 96.

At the level of compensation funds themselves, there might be need for reform. Within each country, the compensation funds are regulated in a different way, based on acts and decrees that are created especially for that specific fund, and there is no general 'act on compensation funds'. This creates a lot of divergence, sometimes without justification. The diversity of funds is translated in the calculation of damages, the amount awarded, the finance source and the conditions victims are required to fulfil.

The reason for this diversity lies in the origin of these funds since they are, generally speaking, created at a moment of need. As a consequence, they are adapted to the circumstances of their creation. For instance, when victims are suffering from long and exhausting legal procedures before the courts or with insurers, a focus will be placed on introducing a fast procedure, rather than on full compensation. Also, the characteristics of the funds are the result of weighing up different stakeholder interests, including victims, players in the field (e.g. industry, healthcare practitioners and insurers) and the government (the State's legal and moral responsibility and political interests). Streamlining compensation funds can therefore be a trickier exercise than one might expect.

Challenging as it may be, some form of streamlining is not impossible. Throughout the chapters in this volume different attempts to streamline the law of compensation funds have been seen, resulting in some harmonisation and unification.

- Germany has not yet implemented harmonisation between its compensation funds, which can be explained partially by the rather limited importance of compensation funds, compared to the other countries. This has left the country with a patchwork of structural and *ad hoc* compensation funds.[71]
- The UK had several occasions where it explored the possibility of creating new and extensive compensation funds (e.g. for medical accidents) and even a New Zealand-style compensation reformation. However, those ideas never got off the ground. Nevertheless, unification has proven successful in the field of contaminated blood and vaccine damage. The former trust funds are abolished and the compensation

[71] Knetsch, p. 63.

schemes have now been appointed to the NHS Business Services Authority that runs all schemes in a unified manner.[72]

- In the Netherlands, the WTS compensation system is an attempt to create a unified legal structure, initially intended for all natural and man-made disasters, in a structural way. Although it succeeded in unifying the law for natural disasters, it quickly became apparent that the system's scope was too limited to include man-made disasters.[73] Streamlining in the Netherlands happened via unified law yet failed (partially) in the end due to its restricted scope.
- In France, streamlining compensation funds has been more successful and took the shape of administrative simplification in a single window, albeit also limited in scope. Two major funds swallowed pre-existing compensation funds and other publicly funded schemes: the FGAO and ONIAM. ONIAM absorbed the compensation fund for victims of HIV-contaminated blood transfusions and the public scheme for damage by vaccination.[74] The FGAO acquired technological accidents, mining accidents and compulsory insurance default.[75] These mergers did not result in unification of the law, however, since different procedures and calculation of damages might apply, depending on the cause of the damage.
- In Belgium, the Belgian Common Guarantee Fund added compensation for technological accidents to its core task, traffic accidents.[76] The Workmen's Occupational Accidents and Diseases Fund are merged together into one fund, *Fedris*.[77] This was a simple merger and did not have implications for procedure or for the measurement of compensation. Therefore, it was a mere administrative simplification.
- In Spain, the Insurance Compensation Consortium functions as a compensation fund for different kinds of accidents and disasters (extraordinary risks, car accidents, damage to volunteer firefighters).[78] Although accidents from multiple sources are covered by this fund, it does not encompass all compensation funds in Spain. Similar to France and Belgium, different rules apply according to the relevant regime.

72 Oliphant, pp. 174–175.
73 Faure, Hartlief and van Maanen, pp. 70–72.
74 Knetsch, p. 49.
75 Ibid, p. 47.
76 Vanhooff, pp. 18–19.
77 Ibid, p. 16.
78 Garcia-Teruel, pp. 140–141.

- New Zealand took the furthest step in streamlining compensation law by effectively abolishing accident and injury tort law and replacing it with one single compensation fund for almost all cases of corporal damage.[79]

These initiatives for streamlining are a step in the direction of a more simplified and coherent compensation law since they guide victims to the right compensation source, whether it is a fund, insurance, or social security benefits, and should be encouraged as such.

As one cannot lose sight of political and ideological differences between and within countries, the best hope for a more coherent development of compensation law is to focus on good procedure and decent system designs rather than proposing that jurisdictions implement a certain loss allocation model that might not fit within the larger legal picture of their jurisdiction. As a first step (and maybe final) this can be reached by proper legislation for every compensation fund and a well-thought-out system that befits the country's view on compensation. For indeed, one should not seek harmonisation for the sake of it. Compensation law and the specific role compensation funds play in that whole should be construed in a way that can be properly tested as a legal principle and withstand human rights and access to justice challenges.

7.2. INTERACTION BETWEEN COMPENSATION FUNDS AND HUMAN RIGHTS

A key issue that remains to be resolved is the interaction between compensation funds and human rights legislation. The matter is touched on briefly by Vanhooff and Knetsch in their chapters.

By awarding a unique compensation to a clearly defined group of victims, compensation funds arguably lead to the fragmentation of the legal compensation system and may interfere with human rights, such as the principle of non-discrimination (art. 14 of the European Convention of Human Rights ('ECHR')) and the right of access to justice (arts 6 and 13 of the ECHR). Due to the limited scope of application of funds, some victims can rely on a fund and others cannot. Consequently, victims

79 Watts, pp. 91–92.

with damage that occurred in comparable circumstances will not be treated similarly. Whether or not this obvious difference in treatment is discriminatory is still unclear and requires further consideration.[80]

Moreover, a European version of a New Zealand-style universal compensation fund that turns tort law on its head and prohibits access to court could infringe the right of access to justice (arts 6 and 13 of the ECHR).[81] Even narrower funds that preclude a victim's access to court, such as Belgium's Fedris and Asbestos Compensation Fund, give rise to similar concerns. The right of access to justice is safeguarded in different treaties, among which the ECHR is the most prominent source (arts 6 and 14 of the ECHR). Compensation funds could thus infringe this right, and further study is required on this point.

8. THE FUTURE AND WAYS TO IMPROVE EXISTING COMPENSATION FUNDS

The immediate future of compensation funds in the jurisdictions analysed will be shaped by the success (or otherwise) of the performance of existing compensation funds. There is a huge difference between, for example, the very cautious and limited approach in Spain and the more expansive examples of compensation funds seen in France. In the common law world, the *ad hoc* and unprincipled use of compensation funds in the UK is at odds with the wholesale replacement in New Zealand of personal injury tort law compensation by the ACC Scheme. The development of compensation funds in each jurisdiction will be heavily dependent on the surrounding tort, insurance and social security landscape. It can generally be concluded, however, that the streamlined procedural advantages of compensation funds and their ability to address uninsurable and un-litigatable risks will lead to their continued, and possibly increased use, in all the jurisdictions analysed.

An obvious failing of all the compensation funds analysed in this volume is the discrimination exercised against very similar categories of individuals who have suffered loss. For example, individuals who

80 Janet Esther Van de Bunt, *Het rampenfonds* (Wolters Kluwer 2016), p. 91.

81 Jonas Knetsch, *Le droit de la responsabilité et les fonds d'indemnisation* (L.G.D.J. 2013), pp. 54–59.

suffered loss as a result of a terrorist attack in France are entitled to access more generous compensation via the relevant compensation fund than a person who suffers similar levels of injury, hurt and anguish as a victim of a non-terrorist crime. In the UK, Belgium, the Netherlands, France, Germany and New Zealand an individual who has a shortened life expectancy due to an industrial dust disease like asbestos will be able to claim enhanced compensation compared to a person who has shortened life expectancy due to stress-related heart disease or strenuous work. As the authors of the Netherlands chapter ask, every threshold created by compensation funds will create inequalities and disappointment – is this fair?[82]

The answer to this dilemma would appear, at first glance, to extend the reach of compensation funds to address many different types of loss. The New Zealand ACC scheme is the most obvious example of this. However, this is not a real answer to the problem of discrimination between eligible and non-eligible classes of victims – an extended compensation fund simply shifts the border of discrimination a little wider. For example, the New Zealand scheme has always discriminated against individuals with non-worker sickness and disability. These individuals can only access meagre social welfare support for their losses and ongoing needs or must consider the likelihood of a successful damages claim in court. There is presently a push by disability advocates in that jurisdiction to extend the scheme further to encompass all types of misfortune.[83] But again this simply moves the border of discrimination – what about, for example, individuals who suffer uninsured economic and property loss? The potential to extend compensation funds is limitless – what about compensation for younger generations denied similar economic opportunities to their parents due to increasing inequality and sluggish economic growth? What about compensation for the effects of climate change and air pollution on individuals' health and quality of life?

The argument for comprehensive expansion of compensation funds is therefore an unrealistic position to take. As leading accident compensation law commentary has noted, it is surely better to accept the reality of distinctions between different categories of individuals, and properly design a scheme around justified differences in treatment

82 Faure, Hartlief and van Maanen, p. 86.

83 Forster & Associates, 'Expansion of ACC' <https://www.forster.co.nz/beyond-injury/expansion>.

that reflect acceptable priorities for the use of public funds and other social resources.[84] A stricter approach to the relevant procedure for the scope, design, operation and management of compensation funds is a better way forward than simply advocating an expansion of the victims they aim to compensate. The tool that is described as a 'compensation fund' should no longer be regarded by legal literature or legislatures as mysterious, a quirk, or an exception. This kind of eccentric categorisation allows compensation funds (and the public authorities that create and manage them) to escape rigorous legal scrutiny. It also implies that compensation funds do not have the same importance as court, insurance and social welfare methods of compensation, when in fact they often have an equally important role to play in helping victims to recover from losses and traumatic life events.

---

84 Cane and Goudkamp, *Atiyah's Accidents, Compensation and the Law*, above n. 62, pp. 446–447.

INDEX

ABOUT THE EDITORS

Thierry Vansweevelt is a Professor and former Dean of the Faculty of Law, University of Antwerp. He works in the fields of liability law, insurance and health law and for this has been awarded the Fernand Collin Prize and the Antwerp University Research Council Prize. He is an advocate at the specialist healthcare law practice Dewallens & partners and has been appointed as member of the Royal Academy for Medicine of Belgium and as member of the board of governors of the World Association of Medical Law.

Britt Weyts is a Professor of Law at the University of Antwerp. Her work focuses on the law of obligations and insurance law and has been awarded the Fernand Collin Prize. She is the spokesperson of the research group on Personal Rights and Property Rights also works as an advocate at Verbist & Vanlerberghe Omega Law.

www.ingramcontent.com/pod-product-compliance
Ingram Content Group UK Ltd.
Pitfield, Milton Keynes, MK11 3LW, UK
UKHW021012120926
8556IPUK00039B/1043

9 781780 689425